BOYHOOD,
GROWING UP MALE

BOYHOOD,
GROWING UP MALE

A Multicultural Anthology

Edited by
Franklin Abbott

Second Edition, With a New Foreword
by Michael S. Kimmel

The University of Wisconsin Press

The University of Wisconsin Press
2537 Daniels Street
Madison, Wisconsin 53718

3 Henrietta Street
London WC2E 8LU, England

1 3 5 4 2

Printed in the United States of America

First published in 1993 by The Crossing Press

Library of Congress Cataloging-in-Publication Data
Boyhood, growing up male: a multicultural anthology / edited by
Franklin Abbott. — 2nd ed. / with a new foreword by Michael S. Kimmel.
296 pp.   cm.
Earlier ed. published: Freedom, Calif.: Crossing Press, c1993.
ISBN 0-299-15754-7 (alk. paper)
1. Boys—Psychology—Cross-cultural studies. 2. Men—Socialization
—Cross-cultural studies. 3. Masculinity—Cross-cultural studies.
I. Abbott, Franklin.
HQ775.B63   1998
305.31—dc21   97-47771

Since the first edition was published in 1993, two of the contributors to BOYHOOD have died. Jeff Beane, an activist for many causes including the pro-feminist men's movement, gay rights, and HIV awareness, died of AIDS in San Francisco in 1994. John Gill, deft poet and publisher of many fine books with his partner Elaine Goldman Gill at the Crossing Press, died surrounded by loving family and friends in Santa Cruz in 1995.

This edition is dedicated to their memory.

CONTENTS

BEING A BOY IN THE WORLD

BOYHOOD AND THE SOUL

HOW TO USE THIS BOOK

FOREWORD

"The child," wrote Wordsworth, "is father of the man." Our experiences as boys indelibly brand who we become as men.

When I lecture to college age audiences around the country, I invariably encounter a question or comment about the need to reach boys at younger ages—high school, junior high school, and even elementary school boys. How can we enable young boys to develop a secure and confident sense of themselves as men without resorting to violence, rape, and war. How can we encourage the nurturing fathers, the compassionate lovers, husbands, and friends, that we so desperately need?

While these questions are occasionally prompted by a desire to abdicate responsibility for one's own actions, as if one cannot challenge and transform patterns from earlier ages, I think it more often expresses what I believe is one of the more crucial issues of our times: America has a boy problem.

Unfortunately, this "boy problem" remains relatively invisible. We know it as something else: teen violence, urban gangs, guns in school, elementary school sexual harassment, suburban violence, fraternity gang rape. Just who, exactly, is doing it? Girls? These are boys desperate to prove something, to show they are real men. Because in this culture, being a real man is vital to every boy.

I remember one little childhood game called "Flinch" we played in the schoolyard. One boy would come up to another and pretend to throw a punch at his face. If the second boy flinched—as any *reasonable* person would have done—the first boy shouted "you flinched" and proceeded to punch him hard on the arm. It was his right; after all the other boy had failed the test of masculinity. Being a man meant never flinching.

What else does growing up male in a male-dominated society mean? As readers of this important volume will see, it means many things, all at once. It means the crippling coercion to conform to rigidly defined ideas, ideas that may feel as foreign as wearing someone else's skin. Growing up masculine may mean the brutality of the schoolyard bully, the nightmare of sexual abuse by a trusted elder, the yawning emptiness of longing for a distant father, the isolation and chronic anxiety of having to prove your manhood every second. Boyhood is a constant, relentless testing of manhood.

It also may mean the exhilaration of physical challenge and athletic triumph, the blushing, tentative thrill of first sexual exploration, the freedom of movement, the carefree play—what Wordsworth called "the coarser pleasures of my boyish days" with all their "glad animal movements." Boyhood is a freedom from responsibility, the constraints and compromises of manhood.

And it also means the entitlement to get your way, to be heard, the often invisible privileges that come from being a man, the ability to see your reflection (at least if you are also white and heterosexual) in virtually every television show, action-hero comic book, and movie, and seated at every board room in the nation. Boyhood is the entitlement to, and the anticipation of, power.

Boyhood means all these—some, understood; others, unexpected. I think that my first experience of masculinity as a boy, my first taste of what manhood meant, was safety.

I was three years old, and at the beach where we spent every summer of my youth. One sunny summer afternoon, my father and I were playing by the shore, watching the waves. He waded into the water a few feet, where the water gently lapped at his feet, and I followed, tentatively, hesitant, frightened. When the water was calm, we splashed each other, and I giggled, almost uncontrollably. Gradually, my father and I had moved further and further into the water, now up to his knees, my chest. It was deeper than I had ever gone before.

Suddenly several large waves broke nearby, and I tried to run for the shore, terrified. Of course, I could barely move, and I was about to cry in panic as I fought the water to get to the shore. Just as the wave was about to break over me, my father reached down, swooped me up and held me so close to his chest. "It's O.K.," he said, his voice soft and reassuring over the crash of the water. "Nothing is going to hurt you."

Today, almost half a century later, I can still feel the power of his arms, the hair on his back and shoulders, my head against his chest. I knew I was safe, secure, protected.

The essays in this book give us a window into remembered boyhood and outward to its adult expression, a prism through we see how boys become men. They suggest the wide range of experience we take from our childhoods, and therefore the wide range of possibilities we bring to adulthood.

Books about boyhood are always about hope. They imply growth, change, possibility. But such hopes must be based on the realities of our lives as children, not the sanitized and prepackaged memories provided for us by a culture desperate for the comfort of amnesia.

Franklin Abbott's brave and caring collection gives us genuine hope, because the authors, like real men, look at their lives squarely and honesty. And they do not flinch.

New York City   MICHAEL S. KIMMEL
March, 1997

ACKNOWLEDGMENTS

First, I want to thank Kay Harrison for suggesting the focus for the anthology. I am grateful to the following people for their assistance in locating contributors to the anthology: Assotto Saint, Don Shewey, Jeff Glauser, Ike Anyanike, Jean Caiani, Walt Bresette, John Gilgun, Terry Kupers, Gus Kaufman, Essex Hemphill, Michael Kimmel, John Gill and Andrew Wicker.

Thanks also to John Gill, Adam Rostoker and Cal Gough for their editorial help. The anthology could not have been created but for the courage of the contributors. Most of the essays and poems are published here for the first time.

I want to thank John and Elaine Goldman Gill and the staff of the Crossing Press for their support and patience, and Shelly Robbins who typed a large part of the manuscript. I also want to thank Felice Picano, who introduced me to Raphael Kadushin, editor at the University of Wisconsin Press, and to Raphael and his staff for their work on the second edition of this book.

Finally, I would like to thank my friends and mentors, particularly Naunie Batchelder and Earl Brown, who offered encouragement during the difficult times that interrupted the work on this book.

BOYHOOD,
GROWING UP MALE

INTRODUCTION
Reclaiming Boyhood and Saving Our Own Lives

"What's past is prologue."
—Shakespeare, *The Tempest*

Central to three of the world's major religions—Islam, Judaism and Christianity—is the story of the Adekah, Abraham's near-sacrifice of his son Isaac. Acting on a vision from God, in a test of his faith, Abraham prepares to sacrifice his precious son. Isaac submits to his father's will but is saved at the last minute by the command of an angel sent by God.

What is celebrated through the centuries is neither the role of the son nor the role of the angel, but the faith of Abraham. The sacrifice of sons by fathers for king, country or creed continues to this day. Except in this century, the sacrifice of sons in war has rarely been questioned. And while most "civilized" people embrace the ideal of peace, our history and mythology are still powerful forces. As Leonard Cohen wrote in his "Story of Isaac," "When it all comes down to dust/ I will help you if I must/I will kill you if I can."

In order to understand how this myth propels us toward destruction, it is important to return to the time in our lives when it was learned. This particular anthology focuses on men's experiences. Women's experiences are different in many ways. Girls are raised to "keep the home fires burning." Boys are raised to do battle. And preparation begins very early, as early as a boy's first toy gun or competitive game.

Myriam Miedzian explores the connection between violence and masculinity as it begins in boyhood in her well-documented, if somewhat homophobic study *Boys Will Be Boys*. A particularly relevant chapter is entitled "When the Toy Store Looks Like a Military Arsenal." According to Dr. Miedzian, toys, sports and mass media all reinforce violence in male children. Her research is easy to verify: visit a toy store, watch Saturday morning TV aimed at young audiences, or check out boys playing team sports. The message is clear: the road to manhood is fraught with endless initiations in violence.

Men in general have benefited from social movements that question the prevailing politics of gender (such as feminism and gay liberation) in that society has become less and less accepting of man's traditional role as good soldier. That men are as locked into roles as women are is a painful revelation. Understanding how men pay for their privileges is equally painful. Mary Robinson, the feminist president of the Irish Republic, is very clear on this issue. She states, "In a society where the rights and potential of women are constrained, no man can be truly free. He may have power, but he will not have freedom."

Trying to free ourselves from prescribed learning and early gender roles has given rise to what is referred to as "the men's movement." The men's movement is actually many movements. A small but spirited pro-feminist men's movement predates the more popularized mythopoetic or "wild man" groups by more than a decade. In most of the different versions of the men's movement, there is a strongly felt need to explore the origins of masculinity in order to transform it into something better.

Social and historical issues have been examined by numerous authorities, including Robert Brannon, Harry Brod, Michael Kimmel, Tom Mosmiller, Joseph Pleck, John Stoltenberg and Sally Roech Wagner. Sam Keen, John Lee and Terry Kupers have written about the psychological effects of traditional masculine roles. Shepherd Bliss, Robert Bly, James Hillman, Michael Meade, Robert Moore and Malidoma P. Somé have written and spoken about male archetypes, myths and symbols in search of the "deep masculine."

The desire to understand and change men for the better is implicit in all of these varied approaches. At a deeper level, the intent is to save men's lives, to stop the war against women and to give future generation of boys a chance to be free in a world where the sexes work as equals.

A crucial but understudied aspect of our new knowledge of gender is the study of how gender is explicitly and implicitly taught in childhood. The experiences of girls and boys are different. Poet Adrienne Rich asks, "Are you a daughter, are you a son? Strange trade-offs have long been made." This anthology seeks to examine some of the strange trade-offs made by boys in order to grow and survive into manhood.

Gender evolution is an essential aspect of the "deep masculine," of the social and psychological factors that have made us into the men we are. In his own life, each man echoes Wordsworth's observation, "The child is father to the man."

This book aims less at analysis and more at experience. Women and men are likely to read it differently. For women, I hope it offers understanding. For men, I hope it provides a stimulus for memory.

In compiling the anthology and approaching men for essays, I was surprised at how many men said they remembered little or nothing of their boyhood. Some were aware of a wall of fear that kept them separated from painful recollections. Others reported a haze that clouded over any clear sense of what it was like to be a little boy. Part of our "forgetting" has to do with how hard it still is for men at any stage of life to be vulnerable, even with themselves. Part of it is wrapped tightly in old macho conditioning that tells us not to admit loss. If we don't own our losses, we cannot grieve them. The inability to grieve necessitates defending a version of reality that lends itself to nostalgia on the one hand and abuse on the other. Historian C. John Sommerville in his *The Rise and Fall of Childhood* notes that adults who have not reckoned with the reality of their childhood experiences project them onto children. Children are seen then as objects to be idealized or exploited.

In recent popular psychology, there has been a great emphasis on what is termed "the inner child." This concept of the child is often portrayed in a pure light as the embodiment of innocence and love. Adults are generally seen as manipulative, negligent or abusive; the inner child is the victim.

It is not the intent of this book to portray boyhood in such a light. Perhaps the men who read it will be able to reconnect with the little boy who lives inside their psyches. That little boy is no simple cherub, but a complex being who struggles as much with the giants of the adult world as he does with his peers. Whether at home or in the world, whether experiencing wonder or terror, the boy is real, alive and acutely sensitive to psychological and social forces he rarely controls but often control him.

In this anthology, many different stories are collected from men of various races, ages and backgrounds. I commend my contributors for the courage they demonstrate in sharing their memories. I hope each man who reads this book will add to this body of experience. Each of our stories is important, not just for ourselves, but for our sense of shared intimacy with each other.

And there is something more. In *The Untouched Key: Tracing Childhood Trauma in Creativity and Destructiveness,* psychoanalyst Alice Miller speculates on how Isaac might rise up from the altar Abraham has set for his sacrifice. She says for the Isaac in each of us to rise, he/we must "love life more than obedience." This new Isaac, "with his question, with his awareness, with his refusal to let himself be killed, not only saves his own life but also saves his father from becoming the unthinking murderer of his child."

In moving back into the awesome terrain of boyhood, we can begin to allow the Isaac in each of us to loosen the bonds that tie us to the sacrifice. Mohandas K. Gandhi, writing on nonviolence, said, "The moment that the slave resolves that he will no longer be a slave, his fetters fall." Part of our resolve to no longer be a slave is to become conscious of ways we are one. This isn't easy, especially for those of us who are deluded in our choice of power over freedom. But if we can stay with the pain of this newfound consciousness and share our experience with other men and women who seek freedom instead of isolating ourselves, if we can find the patience that is required to cultivate understanding, we may hear calling from somewhere deep inside ourselves the voice of a boy whose love of life frees us from the cycles of fathers who murder their sons and sons too dutiful to save their own lives.

The anthology is divided into sections that speak to four major aspects of boyhood: *Getting Gendered, Being a Boy in the Family, Being a Boy in the World,* and *Boyhood and the Soul.* Short introductions to each section help the reader grasp the unifying elements. Many important aspects of boyhood experiences are not explored in depth or even mentioned. This book does not seek to be authoritative but rather indicative. Each section presents constellations of experiences, constellations that reveal the boyhood worlds that have shaped the men we are today.

This is *Boyhood*'s second edition. The reprint of this book attests to the continuing need to examine the roots of masculinity. Every effort was made to reprint the original in full. Finding all of the original contributors was a task for a private eye. All but three are back in these pages.

Atlanta, Georgia   FRANKLIN ABBOTT

GETTING GENDERED

Is it a boy or is it a girl? The second thing they always check after seeing if a newborn is alive is gender. It is significant in the study of gender to note that, in most cultures, males are more welcomed and celebrated than females. Feminist studies have shed light on what this does to women individually, in relationships and in societies. The effects of male supremacy on men have been studied less and conclusions are less clear. Also, significant variables such as ethnicity and sexual orientation in relation to gender are newly opened fields for inquiry and reflection. The play of gender against nature often evokes the absurd and the unjust. Paul Goodman and Ivan Illich have written extensively about how social needs for control oppose the needs of the young for growth and support. The argument of nature vs. nurture is played out by many authors writing about men. Are men natural aggressors who are socially propelled to learn competition in order to protect themselves?

The personal accounts that follow chronicle the ways in some men's lives in which gender is taught and learned.

By the Beautiful Sea

by Sy Safransky

Soon we'll be by the sea again.

Like pilgrims we come each year, my wife and her son and my daughters and I. It's a family tradition for our sometimes-family. Each summer, for a week, for seven days to which our coming gives a shape, we live together by the sea, giving to our oddly separate yet intertwined lives a shape. A family we are, here to have fun, before saying good-bye to the waves and the summer and each other: Jaime going back to his father in New Jersey; Mara and Sara going back to their mother in the mountains; Norma and I going back to an unencumbered life which full-time parents sometimes envy, but not as much as we envy theirs.

What is there to envy, though? We think we understand someone's life but we never understand; our joys and griefs can't be compared. Only from a distance, and through the haze of ignorance, do we judge and praise and condemn.

See us walking along the beach on a hazy morning, a family on vacation, Dad and Mom and the kids.

My arm is around Norma's waist; the curves of our bodies fit. The children are lithe and healthy-looking. They search for shells; they watch a gull skimming the waves; they're happy here.

We walk, I talk: about something I've just read or am worried about. I'm on vacation, but not from myself. Norma half listens, wondering why I tax my mind so, wishing I were more fully here with the sky and the sea. She bends to pick up a shell—dark, wet, near perfect—and hands it to me.

The children want to show me their shells, too. I look at each one of them, marveling at their strange beauty, with the waves breaking and roaring nearby and the water hissing around our feet. I think, for a moment, how important Norma and I and the children are to each other, yet, in this vast landscape, how insignificant; how loved we are and how lonely, family and speck. There's an old Hasidic saying that a man must have two pockets in which we can reach. In his right pocket, he must keep the words, "For my sake the world was created." In his left, "I am dust and ash."

There's another paradox for me in being at the sea, less cosmic but more compelling, spiraling like a conch shell from an event nearly forty years in my past. Like the sea, ever-changing and never-changing, I come back each year different but the same; the fear is the same, so old it seems a part of me, like my hands or my face. The paradox is that I love and hate the sea—that I'm drawn to it with a passion, but won't go in above my knees.

Silly, isn't it? It's like having a beautiful lover you won't talk to or kiss. It's like sleeping without dreaming. The thing is, I never learned to swim.

I nearly drowned as a child, or so it seemed to me. What really happened—since my father is dead now—will always be a mystery.

The family was on vacation, at a lake in the country surrounded by trees. In the middle was a raft, one of those old-fashioned, wooden, weather-beaten things. One day, my father hoisted me on his back and swam out to it with me.

He was a fat man but a strong swimmer; I loved the way he moved, the feel of him beneath me, the long, powerful strokes. At the age of four or five, I loved everything about him, though.

The raft, when we got there, was already crowded. He treaded water, his arm around me, while he and the other swimmers talked and joked.

Suddenly, he let go. It was unbelievable, like a dark door appearing out of nowhere, opening and then shutting behind me, leaving me in a room of water without ceiling, walls or floor. I was astonished, terrified. I started to sink. My thrashing brought me up like a buoy. I gasped for air; I started sinking again; I thrashed some more.

I don't know how long this went on, but I remember vividly the panic, the helplessness, the disbelief. What had happened? Did something distract him? How in the world could he have let go?

Hands reached out for me; to this day I don't know whose. Maybe they were my father's, lifting me out of the water, but they felt like a stranger's hands, comforting me, not sure where I belonged. By this time, I was crying hysterically. I heard my father's voice, and looked up, and he was holding me. Between sobs, I pleaded with him to take me back to shore.

I was still crying when we got there; my mother asked what was wrong. It was "nothing," he said. Someone had splashed me and I'd "panicked." I looked at him dumbfounded. "But Dad! You let go!" He shook his head. He said I was "making a big deal out of nothing," and told me to stop crying. Something sank in me then, swifter than my own body in the water, down to the bottom of my heart, where it settled like a stone.

I still don't fully understand what happened that day, either in the water or between us as father and son.

His story was implausible, less convincing than a fairy tale, but it was frightening to admit, even to myself, that he might be telling a lie. To be unable to trust him was as terrifying, in a way, as drowning. As children, we need to believe our parents; it's impossible for us to understand they're still struggling with childhood fears of their own.

The dilemma comes when we have to choose between them and ourselves—between their "truth" and our reality, their idea of what "love" is and our injured heart. Something we know, some feeling we have, *who we are,* isn't acceptable to them. The pain of that is enormous—for a small child, it's too great to live with. So it's buried. We build up a defense against it. We assume a false self that fits in with their beliefs.

For me, being afraid all these years of the *water* was safer than being afraid of my *father*, than acknowledging the pain of his betrayal, his unwillingness to be honest about a mistake.

How many of our fears are like this. How much pain there is in all of us, in the wounds we received as children from parents themselves too wounded to give us the love every child needs. We grow up. The wounds scab over. But life picks at the scabs; for me, it happens every year at the sea.

Sy Safransky is editor of The Sun, *a monthly magazine published in Chapel Hill, North Carolina. He was born in New York City in 1945 but these days goes there only in his dreams.*

My War Story: A Child's Trauma

by Shepherd Bliss

I was born in California at the end of World War II to a young soldier and his new bride—a farm girl/woman from Iowa and a Southern boy/gentleman from a prominent Kentucky military family. Whenever I get close to war a great pain emerges that goes back to my childhood. I have come to understand this pain as my war trauma.

War's shadow seems to have stalked me throughout my entire life cycle. As the son of a career soldier, I spent my childhood on military bases, always on alert for war. As a teenager, I went into the U.S. Army during the Vietnam War, though I never saw combat. As a young adult, I lived in Chile during the military coup which destroyed its democratic government and killed many, including some of my friends. During my mid-life, the U.S. invaded Panama, where I spent part of my childhood, then Iraq, brutally killing hundreds of thousands and wounding others. For nearly fifty years now, from the time of my birth, war and the warrior's way have been defining factors in my life.

Pounded by war and the preparation for war, my soul has been a casualty. I feel like a war casualty. No bullet penetrated my skin, but my soul was damaged. War's violence reaches far beyond combatants, touching the sons and daughters of the military and many others. War's impact is deep and long-reaching. Those killed and wounded, soldiers who fight, their families and those who witness war in person or on television are all casualties.

The Persian Gulf war re-stimulated my war trauma, as I watched pictures of children devastated by war, and remembered my childhood on military bases. Upon hearing of the bombing of Iraq, I doubled up in pain. A deep, uncontrollable sound of grief leapt from my psyche. I began shaking. I was suffering war trauma. Though physically safe from the war zone thousands of miles away, I felt a shock to my body. I am a war survivor and experience flashbacks to earlier traumas. Even from a distance the impact of war upon a child can be enduring. I still jump at loud sounds and am always on alert for a potential "enemy." It used to be called "shell shock," a defensive mechanism which numbs the psyche so it can survive devastation. I hold within me lots of unfelt experience. That is to say, things happened, but I did not fully feel them. One might consider this a form of post-traumatic stress.

This is my war story. I tell it to illuminate war's consequences for families and to free myself from continuing to sit upon these feelings alone. I write to heal war trauma through storytelling. For five years now I have met weekly with the same group of guys to tell our stories. We have come to know each other well and care for each other. We call ourselves the Sons of Orpheus, after the Greek father of music and poetry who taught followers to take no lives and eat no meat. Orpheus was an ancient pacifist and vegetarian. On some nights in "The Sons," the room is playful, humorous and upbeat. On other nights, it is incredibly sad. Hearing other men's stories can help transform feelings of isolation into intimacy. As I witness other men struggling with their pain, I am brought into contact with my own and with our common ground as men. Within the context provided by the mythopoetic men's movement, more of my story is able to emerge, thus healing my trauma.

During my nearly fifty years I have spent almost as much time inside the military—during those crucial years of infancy, childhood, adolescence and early adulthood—as I have outside as a civilian. The military and civilian worlds are as different as Earth and Mars. I left the U.S. Army in my twenties and stepped away from my family military legacy, which remains within me. De-militarizing my life has been a long and still-continuing process. Some characteristics of the military remain, including secrecy, stoicism, denial and the compulsion to control.

My father, away on war maneuvers, was not present at my birth. My father was absent! I still feel pain, rage and sadness at his initial absence. The women were there—my mother, her sister, and my father's mother—but not my dad. At that crucial moment he was gone. His absence continued during my infancy, boyhood and adolescence. My dad spent time away from the family, sometimes overseas. When he was home, he was emotionally distant. I never remember him touching me, except in anger. No playing ball or taking me fishing. I followed his model by taking off as soon as I could. I have been away from home now for over thirty years. Writing this is a form of homecoming; it has not been easy to revisit these memories and feelings, even from the safe vantage of mid-life.

I do not remember much from my early years. Feelings I do have from that time are not pleasant. I was a "military brat." Our lives were ordered, disciplined, contained, regimented; not spontaneous. Meal times were not fun: "Please pass the butter, sir." Stiff-backed, stiff-necked, with my little fingers I lifted the utensils correctly to my mouth, never my head to the plate. Or else! No talking was the rule. One of the rules. There were many rules. Ours was a no-talk family, then and now. But the sounds that surrounded us were loud—airplanes, men marching, and my dad yelling at us, yelling at us, yelling at us. I still hear his voice, not only in my head. I still feel him in my body today, bending over to receive his belt on my bottom. My father is thousands of miles away now, and has been for thirty-five years, since I was old enough to leave. Today he is an old, crippled, powerless man. But when I hear loud sounds, like yesterday a woman yelling at her dog, I look around to see if anyone will hurt me.

I was born Walter Shepherd Bliss III. As the third, I was expected to continue the military dynasty. But I fooled them. When I left the U.S. Army in my early twenties, my first act as a man, I dropped the name Walter which means "warrior." I turned away from my father's military legacy. Shepherd is a family name on my maternal side. I am proud to be called by my great-grandmother's name. In my thirties, I even threatened to drop my father's last name and become a single-named person. The things we do to our parents to get back at them! I wrote a rough letter to my father denouncing him and his names. But I never followed through on dropping the last name. As my father moves about in a wheelchair from a stroke, near Strategic Air Command headquarters in Omaha, I even consider regaining Walter, which I recently discovered also means "woodsman." I would rather be a woodsman than a warrior.

I never knew Walter Shepherd Bliss, Sr. Nor did my father. My grandmother contended that her husband abandoned them when my father was an infant—going to the Indianapolis 500 race and never returning. That was her story. We all thought my grandfather must be dead. In my thirties he wrote to my father. My dad refused to answer his dad. "I'm too old to start having a father." I answered, instead, "I bear your name and would like to get to know you."

My grandfather told a different story regarding the family separation. He did go to the races, but returned on schedule. My grandfather claimed his wife abducted their son. He looked for them, unsuccessfully. He sent me many letters which he had written through the decades to officials trying to locate his first-born son, whom he finally found only shortly before he was to die. He never saw his son, except as an infant. According to his other children, my grandfather longed for decades to reconnect to the son who bore his name. The man who originated my name then married his high school sweetheart; they stayed together and raised a good family. Years later my father admitted, "Not answering my father's letter was the biggest mistake of my life."

So we have two distinct stories. Which is true? Whom to believe? There was a split. Was only one side to blame?

I am a product of that split. My father was raised without his father at home; he never learned how to father. He followed the model he did have, which was to be absent. My father was also born during a war—at the end of World War I. My grandfather served in that war, making him absent from my father's birth. The legacy continues: son of a soldier, son of a soldier, son of a soldier. It goes back many generations, including various generals and Fort Bliss, Texas. I broke that legacy by not providing the U.S. military a son to send to war.

I sustained many losses as a boy, as does any child. My first major loss was being severed forever from a sensitive part of my boy's body—my foreskin removed by the brutal circumcision ritual. Most boys are routinely wounded in their first days of life by a knife. This mutilation is an initiation into the warrior cult, which predates its medical and religious meanings. Fortunately, this barbaric practice is no longer common in most parts of the world and is diminishing considerably in the United States. This wounding, early in boys' lives and to such a sensitive part of the body, begins the wounding of our boys into manhood. We would benefit from finding better ways to treat our boys and initiate them into manhood than circumcision's mutilation.

I was raised on military bases, which are always on alert for attack. Our household was always preparing for war. Loud sirens and uniformed men scrambling around interrupted us at all hours of the day. I did not get an adequate chance to rest and relax. Loud airplane sounds startled me by day and awakened me at night. To return home was like entering a prison—guards at the gate, checking our IDs. My father would raise his hand to his forehead in a strong gesture, which other uniformed men would repeat. "Saluting" is the term I later learned to describe this strange behavior. My father made us salute him, since he was in charge. "This is my house. As long as you are under my roof, you will do as I say." I got out as soon as I could. To be the first born carried certain expectations of accomplishment. I was expected to rule, as my father did. It is hard to run a family as if it were a military squad—children and soldiers being two different kinds of creatures—but my father tried. I still rebel against any authority which attempts such domination.

Feelings were considered a threat to national security in my family, not something to be expressed. Perhaps the Russians or other "communists" would overhear them and use them against us to get classified secrets. My feelings were classified as secrets, not to be shared. So I did a lot of stuffing, becoming quite stoic. Even after years of deep bodywork, I still have a stiff "military neck" and military bearing in my body. Secrecy and fear dominated our family. An "enemy" always lurked around the corner. Only later did I discover that not all families are like this, though many military families are. I remember visiting my aunt's family. They had five kids, like us. But they had regular family meetings. And the kids got to speak. What a shock! The children were asked how they felt and what they thought. In the Bliss family we were told how to feel and what to think. That early image of family democracy at my aunt's house has stuck with me.

We moved every three years during my childhood. There were times, like right before my elementary school graduation, when we left with a few days notice. I missed that ceremony and to this day have difficulties with closure and good-byes. My sister was elected to the homecoming queen's court, but we had to move before she could be honored; that trauma damaged her. Among the legacies of my military heritage is a lack of a sense of place. I was born in California and left the state within weeks. I never learned a particular place well. I cannot remember a particular tree or hill with which I had a relationship. I communicate with no one from my elementary, high school or college years. I know no one outside my family who knew me then. I am in touch with only one person from my years of graduate studies. My past is not well-anchored in specific places, persons or things. Thinking about these realities I feel lonely, isolated, and out of touch with myself and others.

I continued the compulsion to move—to fly off. At my twenty-fifth high school reunion I won an award for having lived in the most places since graduation. I have met many people in my life; I have stayed with few. My personality is constructed around being able to detach and leave, one foot out the door, even when attaching and staying would be healthier. Making human relations that last is hard for me. I expect the other to leave, or I will leave. So I am good at starting up in order to survive, and less effective at remaining. Who gets to leave first? I am tired of starting up, again and again.

Did you see the movie or read the book *The Great Santini*? Pat Conroy accurately described our family—right down to the five children and the 1955 Chevy station wagon. Like the teenager in the story, the only way to get my father off my back was to beat him up. I finally grew big enough and fought back, like millions of other military brats have done. To understand how the military affects children and families, read Conroy's powerful novel, or Mary Wertsch's excellent non-fiction piece, *Military Brats*, subtitled "Legacies of Childhood Inside the Fortress." I thank Wertsch for her excellent account and for stimulating my own mid-life re-evaluation of a military childhood.

I also want to echo Conroy in his introduction to Wertsch's book: "We moved every year, preparing for that existential moment ('this is no drill, son') when my violent father would take to the air against enemies more fierce than his wife or children. I grew up thinking my father would one day kill me." Conroy feels like a brother when he writes, "I am accustomed to order, to a chain of command, to a list of rules . . . and everyone in my world must be on time. Being late was unimaginable."

In contrast to this military heritage, I fortunately had an uncle and aunt with whom I lived one summer as a teenager. Their Iowa farm presented a different option—a rooted life. I recall a clear feeling of connection and relationship in my Uncle Dale and Aunt Elva. Their farm was a great place to run after chickens, throw rotten eggs into the creek, watch animals being born and dying, drive tractors in the fields, and stack hay. These were my best childhood memories, on which I have been able to build my recovery from war trauma. Dale and Elva were the first humans I ever saw cuddle on the sofa. They actually touched each other—affectionately rather than angrily. No electricity yet, so no TV. Without TV, they were left to themselves. They did quite well, actively telling stories at night, rather than passively absorbing television. They were both tall—he white-haired and she jet black. He must have weighed 300 pounds, whereas she was slightly over 100 pounds, or so it seemed when I was a little boy. But they fit together well.

As I move these days from the urban San Francisco Bay Area to rural Sonoma County in northern California, positive memories of living with my aunt and uncle emerge. When I open my inner eye, I see Dale and Elva cuddling. They both died last year, within months of each other, after sixty years of marriage. Dale, my mother's brother, was the father I wanted. We usually did not get the father we want. Nor do fathers usually get the sons they would choose. Some of Dale's children were not too happy with him. I was. Instead of trading baseball cards, could we trade fathers?

I did become a man, in spite of the obstacles in my childhood and the lack of initiation and guidance in adolescence. I even entered the military myself. As I work on my war trauma, my yearning for a partner increases. Now I feel more ready for a committed relationship. War and the warrior's way stunted my growth as a man able to love and surrender to another. My fear has been that the other would leave. My manhood has been constructed around war and the military and their peculiar ways of being.

My life's work opposes a rigid military establishment, though I support appropriate national defense. The military also made some positive contributions to my life. From the military I learned discipline, teamwork, a sense of mission, loyalty to something beyond the self and a capacity to get things done. I advocate a "Century of Peace" to follow what historians describe as our "Century of Total War." The next war, given our advanced weapons, could be the last war, the end of human habitation on this planet.

The warrior ethic has damaged us. As we move into the twenty-first century we need to mature beyond war and warriors. I disagree with those men's movement writers and activists who speak so highly of the warrior. I appreciate some of his traits—like courage, teamwork, loyalty—but the archetype itself is bankrupt at this point in history. We surely need guardians, boundary-setters, husbandmen, and citizens. If we are to survive on this planet, so threatened by war and warriors, we must get beyond the obsolete archetype of the warrior and value images such as the peacemaker, the partner, and the husbandman who cares for the earth and animals. Though the U.S. is currently not at war, preparations continue. The weapon designers and manufacturers silently continue their deadly work and the military continues to try out their new toys, as the U.S. did in the Iraq massacre.

Our 1990s version of war—America across the seas—was in the Persian Gulf. Not quite as long as other wars, it lasted months for some

500,000 men and women. Their children were all affected by their absences and will grow up being what we might consider "war casualties." They will grow up without the presence of their fathers or mothers at critical times in their growth. My son did not fight in that war because I remain childless. I successfully broke the Bliss legacy, but at considerable personal cost.

Children deserve the positive attention of their parents at home, rather than overseas at war. Children flourish with the touch, gaze, support, and comfort of adults. They are diminished by their absence. I am a child of trauma, a specific kind of trauma—military trauma, war trauma. Healing the wounds of war and the warrior's way is possible, once we identify them as part of our problem. Having now identified my trauma specifically, I can work on recovering from it. Writing this essay is a form of healing for me—breaking the silence and recalling memories, even painful ones.

Walter Shepherd Bliss III was born in California during World War II on federal property and was transferred within weeks, initiating a lifelong pattern of constantly moving. He left the U.S. Army during Vietnam, dropping his first name, which means "warrior." Shepherd directs The Kokopelli Traveling Lodge, which tours the U.S., Canada and Europe offering storytelling, drumming, poetry and ceremonial arts at gatherings.

Arms and the Boy

by John Gilgun

I was six years old on December 7, 1941. I remember that Sunday and
a nightmare I had shortly after. In the nightmare, a curtain is blowing
into our parlor from an open window. The cathedral radio with its
Gothic front—from which had issued the news about the bombing of
Pearl Harbor—is directly in front of the tossing curtains. Through the
open window I can perceive nothing but a terrifying blackness. On the
evening of December 7th, two of my mother's brothers, Kenneth and
Bob, came by in their uniforms. They were already in the reserves and
would be called up first. My mother's nickname for Kenneth, her
favorite brother, was "Army," and I think she envied him. She herself
would have liked to go to war. She really wanted to be a man. But after
they left, she went into the kitchen and cried. I took the Sunday paper
in to her—it was the Hearst "Boston American"—and said, "Don't cry.
See! It says here the war is over and we won it!" I pointed to the
headlines. But at the age of six, I could not read.

It was a movie war and I didn't like war movies. Inevitably,
however, I found myself sitting through them. I always left the theater
upset and fearful. I remember one about submarines in which Tyrone
Power drowned in flaming oil. After being treated to an hour of bucolic
American boyhood in Waterloo, Iowa—the Tom Sawyer/Norman
Rockwell version of American boyhood the movies were promoting in
the forties—I saw all five of the Fighting Sullivans blown up in their
ship in the Pacific. They drowned. For me, the reality was their
collective death. The final sixty seconds in which they are shown
walking through the clouds toward heaven, with the youngest one
yelling, "Hey! Wait for me!" did not mitigate the horror of their
extinction. But you were not supposed to feel the way I felt. It meant
you were a sissy. Well, I really was a sissy. I couldn't hide it. I hated
killing. I hated war. I hated fighting. I hated violence. It meant there was
something wrong with me. I didn't play with guns. I played with dolls.

I remember a film about the French Resistance. A woman who is
a nurse in occupied France has a brother in the Resistance. A German
general comes to her for treatment and she must give him a shot. She

can put poison in the hypodermic needle and kill the man, but she has scruples. Just before she must make her decision, a truck pulls up in the street below. A German pulls a curtain away from the rear of the truck revealing the woman's brother, strung up from the roof of the truck. They have captured him and tortured him. The reality of this for me was the pain the man was suffering and I hated the film. The following day when my cousin Freddie told me how much he had enjoyed this film, I just stared at him. What had there been to like? Well, it was mean and bloody and cruel, he told me, which made it good.

In those days, you shared tables in restaurants with soldiers, sailors and marines. It was just something you did to show you approved of them. These men were "our boys" and they were protecting us. My mother's sister took me to a movie in which some men are blown up in a bunker on a Pacific island. One of the men—it was probably William Bendix, who turned up in these films for comic relief and ethnic identification—had a dog which had had puppies. As the bunker flew apart, I could hear the puppies yelping. They had been blown up, also. I was horrified. My aunt took me across the street to Thompson's Spa were we sat at a table with two sailors. One asked, "Are you going to join the navy when you grow up?" I replied with an adamant "No!" "Ah, then you'll probably join the army." "No!" "How about the Marines?" "No! Never! Nothing!" They laughed nervously. My aunt was furious. She took me out onto the sidewalk, shook me up and down and shouted, "Don't you ever say anything like that again!" But I wasn't about to get involved in anything where men blew up puppies. It seemed even worse than men blowing up other men. "Are you going to blow up other men when you grow up?" "No! Never!" What was wrong with me anyway? Why couldn't I learn to act like the other boys?

John Gilgun was born in 1935 and ceased to be a "boy" about 1950. He was born in Malden, Massachusetts to an Irish-Catholic working class family. His mother was a waitress and his father delivered milk. He was educated in the public schools. He is now a tenured full professor at Missouri Western State College in St. Joseph, Missouri, where he has been since 1972. He is the author of four books, including Music I Never Dreamed Of *(Amethyst, 1989),* The Dooley Poems *(Robin Price, 1991), and* From the Inside Out *(Three Phase, 1991).*

Reflections on a Biafran Boyhood

by Ike Anyanike

It was January, 1964, a Saturday, and I had just celebrated my fourth birthday three months ago. Mum was busy dressing up the two-room apartment we occupied in a large block of about thirty other apartments. She would do the beds in the newest bed linens, scrub the nooks and crannies of the rooms, fold all items of clothing strewn around, wash all utensils and leave the rooms sparkling. When done, she washed my younger brother and me, dressed us in the best of our clothing and took time to tend to her pregnant self. She delivered a few days later. Meanwhile, Dad was reveling in banter with his friends, after having cleared up the drains and cut the grass around the block. When all seemed set, a kind of quietude swept the entire block and all now talked in hushed voices. Mum momentarily broke the silence, telling us to rehearse for the last time the greeting that we were expected to practice soon, while Dad was at the door awaiting the visitors.

Soon Dad would stamp his feet in attention, barking out his name, announcing how many people were in his household and informing the strangers that he was ready for inspection. Everything he said ended in "Sir," and all his replies to the visitors were "Yes, Sir," executed in a very sharp tone that reflected his alertness.

After the exchanges at the door, the visitors in the dark uniforms I had recognized as the officers' uniforms of the police force would saunter into the apartment, inspecting, upturning, rummaging into everything Mum had so neatly packaged. They would also turn us around to see if we were primly dressed. They often felt satisfied and instantly commended Mum for being a very good housekeeper. On reflection, I now know that such commendation encouraged Dad to think that Mum could not fit into any other role than being a good mother, perfect wife and housekeeper.

I later came to enjoy this routine, as I later understood it to be a monthly inspection of the barracks to ensure that the policemen kept a minimum standard of hygiene and cleanliness. We also learned that those with good grades got regular promotion, so the entire household worked hard to see that Dad retained a track record that would ensure him steady promotion and us a higher standard of living. Living in the sheltered life of Falomo Police Barracks, Lagos, my vision of the world became very predictable. It was my belief that everything had its own version of inspection. Again, I thought it was the lot of the adults to say how things went. It was especially the lot of the women to look into the finer details of the ordered world.

We saw Dad off for work and greeted him with the usual singsong on return. While all other needs were catered to by Mum, Dad would occasionally take us on a walk close to the Atlantic Ocean inland shores, positioning us right on the brink of the ocean. Talk about dangerous excitements! The sense of orderliness and responsibility I thought intrinsic in every adult was shattered when one evening Eze, the latest addition to the family barely a year old, picked up a razor blade to manicure himself in the full glare of an Auntie who had come to live with us. Eze chopped off much of his finger. I watched in horror as he screamed to high heavens and blood freely flowed. I dashed out to fetch Mummy. Mum couldn't understand why an adult could sadistically watch this and not intervene. She didn't flinch in telling the Auntie off, but, surprisingly, the Auntie had a defense. She didn't know what was going on, and at any rate, it was not her responsibility. This encounter wised me up for a lot of issues I was to face later in life. I started to appreciate that the world went beyond Falomo Barracks, that every unassailable argument is debatable, and that life is a bundle of contradictions. With this knowledge firmly in place, I gave vent to the contradictions within me. I thought I should go out and explore the world, but was not ready to be ruled by the world. Dad probably enjoyed doing the drains and Mum doing the beds, but I enjoyed both. Neither Mum nor Dad should tell me which to do. Now, exploring, I happened upon many children. But being a latecomer, I only sat and watched while the "wiser" children called the shots.

We only played the games they chose. Their assertiveness manifestly contrasted with my gentility. They obviously knew I was not docile for the adults thought I was smart and caring—qualities they would want in their own children. This provoked the envy of the boys, and one boy, Innocent, decided to teach me a lesson. He engaged me in a game but cheated. I protested. He decided to settle the score by bullying me but was surprised when I put up a good fight. That settled their myopic view of my sensitive disposition. Without ceremony, I was initiated into the clique of boys. I could never imagine that at that age we could reason and make decisions for ourselves. So far, Mum or Dad had sanctioned all I did. This encompassed everything from stepping out of our home to leaving the block and entering other people's homes. What I dared not do was eat outside. Since my peers did all these without obtaining permission, I thought it was a harmless choice.

Our adventures started happening further afield. The other boys and I made forays further into Ikoyi, the upper-class settlement, to crab and fish in the backwaters of the swamps. Ikoyi is set at the precipice of the Atlantic Ocean, so it was no wonder that there was so much water around and within its grounds. While we lived in a barracks containing thousands of people, I could not reconcile the fact that those in Ikoyi lived in houses as large as the entire barracks yet containing a single family each. Peeping through the flower hedges into any of these compounds, whose occupants were mostly white, I saw lush gardens and bright flowers with a kind of quietude I only felt in dreams. I didn't know what the occupants did, but I thought my father's occupation was more relevant to the society. However, I didn't wish to trade places with the people of Ikoyi, for life there was more artificial. I couldn't imagine a life where the children did not come into the street to play, where you wouldn't hear the cars whiz past, where the children wore stockings and shoes even when they were home. In fact, a place where there were no entirely separate children's groups. All the children that came out from there were usually chaperoned by their parents or some adult maid.

Drifting with my peers, we happened into the room of a policeman in another block. Apparently he was a good friend of my friends. As we were so young, I couldn't make out whose friend in particular he was. While we were there, he busied himself with other matters while we chatted away in our own world. He would later buy us a drink from the Cola stable. This apparently was the delight of dropping by his place. Entertainment then was a special affair either at home or outside it. You hoped for lavish entertainment at home during your birthdays or after a good performance in school. Some of the liberal fathers like mine made sure that our Sundays included entertainment. So, as we all knew this man was generous with entertainment irrespective of the occasion or day of the week, we made it a general routine to stop there. Soon enough, he began taking special interest in me. He would buy two packets of biscuits, share the contents of one among all the boys and then give me one full packet. To ensure the other boys did not get envious, he invited me into his inner room. On two occasions he fiddled with my body generally. I excused it as a sign of his fondness for me.

It didn't hold any other meaning and I enjoyed it. On those two occasions, he exhorted me not to tell anybody and I assumed he was referring to the unequal share of my biscuits. But how could I not let the other boys know that I was better than them? I would blab as soon as we left the house, and the looks on the boys' faces often massaged my ego. They, too, could not understand why I, who had just gotten to know their friend, got preferential treatment. They decided to cut my unfair advantage. Already knowing how strict my parents could be with some rules, they decided to tell Mum that I always ate in people's houses. They particularized the fact that I ate and drank each time we visited the policeman even when they, the good boys, often said "no" when invited. That earned me a ban from going to the man's house. On the one occasion I tried to break the ban, our house help came to fetch me from the man's house and Dad gave me a beating that bruised my body all over. I attributed the beating to the man and never visited him again. I didn't, however, make any correlations between his amorous advances and my calling it quits with him. I enjoyed the warmth, and craved it, but thought I could have been doing the wrong thing when it was severed.

Relishing the more organized adventures within the barracks and the occasional forays into deeper Ikoyi, I could not think of joining in the rough and mad boisterousness that characterized my infant/ primary school. St. George's Boys School, Falomo, was a boys school, though we had our sister school within the same compound. I did not really think about the logic of the segregation. I simply came to believe that it was the usual way of doing things. Our boys were rough. During recess, they had all kinds of dangerous adventures—climbing very tall trees, scaling walls and fences, running about aimlessly and shouting at the top of their voices. I could join in any of these things but was hard put to enjoy them.

Once more, I put on my garb of a sheltered life and watched what was considered normal life pass me by. This was mistaken for weakness by Toyin, a boy in my class, who stole my rain cape. I gave Toyin a hot chase. All the boys applauded as we engaged each other in a marathon chase around the school compound. Toyin, being very daring, dashed onto the highway and made his way home. I ran straight to his home after school hours. He denied taking my cape, of course, and I couldn't face the interrogation of his parents. The incident made me shed some of my gentle, "home-grown lad" demeanor. However, I still thought it was better to remain the good boy no matter the odds, and to fight occasionally when unbearably provoked. Little did I know that my wide interests both at home and at school were preparing me for a bigger role.

On a fine mid-morning Mum went into labor at home. I was barely seven years old and the oldest person at home. It being her fourth childbirth, Mum was familiar with what needed to be done. I waited on her, assembling whatever she instructed. I was filled with excitement and fear, as I didn't know what role was expected of me at the appointed hour. Again, Mum was determined to do everything herself and I wondered if she could cope. She had always traveled out for her previous deliveries. To my relief she sent me to call Mrs. Eneh, her friend. In a jiffy I was back. Mrs. Eneh had seen the urgency written all over me. With the emergency midwife around, I hung out in the sitting room awaiting instructions from the inner room. Soon my first sister arrived in this world. I was thrilled to be part of it all. Dad was phoned at work and he raced back and was delighted to show off his latest offspring while entertaining visitors. Meanwhile, Mum and I were busy doing the chores, and I kept on secretly wondering about the contribution of Dad to the whole process. He was nice to us, no doubt, and made sure we had all we wanted, but why didn't he join in chores other than polishing his boots and belts and shining his buttons with Brasso? Later I was to realize this was the nature of a patriarchal society.

Earlier in 1966, the first Nigerian military coup had occurred. To prosecute the war that eventually followed in 1967, all adult males of the civilian population were enlisted in the army. We, the younger ones, learned war drills, diving for cover and holing up in bunkers. Everybody was involved. Dad naturally continued in the police force, but this time for our new nation. Though we retreated to our village, Dad's duties kept him away in the administrative divisions of the constituent parts of Biafra.

As the war progressed, the Nigerians had to wage an economic blockade. Hunger bit everyone and structural economic adjustments had to be made. It was at this point that all despicable rodents, reptiles and mushrooms crept up to the dining table. There was indeed an overhauled nutritional agenda. Mum started trading. She was a bit relieved of the drudgery of housework, which took about sixteen hours of her day. However, as the eldest child, not "lucky" enough to have an immediate or grown sister, I inherited the full weight of the chores, which included cooking, fetching water from distant streams, hewing firewood, fetching livestock fodder and taking full care of the younger ones. Indeed I was transformed into a "mother and housekeeper." Other boys did similar jobs but they complained often that they didn't enjoy it and thought they were women's jobs. They would rather go hunting and fishing. Mum didn't consider the jobs feminine. Neither did other elders in the village. The joy and precision with which I did my jobs endeared me to the villagers. Everybody wanted their sons to be like me, while most hoped I would marry their daughter. I was used as an index in most homes and the other boys started feeling uncomfortable with me. When we met at the stream, they would make jokes and cajole me. Nobody, however, laid a hand on me. They ended up branding my work habit as that of a "lady." This, however, did not agree with my makeup, as I was muscular and not particularly effeminate. I fought the labels. The boys eventually dropped the names and became friendly.

As I hardly acknowledged any gender differences, I played any roles that came to mind in anything I did. I switched from one stereotyped role to the other but never attempted or thought anything of sex during those years. For me, sex was an adult affair and even at that, was sinful. Religion and tradition curtailed such thoughts. We generally termed sex *ife alulu ani*—an abomination. I publicly broke the gender barrier when one day at the village school the entire school erupted in a traditional song in a wide circle. It was the young maidens' song in praise of manhood. All the pupils were dared to dance. Anybody who opted to would get into the center and dance solo to the delight of the entire school. Girls were expected to do that, as the boys would feel ashamed to show the subtle side of them in public. Our traditional dances often exuded grace and delicate, complex footwork. I wanted to dance and I waited, debating within me how my action might be interpreted, for nobody took the challenge. I gingerly danced to the center of the circle and danced my heart out. What I took for fun turned into a celebrity affair. People offered me money, hugged me and poured on their encomiums. The whole idea was ironic. Here were people who would not engage in an activity lest they be seen as weaklings, yet they basked in the honors another boy brought them. The boys started teasing the girls, reminding them that they, the boys, were better dancers.

My interest in home chores brought me closer to the adults, especially women who saw my efforts as sympathetic. They would now confide in me and that was how I first learned the story of procreation.

After I returned home from fetching livestock fodder, my young aunt with her female friend did not mind my eavesdropping on their discussions. When I asked specific questions, they gladly told me how sperm was produced and how women underwent menstruation. Since I was warned not to tell anybody what they had told me, it fortified my belief that issues regarding sex were abominable. I never raised the question again, nor did I show any sexual interest in anyone, boy or girl.

At this stage, I was swinging from the world of adults to that of my peers. I enjoyed the confidence and respect of both and did have the good sense to note that I was changing from a child into an adult. This also meant fortifying my sense of responsibility and fashioning new forms of identity with the adult world with its consequent acquisition of responsibilities. I began to appreciate that the war was not just a holiday that warranted our returning to our roots, but a period of some kind of struggle. For me, all I knew of the war was from the songs and poetry that were composed on a daily basis, and, of course, the regular sighting of warplanes in the sky and the sound of exploding ammunition. In hindsight, there couldn't have been any other literary art form but conscious resistance and struggle, with some propaganda thrown in. This made a serious impression on us children, coupled with the fact that anybody who was man enough had gone to the battlefield. The women and children stayed home and managed the bout of hunger and disease that became second nature. But this population did not become idle villagers and nurses of the sick. The women quickly took over the economic wheels of the young republic and also took charge of governance at home, while a few provided direct support services in the war zone. The intriguing aspect of the women's contribution was the combination of economic forte and military intelligence. They traded far into the enemy zone and obtained very useful information. As the enemies (vandals, as they were called) noted this, they resorted to raping and taking the women captives. Then boys of my age took over. Wandering into enemy lines pretending to be orphaned by the war, the soldiers took them into their confidence and even encouraged them to hawk cigarettes. These boys stealthily passed whatever information they gathered through the established safe paths or chains. This was another test for me to prove my manhood. You were really a "lady" if you did not join the Boys Company, as the group was officially known, even though our ages ranged from seven to twelve. Fired by patriotism and zeal to prove my "masculinity" once again, I mounted pressure on

Mum to allow me to enlist. Mum, however, thought that Dad, who was already in the battlefield, and Uncle, who at the time I didn't know had been killed, were enough sacrifices for one family. To wander far from home was a very difficult step, as one might meet death. Staying at home, therefore, meant more taunting for my perceived unmanliness. If I thought I was a "man," then I should be in the battlefield, not being the good darling boy of the community, even though I was just nine years old. I thought the analogy unfair and justified my not joining the army on the grounds earlier proffered by Mum. But I never missed out in the literalization of the struggle. We often composed songs and anecdotes from whatever information gathered from the rumor mill or the official Biafran Radio. No sooner had my increasing zeal for a taste of the adventure mounted when the war ended and the Nigerian Head of State declared a truce by proclaiming the now famous cliché, "No Victor, No Vanquished."

Growing up was really a kaleidoscope, a window that opened into the real world. I recall the overbearing call to masculinity on every boy. Roles were and still are confused with nature. I have always had problems with this and didn't waste time challenging the baseless confusion. I have now come to interpret father's attitude and jealous attachment to his masculinity as an institutionalized phenomenon. He probably was acting not because he perceived mother as a machine, but because he thought things had to be that way. But then why didn't he challenge it? This also calls to question why Mum did not reject that position. These basic contradictions now form a resource compendium for my activism in the area of women's liberation.

My childhood association with women revealed that there is no work or chore done with genital organs or breasts, areas where women are distinctly different from men, and since this is so, why the gender differentiation of roles? This inherent gender neutrality of roles makes it imperative that one fight to address the injustice that has perpetually put women in "their" place. If I had had an elder sister or even a not too much younger sister, I should have been shielded from doing all the childhood "feminine" chores, thereby stunting my development as a complete human being.

My mother was seen and praised as a good mother, perfect wife and homemaker, yet her ambitions to fulfill her life wishes were probably thwarted because the men couldn't see what else she needed or lacked. After all, she had delivered five sons to her husband. Her husband was pleased with her. Meanwhile, she inherited no property from her "maiden" home because she was meant for another man's family. In that man's family, that is ours now, she expects nothing unless it is purchased by her. "Luckily" she has male children who would inherit land and other real property. To think that this oppressive cycle awaits my sister and all women betrays my childhood experiences if I don't put up a fight.

Ike Anyanike was born in 1959 in Lagos, Nigeria, and lived through the Nigeria-Biafra war of 1967–1970. He later became an attorney actively involved in human rights issues.

Wrestling

by Eric Kupers

"O.K., Eric, we want you to wrestle now. You always watch and I think you should have to do it, too."

I froze. Me? I had never wrestled before. The idea also shocked everyone in the room. I was the nicest kid most of them knew. Aggression and me didn't seem to mix. Very soon, however, their interest pushed them past their surprise and they were enticing me out of the corner.

"C'mon, Eric, don't worry. We'll help you if you need it," the oldest boy assured me. So I wouldn't have to do it by myself? That did make it a little less terrifying, and part of me even rose to meet the challenge. After all, I was already five years old; it was about time for me to act it and prove that I too have strength, agility, and inconsiderate toughness. But still, I could get really hurt, maybe killed, or embarrassed, and I think I would rather live as a nice wimp than take such a risk. So my decision was, no, I would not wrestle.

"Eric, you wrestle with Marco," the oldest boy ordered. I panicked. It was looking like I didn't have the choice I thought I did. But wrestling with Marco seemed like the best way to go if I had to do it with someone. Me against him would mean everyone rooting for me. No one would be mad at me if I hurt him and I was sure everyone would help me.

Marco was the unofficial scapegoat for our after-school group. He was weird-looking, wore glasses, was fat and hyper, did gross things, talked a lot of Spanish, and was tough enough to survive all the abuse we dealt him. Basically, whenever we wanted to make fun of, hurt, or trick someone, we picked Marco. If it looked like this weirdo was hurting me, the precious, soft, vulnerable guy, no one would stand for it.

For these very same reasons, I didn't want to wrestle Marco. Up until now, although I hadn't actively defended him, I hadn't done any direct meanness to him. But it was too late. The group was too hyped up. A few of the guys subtly pushed me out into the improvised ring, where Marco reluctantly met me. Someone yelled, "Go!" I grabbed Marco. I couldn't play the weakling now, I had to survive.

"Go, Eric! All right! Get him!" I heard outside of my intense focus on protecting myself and overpowering this guy I had hold of. We were locked, hands clenched in a pushing battle as I struggled for some leverage to overpower him. Marco was stronger than me and he manipulated me onto the ground. Shit! I was losing. "I really am a weakling," I thought.

"C'mon, Eric!" the others were saying. I couldn't be embarrassed like this in front of everyone. They probably wouldn't like me anymore. Anyway, this was my chance to show off, without worrying about hurting someone who anyone felt protective of. I could get away with letting out my violence, finally. From some deep anger in me came a wild strength. I remember tearing at Marco, and wrenching him under me. But I don't remember if it was just me who overpowered him or if Frank, the oldest boy, and some others helped me by ripping Marco off me and onto the floor. Either way, Marco was pinned and I was on top of him.

The others all cheered. They wanted more. The count started, "1—2—3—..." Marco was starting to cry. I sort of wanted to stop, but the power and acceptance felt so great that I didn't. I was finally "one of the guys" at that moment. Every time Marco started to get up, someone would jump in and keep him down. The count continued, "4—5—6—7—..." The after-school group was cheering louder, egging me on, and initiating me into boyhood. "8—9—10—Yea!" I had won. But what now? Almost everyone cheered and laughed some more. I was still pinning Marco down. I didn't know when to stop. I looked to the others for some kind of cue, but none came. Marco was crying harder. I was really hurting him, but was scared to stop at the wrong moment because I might lose my "cool" status if I misjudged.

"Lunchtime!" Linda, our teacher, called from downstairs. I was saved from a decision and I got up relieved. As everyone filed out of the room, Marco got up, sniffling and wiping away tears. I felt terrible. How could I have gotten so caught up in beating him? The me that wrestled seemed very scary to the me watching Marco now. Why was everyone leaving so fast? They were all so supportive when I was wrestling, but what about now that I felt so horrible? No one was comforting me or Marco. They were all heading straight for lunch. As I stood there feeling guilty for what I had done, my status as "one of the guys" was slipping quickly away. The other guys wouldn't have cared if they had hurt Marco. They always seemed happy after they did.

Marco was alone. I was alone. I watched him pull himself together.

I wanted so much to reach out to him as we both stood still in the moving crowd. I think I went up to him and apologized, but I might have made that up because since then I've wanted his forgiveness so badly.

I don't remember the rest of that day or even how Marco and I got along after that. I know him now, and there's a mistrustful awkwardness between us still. It might be because of our wrestling match, or another incident. I don't know. But I am haunted by the memory of my participation in bullying Marco, and of my feeling so rotten for hurting a friend—a fellow misfit kid.

Eric Kupers grew up in Los Angeles, California, with his mother and younger brother, living part-time with his father, stepmother and stepbrother in Oakland, California. He presently attends the University of California at Santa Cruz, studying religion and modern dance. He is an avid Buddhist meditator and personal growth worker, and is searching for a way to take part honestly in the struggle for a better world.

Schoolyard Fights

by Terry A. Kupers

I was not prepared for schoolyard fights. I had brothers, and we would fight. But there was an unwritten code at home that you never actually hit a brother, especially not in the face. So our fights were usually ninety percent wrestling, and when we did swing at each other we always made sure we missed. Somehow older brother taught the code to younger, even though no words were ever spoken.

In the third grade, I was in an argument with another boy that led to some pushing and shouting. Suddenly, certainly without my ever expecting it, he swung and hit me in the face with his closed fist. I cried. I think some of the tears must have been on account of having to give up the reassuring illusion that all boys played by my family's unstated code. I learned the more universal code of the schoolyard. Boys don't cry. Boys don't walk away from fights. And if you do either, you're chicken, a sissy, or queer.

After recovering from that incident, I, like all grade school boys, had to make a decision about how I would respond in the future when called to fight. I happened to be fairly strong, and, with a certain amount of practice wrestling at home, I could grab most boys my age and throw them to the ground. The problem was that other boys watching the tussle would not then consider the fight over, and did not consider me the victor. You had to punch the other guy. I, on the other hand, had not given up entirely on the original family code, nor did I particularly want to hurt anyone—or be hurt. So I could not bring myself to hit very hard. In two other memorable fights, I threw my opponent to the ground, pinned his arm behind his back and tried to hurt him just enough to make him give up. He and the other boys would say I was unwilling to really fight. Some said I was chicken. And I think a kind of truce evolved, they feeling superior to me because I did not want to "really fight"; me feeling a little safe knowing I could throw most of them to the ground and that few of them wanted that to happen. Even though this meant I had gained some respect from the other boys, I continued into adulthood to harbor a nagging suspicion that I might really be chicken. I discussed none of this with my brothers, of course—that would have been a violation of the family code.

I have always felt at a disadvantage among writers because my early family life was relatively harmonious. It often seems as if, to be a good writer, one has to have had an alcoholic father, a crazy mother, have been beaten or deserted at an early age, discovered the body when a parent committed suicide, or have run wild through the streets and served time in houses of detention. How can my personal story merit narration—and writing is a very public way to narrate a life—when, in the house where I grew up, there was no alcohol, no abuse, not even any significant violence of any kind? Everyone was very nice—too nice.

My parents were kind to their children and very nurturing. In return, they were treated with respect. It was out of respect for them that we all silently agreed not to fight. And we weren't to come home with bad grades. In fact, the grades tended to be A's. My parents never asked any of us the big question—"Why couldn't that B+ have been an A?"—they did not have to ask, we had long ago internalized the message, even before we could have explained it in words. All of my siblings are high achievers. Everyone was obsessed with unwritten rules and, consequently, the problem with so much harmony was an insufficiency of play and passion.

Our house was suffused with quiet. Psychiatric researchers are discovering that a significant proportion of severely disturbed adults grew up in homes where there was an overabundance of "expressed emotion"—the most damaging being inappropriate and disproportionate explosions of rage. In terms of expressed emotion, our house was very quiet. We did not say much to each other. We discussed tasks, of course, or a movie the family might want to see. Our parents tended to explain things to us more than they listened to our concerns. And we were very nice to each other, we talked about the tasks we did around the house, and, later, who would get a car for the evening. But we did not talk to each other much about how we were feeling. Though we ate dinner together every night, I cannot remember anything we talked about.

I didn't talk much with my father, either. While still in elementary school, I was out on an errand with him when he nosed into a parking place just ahead of another car that was heading for the same space from the opposite direction. Before we could open the door, a large man leapt out of the other car and approached our driver's side menacingly. He demanded my father get out of the car and fight. My father muttered something about not having any reason to fight, and rolled up his window. The man slammed his palm on the fender, yelled at my father for another minute, threatened to break the window and haul him out of the car, and then turned, got back into his car and drove away. My father said very little to me, got out of the car and ran his errand. In retrospect, he might have shared his feelings with me and that might have given me an opening to talk with him about those schoolyard fights.

With my mother, there was another kind of silence. A nurse, she left work to be home and raise the six of us. She was always very efficient, hurrying to get us dressed, or fed, or driven somewhere, or put to bed. And she treated us absolutely equally. There was an allowance for each age level, and when we reached that age we received that allowance, just as all older siblings had. When my mother found a shirt on sale she thought one of us would like, she bought one for each of us—we never wanted to appear unappreciative, but, of course, she was totally oblivious to the embarrassment attached to being seen in public with a shirt that matched one's brother's. Her attention was evenly measured; none of us ever got more than our share.

When I was eight I developed viral meningoencephalitis. My father was out of town. Our pediatrician, a family friend, permitted my mother to keep me at home with an intravenous drip running so I would not become dehydrated. I was very febrile and my mother moved my bed into her bedroom so she could keep an eye on me. I remember being very well cared for. If I would have become someone who used physical illness to get a woman's attention, there would be an interpretation of Oedipal victory to make—but that's not really how it was. Actually, my mother didn't spend much quality time with me at all during that illness. She nursed me to health while continuing to run around doing all the other things she regularly did to keep my brothers and sister on track and the house in order; in fact, I believe, she even led all the siblings to believe I was getting no special attention on account of my illness. Later, as a medical student, I learned how serious viral meningoencephalitis can be, and realized how much anxiety she must have been containing while I was sick. She never let on.

It was not until I was in a leaderless men's group that I finally felt safe enough, and sufficiently compelled, to relate my story about schoolyard fights. The group met for about five years in the late seventies. At the end of one weekly meeting we agreed to discuss schoolyard fights at the following meeting. I remember the anxious anticipation. Would they consider me chicken? The evening came, we told our stories—some of the men had been fighters, some had avoided fights at all costs, one had "chickened out," and I believe one confessed having been a bully. But it didn't matter. The men in the room listened attentively to every man's story, sympathized (we found out no one really liked the schoolyard scenario, not even the bully), and we all laughed about how serious it had been once. Men's groups, like psychotherapy, provide a safe place for taking chances, and often, when one is willing to take chances and expose a part of the inner life that had been painfully secret, great things can happen. Is it any surprise that so many men find that they end up talking in men's groups about their relationships with their fathers?

As one after another member of my men's group talked about his father, I noticed that it was easier for the sons who had been severely abused to blow the whistle on their brutal fathers than it was for the sons who were treated pretty well to come up with a list of grievances. Lacking the venom, one is left to wonder what use there is in exposing all those embarrassing things about one's father. But I took a deep breath and began my story: As a youngster, through my teens, I idealized my father and had little bad to say about him. I wanted to be like him, a physician who cared more about his patients than about making a profit. The model came from the novel *The Last Angry Man,* which was made into a movie in my formative years. (It wasn't until my third year of medical school that I realized that, though I loved the image of "the last angry man" battling the medical establishment, the actual practice of medicine held no appeal for me—that realization led me to specialize in psychiatry so I could spend time talking to patients without having to be too concerned about their medical problems.)

It was in early adulthood that I finally acted out my Oedipal rebellion through radical politics—not that my social activism is entirely attributable to unresolved inner conflicts; it was also based on a well-informed social analysis and sense of social responsibility that I retain to this day. But the sixties were a good time to do battle with one's father for all those leftover and unexpressed grievances, and that we did. I remember a meeting in a restaurant with my parents where they were arguing that my political activities were dangerous and would ruin my career. For instance, I was serving very publicly as the physician for the Black Panther Party and they worried lest I be arrested and my license revoked. I countered self-righteously that their politics were neolithic and that was why they were incapable of understanding the importance of my risk-taking. Things got so heated my father stormed out of the restaurant, crashing into a panel of glass he mistook for the door.

I have been closer to my parents in recent years, but have carefully avoided discussing our political differences. Recently I was interviewed on radio in the city where my parents live about the mass psychology of the war in the Middle East. They listened. A few days later I received a long letter from my father complimenting me on the eloquence of my argument against the war and the passion and sincerity of my commitment. Of course, he did not entirely agree with my position. But what brought tears to my eyes was that he had obviously listened very closely, realized how my political stance was based on deeply held principles, and was able to let me know he respected my efforts to live by the principles I held dear. Until that exchange, while I knew in general that my father loved me, I never knew if he really understood who I was—maybe his love was based solely on the accidental fact that I was his son. Earlier, when it had come time in my men's group for a listing of grievances against fathers, I had said I wished my father would have known more about the person I was becoming, and would have backed off earlier on giving advice about how I should live my life. Now, after our exchange about my radio interview, I finally felt recognized—in spite of political differences—and that recognition gives me strength to face all the schoolyard fights to come.

After five years in a men's group, many years of personal psychotherapy, more years spent practicing therapy, and a certain amount of familiarity with the literature on gender and masculinity, I have evolved a properly adult interpretation of childhood events. (Isn't the retrospectroscope wonderful; if only we could have known all this then!) For instance, boys are taught on the schoolyard that there are only two positions, top and bottom. Either you fight or you're a sissy. The one who wins is the victor; the loser a weakling. Top and bottom—there is no third alternative. My problem in grade school was that I was not yet sufficiently formed as an autonomous individual to design a tenable third alternative for myself. I did find an alternative to slugging it out— wrestling my opponents to the ground—but, perhaps because I was unable to exude enough confidence in my alternative stance, the other boys were able to make me doubt my manliness. And boys who were having the same difficulty were unable to support each other at that time because all of us believed "real men" just did not do that sort of thing. For most men, the idea that there is a tenable third alternative to the drama of top and bottom is a revelation that comes much later. The early years are dominated by the either/or theme.

I am learning a lot about men—things my father and his father never had the time or inclination to talk about. But all that advanced understanding of masculinity, and all the skills I have developed being intimate with other men and being a therapist, do not always provide all the wisdom I need to raise my own three sons. They seem to need to go through their own schoolyard dramas, and all the other boyhood traumas, in their own ways, each evolving a different stance. And even though there are many more opportunities for my sons and me to talk about such things, there still comes that time when I, the father now, am not slated to know what my son is going through. And there are those moments when neither father nor son has the foggiest notion of how to proceed with the relationship.

Terry A. Kupers grew up in Los Angeles in the forties and fifties as one of six siblings. He practices psychiatry in Oakland, California, and teaches at the Wright Institute in Berkeley. He is married and has three sons. He is the author of Ending Therapy: The Meaning of Termination *(New York University Press, 1988) and* Revisioning Men's Lives: Gender, Intimacy and Power *(Guilford, 1993).*

A Personal Exploration into the Politics of Boyhood

by Paul B. Seidman

I

As I write this, I am thirty-one years old and just over 5'11". But when the sibling sensations of terror and vulnerability hit, I am young and small, returned in a fear flash to my childhood of daily survival in men's war against women and children. Some incest survivors call these flashbacks post-traumatic stress disorder, or P.T.S.D., which is what the Vietnamese have—the boys who saw their families shot and burned, the girls and women who were prostituted and raped by U.S. troops. We have trouble, at times, separating what's happening now from what happened then. The past bleeds into my present with little or no warning.

Terror is not an easy state to describe to someone who has not visited it since childhood. Terror is an unwelcome companion, following me everywhere, taking me over from time to time, trapping me in my past, in locked rooms with feelings too intense and annihilating to let out. Terror is my link to a childhood filled with real-life haunted houses, where children were too petrified to move, too paralyzed to breathe. There are times when my breathing is faint and shallow, not noticeable to the people around me. It is then I remember to unwrap the terror that binds my ribs like a corset, and pull air down into my lungs. You mustn't move, I learned as a child. You must keep very, very still. Then maybe he won't hurt you again. Terror was probably the most effective weapon of the child molester who got me and many other kids in the early 1970s. The fear that he would find me if I spoke about what he had done kept me silent for many years. Terror keeps me silent still, making writing this a very difficult task. But unlike some of the women I know, I have some control over terror. Men learn to control terror by seeking it out and conquering it, first as boys—by telling ghost stories in dark tents, by riding roller coasters without holding on, by going to see scary movies and not covering their eyes— then as men, by terrorizing women and children. My control over terror is not yet perfect. When I went to see *The Silence of the Lambs* (no woman I know would go to see it with me: most women aren't taught mastery of terror is possible, and daily experience reminds them they are supposed to be its victims), I displaced my terror onto an older white man sitting behind me. The entire time I was in the dark theater I thought he was going to stab me. I would have changed my seat, but that was already the fifth seat I had occupied in the first half-hour of the movie. I kept moving to get away from men who seemed unsafe. (If I could hear them breathing, they were unsafe to me.) Never mind the cannibal/serial killer staring at me from the movie screen; I was freaked out by the sixty-year-old man with emphysema.

Feeling terror when I am not, in fact, in danger is just one of the many effects of the childhood abuse. I have begun to list these effects, the events and feelings and beliefs that plague my daily life, in order to piece them together with the specific abuses I remember. Feeling vulnerable sleeping on my back, fear of making someone next to me in bed angry if I move, being afraid of men who are larger than me, all trace back to my childhood traumas. Not knowing appropriate sexual limits, not being able to distinguish love from sex from affection from use, are some of the effects of the incest. The longer the list gets, the more sure I am that I have been abused, and that there are still plenty of wounds which need to be healed.

Abuse causes damage, but in a society that normalizes certain forms of damage—submissiveness, for example—it is often difficult to take seriously what has happened, and to accurately name the damage. Sexual abuse inhibits identity and selfhood in ways that have been socially recognized as harmful only when exhibited by those who are not supposed to be victimized. Depression, eating disorders, and self-mutilation are only now understood as responses to the pain and trauma of abuse, often sexual. As I hear other survivors of child sexual abuse talk about their daily struggles, I am reminded of other effects, other facets of damage. We recognize our pain in each other's stories. Some of us have survived family incest, child molestation, Satanic ritual abuse, sexual torture, fondling, profound emotional abuse and neglect, or sexual violation from trusted adults such as clergy or doctors. The damage varies but is remarkably similar. Sexual abuse, whatever the degree, teaches many of the same things. We learn we are worthless, invisible, contaminated, bad, ugly, stupid, incompetent, out of control, dirty, crazy, wrong, unlovable, unsafe, and alone. We find ourselves in situations which reinforce these beliefs. We carry terror, vulnerability, isolation, shame, guilt, remorse, grief, sadness, loneliness, confusion, anguish, disgust, distrust, desperation, despair, betrayal, contempt, and rage. We find ourselves in situations which elicit these feelings. The situations we find ourselves in, and the directions our feelings go (inward or outward), depends partly on what we have learned is acceptable self-expression. Generally, men learn to rage out; women learn to rage in. Men hate women; women hate themselves. Men cut up women; women cut themselves. Men learn to express anger when hurt or sad; women learn to express sadness when hurt or angry. Men learn to be destructive; women learn to be self-destructive. This system isn't perfect; some men are anorexic, some women do hate men, but, by and large, feelings and actions follow the proper political channels, keeping socially subordinated people down and socially dominant people up (figuratively and sexually speaking).

Incest and other childhood abuse cause pain, rage, and injury to the body and soul. A healthy society would support the constructive release of that pain and rage, but, under male supremacy, boys are systematically shamed for their vulnerability. Those compressed and thunderous feelings are carried into adulthood. Male supremacy directs their paths and points of destination. Child sexual abuse doesn't cause men to be rapists or child molesters; the political system which divides humanity in two, with men on top and women and children on the bottom, causes rape and incest. This male supremacist gender system causes children with penises to be boys and later men, and gives men permission and the emotional/sexual training to act violently against women and children. It is not accurate, therefore, to say that men rape because they were raped. Men rape because they have learned that being a rapist is an acceptable way to express rage. If men who were abused as children were not socially dominant they would probably have eating disorders and self-mutilation compulsions just like women. If women were not socially subordinated their male abusers would probably have to watch out.

II

"Not last night but the night before
Twenty-four robbers came knocking at my door
I asked them what they wanted
And this is what they said
Lady, lady show your slip
Lady, lady do the split
Lady, lady turn around
Lady, lady touch the ground."

So went one of the many jump-rope songs I skipped to with several girls in elementary school. Some of the deepest lessons about life came to us outside the classroom, on the playground, as segregation by sex was enforced with rules and codes that had no textbook. I broke the rules by preferring to play with the girls. The punishments girls and women receive for being female under male supremacy made several appearances in my little boy life because I aligned myself with them, rejecting the ways of boys. I was to be systematically abused—verbally and physically—for the next eight years. The names given to boys who liked girls as friends (who saw girls as equals, not subordinates) reveal the misogyny implicit in the tyranny of male socialization—"sissy," "pansy," "fairy," were terms that linked me to females, to white femininity, in my case. These were the terms that carried the stigma of the female, that brought my superior status as a male down to the lowly and contemptuous status of the female. To be female, as the jump-rope song goes, is to be victimized and violated, by one male or twenty-four. And what they rob is not the silverware, but the self-esteem, integrity and dignity of the female. Inside the threat of their forty-eight fists and twenty-four cocks, the female is forced to submit to their whims, their humiliations and degradations. Inside a system which wanted and needed all males on one side, the side opposing the females, I was coerced into playing the boys' games, and, fortunately for the girls in 1970 in Staten Island, N.Y., the game at the time was softball, not gang rape. Even the male principal of the school came out onto the asphalt diamond to show me how to swing a bat. Leaning over me, his hands engulfing mine, he moved my body the way he wanted it to go, the way a boy's body should go, so that I wouldn't be perceived as a girl. I buried my shame, but not my contempt for the rules of conduct.

III

In childhood, emotional worlds are formed and set in motion. Youth is not so much a time of innocence as a time when terrors and traumas are repressed, so that the child can move out of the neighborhood of devastating neglect, excruciating invisibility, scalding vulnerability, and haunting violation while thinking things "weren't so bad, really." Virtually everything a child ever needs to know about abuse is learned by the time puberty strikes. But the lessons are buried quickly, so one's actions beyond childhood appear mysterious, seemingly without cause or context.

So it was for me. The psychosis, feuding, secret touching and the constant, instant editing and revising (read: "forgetting") of the ten thousand violations and humiliations of life called "my wonderful childhood" left me, at thirteen, quite ready for drugs.

A single volume of literary pornography on the living room bookshelf disappeared into my bedroom often. Masturbating to a world in which self-alienation and violation were both worshipped and eroticized was my ticket to oblivion, emotional numbness, and the world of male supremacist sex in which pain is not pain but pleasure. I rejected other drugs because I associated them with the groups of boys who hurt me. Pornography seemed to be enough to keep the torment of my emotionally and sexually land-mined childhood at bay.

My longest sexual relationship began with some magazines a junior high school friend and I bought at a used bookstore. The owner pimped the images of women and men to us, two thirteen-year-olds, for 25 cents an issue. We were his customers for months. He kept us supplied with a steady stream of objectified, fetishized bodies. We kept his change-purse full. He even led us through the dusty aisles in the front of the store to the musty, dimly lit back room, where the dirtier stuff was kept. We pawed through it all, picking and choosing the magazines that most fit our newly cultivated taste for porn. The magazines that worked best at home were the ones I'd come back for. The pictures that most effectively anaesthetized my pain and gave me a sense of power over myself were the images I pursued repeatedly in the front and back of that store. And among those chosen images were letters, cartoons and stories about incest. So distant was my recent past that I read these as if they were not about me at all. And they weren't, really. In these stories the children wanted it to happen; the whole family was in on the act—no secrets, no shame. The incest I read about was as emotionally and politically truthful as the smile painted across a Playboy model's face.

Pornography is the travel brochure of the world of sexual violence. It maps out who should be targeted for destruction, and how and where and why. Childhood abuse caused me pain. Male supremacy choreographed that abuse and its resulting pain, the limitations of its healthy expression, the directions for its abusive display, against myself and others. Male supremacy supplied me with the drug I found most effective for anaesthetizing the pain. That drug—pornography—was also a textbook, and a document, the lesson plan and recording of male supremacist sex. If everything male supremacist had been extracted from the pornography I used, I would have been left with piles of blank paper.

Fantasyland was the world I most needed to inhabit. I could pretend, as the pornographers wished, that what I was seeing was not the atrocious destruction of human life. I could pretend that what I had just lived through, and would live through for another couple of years, was also not the destruction of human life.

I needed to escape my pain because I lived in a culture which could not bear its honest expression. Pornography deadened my pain and my capacity to understand anything about the ethics and meaning of abuse. Male supremacy thrives on this emotional and ethical numbness. To break through the walls of terror and vulnerability and pain, to understand what happened to me and to those people in pornography, to understand the connections between what happened to me and what is happening to them, is what has saved my emotional and ethical life, and directed my rage away from myself and women, and focused it instead on male supremacy.

Unfortunately for girls, growing up does not bring freedom from sexual violence and violation. Fortunately for me, as I scrambled out of the wreckage of my childhood, I found sanctuary in adulthood. Though old terrors still haunt me, my future will not resemble my past.

Paul B. Seidman was born in the summer of 1960 in Hollywood, California but was raised in West Buxton, Maine and Staten Island, New York. He has lived his adult years in Portland, Maine as an activist against sexual violence, a writer, and a grandson.

"How Do We Eat When We Don't Know We're Hungry?"

by Thomas Weinberg

There is a large population of us out there starving to receive. Part of the problem is that we were taught to deny our hunger, so we continue taking care of others pretending that we in turn are getting fed, feeling guilty if we acknowledge, even to ourselves, that we, too, have a need to eat. And the problem becomes, "How do we eat when we don't know we're hungry?"

As a little boy, I can remember those feelings of starvation very well. It was like an intense pressure of feelings and emotions wanting to come out, but bested by a knowingness that it was not safe to acknowledge my needs. And, as a little boy, I learned to live with this hunger that slowly ate away at my soul, finding this was the only way to survive. I knew that those "big" people out there were already starving and in so much pain and if I turned inward and expressed what I felt, then my family might not make it. So, my feelings became deadened out of the compassion for the survival of my family.

There is a story of a similar little boy who one day comes home crying and terrified because bullies are chasing and throwing rocks at him. He takes that fear and runs into his home and shares that pain with his parents hoping they will comfort him. And immediately his parents let him know there is NOTHING to fear, and to stop crying and go play. And this becomes this child's first experience at knowing what it takes to please these parents so he takes that fear and holds it deeply inside while he plays in denial. And that night he has a nightmare about a monster that is in his closet, so terrifying and so frightening that the little boy wakes up crying out for help. Hearing his terror, the parent comes into his room and, after hearing of the nightmare, tells the little boy, "There are no monsters. Stop being afraid and go back to sleep." The next evening, the boy is afraid to go to sleep for fear of the return of the monster, but, since his parents have told him there is no fear, he finally falls asleep. That night, the nightmare returns. But this time the monster is under his bed trying to reach him and pull him under the bed.

Once again he is unable to hold in the terror and he begins to scream and yell. The little boy tells his parents that the monster has returned and is now under his bed. They let him know that his fears are not real; that there are no monsters. And this boy hears the anger in his parents' voices, knowing that he has caused them pain with his fear, so he makes an agreement to himself never to open up this terror and helplessness to closed walls again. And so, the next night, the little boy has all of a sudden grown up. The silencing of the continued terror of his nightmares causes this monster that began in his closet, and later moved under his bed, to be buried deeply inside of him in a place that no one will ever find.

So you see, our little boy learned very early on to take care of others by silencing his own needs. And in the story of the little boy with the bullies and the monsters, he feels guilty for having these fears for he knows that he is causing his parents pain by acknowledging them. How ironic it is that this befriended guilt, born and conceived in the disowned darkness of demons, is the only unnatural emotion that we carry.

We pay an enormous price for having disowned our feelings and emotions. We repeat our boyhood in intimate relationships with others by taking care of them of while denying our own pain. If we truly want to be of assistance to others, and if we really desire to make a difference in this world, then we must find ways to safely open up our feelings and emotions. For if we don't, this backlog of monsters and demons will eventually do us in.

I remember returning from a lengthy seminar tour just recently and hearing a voice inside me say, "Thomas, you are one of the planet's greatest fathers in terms of helping others find a way to reclaim their forgotten child, but you are one of the planet's worst fathers in taking care of your own inner child." I have had to realize that I, too, have repeated my boyhood patterns. I have taken my greatest gift, which is being there for others, and watched it become my greatest curse as it turned against me, as I used my giving to cover up my own disowned neediness.

I truly feel that for all of us, no matter how painful it may seem, there are moments in our time and history that it may be necessary for us to feel and take part in. To turn away from another's pain is to miss an intimacy that is so precious that the loss cannot be measured. But to give up our own feelings and emotions because of the fear of facing these internal shadows of guilt is to risk never seeing the brightness of day again.

It is for these reasons and more that I see the answers not just in behavioral changes. For every occasion that I have attempted to receive and feed myself, there have been voices trained and imprinted from that era of my forgotten boyhood that have subtly found ways to manipulate me out of receiving, softly seducing me with their familiar, sticky, gooey, guilt-ridden words telling me that there are no monsters, that only others have monsters.

What I have learned is that if we want to be there for others, whether it is lover, friend or family member, or whether it is just someone we care about who is in need, we must find ways to journey into that land of internal monsters and demons and embrace the nightmares by holding our own little boy as he trembles. Then and only then will the nightmares leave. Most importantly, we must remember that it is our responsibility to fight for our own right to heal.

Thomas Weinberg spent his boyhood years in the fifties as a member of the only Jewish family in Coffeyville, Kansas, a town of 18,000. He is presently a counseling psychologist with a private practice in Kauai, Hawaii. He is also an internationally known workshop leader specializing in working with the wounds of childhood.

Picking on the Little Guy:
In Boyhood and on the Battlefield

by Gordon Murray

During the Gulf War, I found myself in a discussion group organized by the Men's Center for Counseling and Psychotherapy in Berkeley. We'd come together to explore our feelings about the war. I was opposed, vehemently and sincerely. Yet I could feel a deeper, darker place—a mean place, a shadow place I'm uncomfortable acknowledging—where picking on the little guy felt good. And I found myself wondering how much of the war was about oil and democracy, and how much about how good it feels to beat someone up.

One of the men in our group, Peter, spoke of Elias Canetti's book *Crowds and Power*, a sort of psychological history, in which he develops the concept of the "sting." When someone more powerful than you makes you do something (a "command") you're left feeling wounded (the "sting") which impels you to pass the command on to another. Here's Canetti describing the process:

"Those most beset by commands are children. It is a miracle that they ever survive the pressure and do not collapse under the burden of the commands laid on them by their parents and teachers. That they in turn, and in an equally cruel form, should give identical commands to their children is as natural as mastication or speech. What is surprising is the way in which commands are retained intact and unaltered from earliest childhood, ready to be used again as soon as the next generation provides victims. . . . It is as though a man pulled out an arrow which had hit him, fitted that same arrow to his bow and shot it again.

"The sting forms during the carrying out of the command. It detaches itself from the command and, as an exact image, imprints itself on the performer. . . . It remains isolated within the person concerned, a foreign body lodged in his flesh. . . . It is very difficult to get rid of the sting. . . . For this to happen there must be an exact repetition of the original command-situation, but in *reverse*. This is what the sting waits for through months, years and decades. . . . When this moment comes, the sting seizes its opportunity and hastens to fall on its victim."

I can remember the sting from my boyhood. One incident in particular illustrates perfectly how I received a sting and then passed it on. Quite often on my way home from school, Reed Lincoln used to threaten to throw me off the bridge onto the railroad tracks. I was, naturally, terrified. The terror lodged deep within me—fifteen years later I still dreamt about the bridge: I cross the bridge on the way home from school with my friend Bob B. We are eating home-made cookies. The bridge is long, deserted, icy. Under it an icy torrent splashes high into the air. I am frightened; we eat cookies as we cross.

My parents understood something of my terror. My father took me to a jujitsu school. I remember him taking me on the "L" to downtown Chicago. I remember a large empty cold room with white mats on the floor. I remember throwing the robust instructor backwards over my head. I imagine they meant to reassure me that I could master a force bigger and stronger than myself. I lasted one session. Perhaps it helped a little, yet I still felt small, cold, afraid.

A few years after I received the sting from Reed, my mother began getting phone calls from Mrs. McNally. Her son Buddy was complaining of being bullied on his way home from school. The bully? Me.

Canetti says the sting wants revenge in a scene much like the original one. Picking on a weak little kid filled the bill for me. To master my own humiliation, I needed to prove to myself I wasn't the little guy anymore, that someone else was. By tormenting Buddy, I was able to fix a little of whatever Reed's terrorism had broken in me. In Canetti's image, I pulled out Reed's arrow that had hit me, fitted that same arrow to *my* bow and shot it again, hitting little Buddy McNally.

All this my mother tells me. But all I remember is the sting. I'd banished the uncomfortable memory of myself as tormentor, passing on the sting.

As I thought about the sting, I remembered a particularly brutal murder here in San Francisco a while back. In this case, the sting was passed on quickly, in a matter of days. A gay man in his fifties named Smoot was found murdered in his apartment. Nothing was stolen; the motive must have been something less obvious than need or greed. They found the culprit, a young man. He claimed in his defense that Smoot had made unwelcome sexual advances towards him. As his story unfolded, it turned out that not long before he murdered Smoot, a group of the young man's peers had raped him with a broom handle.

Gang-raped with a broom handle. To be physically violated, to be invaded in that most utterly private and taboo place, to suffer powerlessly this public ridicule, and, most likely, to have no one in whom to confide this humiliation. What deep unspeakable shame must have lodged inside him at that time?

And so the sting lodged in the young man. The days that passed after the rape may have felt like years. When the chance came to pass on the sting, he took it, ruthlessly, and what is worse, guiltlessly.

So the sting is a way we, as boys and later as men, attempt to heal our hurts. We pass them on to others. What outlets do we have, after all, for our hurts? We learn from the culture that we're supposed to appear strong; not let things bother us; not give in to hurt or pain; not cry. So we bury the hurt, the pain, the anger, the shame—the stings of our boyhood. We forget about them. But when we find someone weaker than us, the buried feelings take their long-awaited revenge. It is our desperate attempt to heal ourselves.

This is not a new idea. Freud spoke of the repetition compulsion in which we find a somewhat disguised way to re-enact old traumas and thereby heal them. Nor is it unique to boys. Perhaps girls have more emotional outlets as children—girls tend to be socialized to cry more easily, they tend to have more cultural permission to show vulnerability, they talk over their problems more easily with dolls and, later, friends—but no doubt wounded girls grow into wounded women and wounded mothers. No doubt, their stings are passed to their mates, lovers, children.

But boys and men put a particular spin on the repetition compulsion. We elevate it to an art form, we institutionalize it, celebrate it. It becomes a ritual of manhood, a rite of passage, a call to war.

Back in Berkeley, where we'd come to discuss the war, we wondered if there were such a thing as a collective sting. As I thought about it, several pieces of the Gulf War puzzle came together in a story that sounds suspiciously like boys picking fights after school, but is really the stuff of headlines and death.

The day after Lyndon Johnson ordered the first bombing of North Vietnam, he made his famous remark about his enemy's penis: "I didn't just screw Ho Chi Minh, I cut his pecker off." Of a member of his Administration who was becoming doubtful of the war, he said, "Hell, he has to squat to piss." Sure, Johnson was a plain-talking Texan, but these sentiments are buried deep in the American male psyche: losers are like men who get anally penetrated, men who are eunuchs, men who are like women. That our elected leader can say such things is simply evidence that homophobia and misogyny are pillars of the

American male's manhood.

Johnson clung tenaciously to his pledge not to be the first American president to lose a war. This unwillingness to back down helped the Vietnam War unfold, like a Greek tragedy, to our inevitable defeat. The sting of that first defeat lodged deep in our collective psyche.

George Bush had been accused of being a "wimp" during his campaign for President. He overcame the accusation by becoming ugly, mean-spirited, ruthless. But even after the election, could doubts about his own manhood be very far under the surface of his own bravado, or our public assessment of him? Was trashing Dukakis enough to rid him of this sting?

When Iraq invaded Kuwait, George Bush found the perfect opportunity to pass on the personal sting of being called a "wimp," and the collective sting of Vietnam. He made our collective sting an explicit reason for going to war: there would be "no more Vietnams." Vietnam had proven a tougher enemy than we'd thought. Bush and the military built an image of the Iraqi forces as powerful and "elite," and prepared us to pounce.

A new generation of eighteen-year-old American boys had been born, come of age, and were ready for initiation into manhood. They were particularly ready to hear Bush's call to war.

So we went to war: we massacred uncounted tens of thousands of soldiers and civilians, while losing a few hundred of our own. Under the surface reasons given for the Gulf War were three powerful forces: a generation of boys were becoming men through the ritual of war; Bush was passing on his personal sting; and, most importantly, the sting of Vietnam was removed from the flesh of our collective body politic and hurled, bloody, deep into a Middle Eastern desert people we understood so poorly. Only one outcome of the war is certain: sooner or later this sting, too, will be removed and passed on, with consequences no one can predict.

So, I wonder, is there a way out? Are we doomed to bury our stings only to have them reappear later? Or are there ways of exposing and expressing the pain so it needn't be passed on?

I tend toward optimism, and see around me many ways men are trying to uncover their wounds and express them in healthy ways rather than live them out through lovers, families, children. Surely, for example, one of the reasons Robert Bly and the new men's movement have been so phenomenally popular is that men find it a safe place to expose personal wounds and experiment with ancient healing techniques: drumming, dancing, storytelling. Easy as it is to make fun of this movement, its wide appeal tells us much about men's need to grieve.

My own path has been through psychotherapy. As a therapist, I see men discover and express their buried stings, and know that this can be a powerful and effective path to healing. Here's a story from my practice:

Robert came to me for psychotherapy because he found himself flying into fits of rage towards his girlfriend for reasons which seemed disproportionately petty. They usually happened when she had left him: she'd get out of the car to run a short errand, take longer than she'd said she would, and he would become enraged. He cared about this person, this relationship; he was afraid his uncontrolled anger would destroy it.

Before long we identified the real objects of his anger: not surprisingly, Mom and Dad. Dad had been a violent alcoholic, falling into unpredictabl· fits of screaming at home or in public. Mom had fallen ill, helpless and dependent; Robert was assigned the task to take care of her from an early age. Many days he stayed home from school, smoked pot, listened to the Beatles. Whatever fear or anger he had towards his unpredictable father and needy mother he buried. How does a child know what is "normal"? What child can stand to consider his parents less than ideal? Robert grew up thinking his parents were a little wacky but pretty cool because they allowed him his independence at an early age.

Decades later, he got to replay the scene with Paula. When Paula would leave him, even for short errands in the course of daily life, the sting of his parents' emotional and physical abandonment stirred. When she returned, the hidden rage erupted, for at last he was in a relationship where he wasn't powerless. Under the rage, we discovered the pain, and through the rage and pain, the healing.

Last summer Robert and Paula had a child. Sometimes, when he is holding the baby and she is screaming inconsolably, he feels a flash of the old rage of powerlessness. At these moments, we both understand how child abuse happens, about the natural tendency to take revenge for old stings, to pass them on from generation to generation. In therapy, Robert had found substitutes—sharing his pain and anger with me, screaming at pillows, punching his punching bag—and so the sting was somewhat vented. And he'd achieved a plateau of self-understanding from which he could watch his rage, recognize the senselessness of passing it on, and simply hold his screaming daughter.

I think of Robert when I find myself doubting if therapy works: it *is* possible to transcend the power of the sting.

But is it possible to transcend generations of cultural conditioning, of collective stings? I'm less sure. The conditioning goes so deep, it's so unconscious. I wasn't paying much attention when I learned to pick on the little guy, any more than the soldiers in the Gulf War were paying attention when they learned to become men on the battlefield. We learn how to be men when we aren't looking, when we think we're doing something else.

Here's a final story from my boyhood, about how I learned some differences between women and men:

During World War II, my mother, like so many American women, kept a Victory Garden. After the war, when I was very little, she started a garden on the edge of town. She would take me there and set me under a large poplar tree whose leaves rustled in the breeze, making the sound of rain. I sat under the Rain Tree and watched my mother work the earth, cultivating, seeding, tending, and eventually pulling sweet things from the dirt. With a gentle tug, my mother pulled from the earth a sweet orange carrot. Raw carrots were a staple around our house; I still love raw carrots.

During World War II, my father, like so many American men, kept a gun, as they fought island by island towards Japan. After the war, each fall he went hunting with his buddies to the Wisconsin woods. Once he took me along. We moved through woods beautiful with bright leaves, air crisp and clear. I shot a bird, a grouse. It wobbled about before it collapsed; perhaps I had to shoot it again. I felt a certain excitement at aiming right, but mostly I felt squeamish. I never liked eating these birds anyway; they tasted strong, and you had to watch out for buckshot. This was my last hunting trip.

Women harvest carrots; men shoot birds. This, I learned, is how the world works. I don't believe it can work that way much longer.

Gordon Murray grew up in the postwar baby boom in suburban Chicago, moving only once in his first eighteen years, and that was next door. He made up for that in his twenties and thirties, traveling and working internationally. Now settled in San Francisco, Gordon is a psychotherapist, group consultant, and faculty member at John F. Kennedy University and New College.

Capturing, Knowing

by Jan Nathan Long

When I was young, I grew up in the outskirts of Washington, D.C. I had few friends there; some kids I played with on the street, but no one I would really talk to about things.

My brother, eight years older than me, was my idol. I wanted to be like him. Sometimes I would go into his room when he was not there and look through his things. I was not searching for anything in particular, just the experience of being in that room where there was something haunting, scary, intriguing. And there was that smell: musty, sweaty. It was a human smell, but slightly removed from the body, lingering, or entrenched. It was the smell of dirty clothes, of sweat, the kind that younger boys do not have.

I could never figure out how he could make his room smell like that; I could never get my room to smell that way. It was something I did not understand, how that smell came about, or why I was attracted to it. I wanted to have it, to know about it, to know the mysteries behind it. I knew there were so many secrets that people worked within and my brother seemed to have insight into all of them. Most of those secrets he treated seriously. But some he intentionally broke down. He always knew how to identify these secrets and how to distinguish them. More than anything, this is what I wanted: I wanted his acceptance, wanted to know and understand the myriad of things that he knew. I wanted no longer to not understand.

So often I would imitate him, hoping that wisdom would fall upon me. For instance, my brother never cut his hair, so I never let mine be cut either. Every time I went to the barber, I would scream and cry. Soon my parents gave in and stopped taking me to the barber, though I was only eight years old. (I was the youngest in a family of four and they were tired of resisting us, I suppose. That was in the third grade and I did not have my hair cut again until the first year in college, nine years later.)

Another thing my brother was adamant about was not having his picture taken. It became clear to me then that I did not want my picture taken either. It was very entrenched in my mind, and I was conscious of a camera whenever it was around me. I never stopped to think about why, though it felt like I was losing something very important when someone got a photograph of me, and I usually cried angrily. I would feel as though something of mine had been captured, taken away, something I wasn't even conscious of myself, but which I knew I had within me. As though others would then be able to see it, know it, use it as they liked.

Back when I was in first grade my family would go out into the country some weekends to a farm in Maryland. One time my brother's friend Eric came with us, and he brought a camera. I knew I was going to have to be careful every moment, because Eric was undaunted, decisive, and he was set on taking a picture of me whether I wanted him to or not. (Perhaps especially if I didn't want him to.)

There were three of us in the back seat of our Chevrolet Biscayne as we took the hour-long drive into the country. Eric was by one window and I by the other. I don't recall who was in the middle; maybe one of my sisters. Eric pretended to fix his camera. I wasn't paying attention until he called my name. And then, before I even realized what had happened, there was a click.

I was silent the rest of the ride, angry, violated. And I avoided Eric, treated him coldly throughout the day, in the way children are so adept at doing. The day passed. I plucked the stink bugs away from the base of the big pine tree by the cabin where I played with toy soldier models, forming forts out of pine cones and rocks.

When it was time to go, I gathered my things and was walking up to the car when Eric appeared again. I was right beside the hundred-year-old boxwood tree when I saw him. There he was, poised and pressing his finger slowly. I jumped right into the tree to avoid him! He laughed and said he had gotten the photo anyway. I didn't believe him.

A couple of weeks later, back in D.C., Eric showed me the pictures. (Was my brother laughing about them?) In the first one, I had this startled, fearful look, like an animal trapped and frozen by the headlights of a car which is racing toward it, like someone whose secret has just been revealed.

The second one is a little blurred—a pale face and dark clothing streaking into a bushy tree. My head is spinning to the side to avoid the camera. Most of my body is a grey, out-of-focus mass. The only parts of my body that are in vague focus are my hands; they are just beginning to position themselves for the landing. At that moment they are bent down, so it looks like I am really fey. It is almost like I am doing a cancan and the camera is just too slow to catch me. It is like telling a future.

When I looked at them I tried to keep them from Eric, but he grabbed me and tickled me into letting them go, threatening that I would have to pay for them to be reprinted if I ruined them. But later in the day I noticed that the pictures were lying in the living room—perhaps he had showed them to my mother who had left them there. So I took the two of me and hid them in one of the volumes of the Funk and Wagnall's Encyclopedia, somewhere in those thousands of pages, in those twenty-eight volumes.

(Why didn't I like the pictures? Perhaps they were just too much for me to take. So, I put them in the books of knowledge, attempting to hide them for a while, until the knowledge became something I no longer wanted to hide.)

Soon after I forgot about the pictures being in there at all.

Being the youngest, I would often go with my mother to the Safeway grocery store, helping her pick out the luncheon meats I would have in school for the rest of the week. I remember the loaves of white bread being four for a dollar. I remember all through elementary school feeling this sense of superiority over the other kids because I would always make my own lunch, while most of them had their lunches made for them. I remember being afraid that the orange juice can in the frozen food section would freeze to my small little white hands and rip off my skin.

I remember poking the plastic-wrapped slabs of meat, sometimes until I broke a hole in them. And I remember the Safeway offering the complete set of Funk and Wagnall's Encyclopedias. **Aa** through **Aug** was the first volume, and it seemed like weeks would pass before the next volume appeared on the shelf. I remember Mom and Dad talking about it and deciding that it was just the thing for all of us children, who were in elementary and junior high school. And so, at $2.77 a volume, we started our collection.

Even before we had come across those brand new maroon-ish fake leather books of knowledge, my parents had had us convinced that Funk and Wagnall's was the "font of all knowledge," as my mother would say.

"Look it up in your Funk and Wagnall's"—a confusing and dead-end retort to any argument. I never knew what "Funk and Wagnall's" meant. I thought it was one incomprehensible word and so I mythologized it as being the All Knowing, the ultimate knowledge. I suppose I was looking for some place to find knowledge, a place where it was captured and held for me, a place that made things clear to me.

I was often sick as a child and that meant that I was frequently alone in the house. I recall opening up the cigarette box that my parents had for visitors and guests and smelling the cigarettes, stale and foreign. I have this vague sense that I actually smoked one, though I do not remember anything about it. I am not sure that I was able to light one, to know that I had to inhale *as* I held the match.

Things that do (not) fit together/three connecting memories:
1. Calling my friend on the telephone but not getting through, because I did not pick up the receiver until after I dialed;
2. Eating an apple in bed and then not finding the core, wondering if I had absent-mindedly eaten the whole apple;
3. Rolling a rock on the hood of the family car and completely erasing it from my memory.

One day when I was sick, I decided to go through the Funk and Wagnall's to see if there were any pictures of naked bodies. I kept a mental list, a file, of all the times I had seen someone naked, man or woman. I tried to remember each time in my head, usually as I lay in bed. I remember looking up **Male** and then **Men**. I don't think I found any pictures or drawings of naked men there. I started skimming through the volume, hoping I would fall upon something.

Pretty soon I came across the listing **Michelangelo** and there was a photograph of the statue, David. I remember staring at it a long time and memorizing the page number. I guess I fell in love with the image, though I was only eight or so.

I thought the experience was unique, unrelatable, until I read a passage of Mishima's *Mask* where he describes seeing a reproduction of Guido Reni's "St. Sebastian":

> . . . I began turning a page toward the end of the volume. Suddenly there came into view from one corner of the next page a picture that I had believed had been lying in wait there for me, for my sake. . . .
>
> That day, the instant I looked upon the picture, my entire being trembled with some pagan joy. . . .

Several years later, perhaps when I was ten or eleven, I was sitting alone in the living room again, just thinking. I must have started thinking about the fact that I seemed to have an attraction to men.

Perhaps I saw the encyclopedias on the shelf and remembered looking up **Michelangelo.**

And somewhere over those years I had learned the word homosexual. At that moment a synapse connected and I dove for the **Haa** to **Int** volume of the Funk and Wagnall's.

As I leafed through the volume to find the word, I knew I was scared: scared that I would find terrible things, scared that someone might walk in and find me.

(Sitting here writing, a part of my memory says that I tried to read the article, but that it made little sense, or it was uninformative. Another part says, no, there was no article there at all. I decide to check, and the later part of my memory is right: there is no article.)

I knew that homosexuality existed. I knew this was a book of knowledge. I knew that it had a picture of a sculpture of a naked man. If that picture was all right, why couldn't it say what homosexuality was? Even if it said it was a horrid, immoral thing, shouldn't it at least describe it? Was it not considered knowledge?

I'm not sure that I thought all that so clearly, but there was a perhaps veiled realization that there were things missing, things left out on purpose. That the objectives of this book were not simply to transfer knowledge, but something else, perhaps an intermixing of motives at best.

I used the Funk and Wagnall's less and less as years passed. They became more outdated, and seemed to give less information about the subjects in the listings, and more and more information about the people who put them together.

Some years later, I remembered the pictures that Erik had taken and that I had put in the encyclopedias. I went back to the books, looking for those photographs of me, for personal knowledge. I flipped through all the books, but I don't recall ever finding the pictures.

And, yet, I have them with me now.

Jan Nathan Long says he felt like an adult much of his childhood, having lived in France for three years, growing up in Washington, D.C. until the age of ten when his family moved to a log cabin in rural Maryland. He currently lives at Short Mountain Sanctuary, a collective farm in central Tennessee, where he plays, bakes, bicycles, writes, etc. He helps produce RFD, *a country-based journal for gay men, and works with the developmentally disabled.*

BOYHOOD
IN THE FAMILY

Mother, father, brothers, sisters and extended family make up the matrix of boyhood. This is the vessel that births the young male into the world as it is supposed to be. Families are complex social organisms. They shift from functioning well to functioning poorly again and again as the boy learns to adapt or maladapt to all that is expected of him. Before he is born, a boy is often given a name and a role. Many of us are named after our fathers or other males of significance to our family. Many of us felt strong invitations from our fathers to do as they do and be as they are. Our mothers taught us many things, some of them silly and some of them wise. Mothers often bear the brunt of psychological criticism because their sins are visibly committed. Our fathers' shortcomings are mostly in the absence of relationships with us. Their sins are harder to see, but no less significant. The brothers and sisters we had or adopted in cousins or peers were fellow activists on the child strata of the family structure. They were allies, enemies and both. On the adult strata, there were often grandmothers and grandfathers, uncles and aunts, sometimes stepparents who played counterpoints or substitutes for our actual parents. This is the mosaic a boy finds himself a part of as he figures out who and what he is.

The Greater God

by Rakesh Ratti

She the lesser god,
a shadow of the greater,
She the fearful,
more powerless than I.
She with sandhur in her hair,
a crimson chain of subservience,
passed from father to husband,
a servant in all houses.
She of the slavish devotion,
of the tongue forever bitten
and words left unsaid.
She of the camphor and coconuts.
She of the soft voice,
that I once saw as insanely yielding,
of the kind eyes
I once saw as timorous.
She who once towered above me
yet looked me in the eye.
She of the divas and bhajans.
She, the central thread
that held the tapestry together.
She who absorbed all pain and sorrow
yet radiated light and nourishment
in every direction.
She of the rituals of mystery
that became for me a way of life.
She whose threats
I often laughed at,
for through the fissures
between her words
flowed the love she embodied.
She who was nothing was all.
She the lesser
was to me
the greater god.

Rakesh Ratti was born in 1959 in Punjab, India. At nine years of age he immigrated with his family to California. He is working on a Ph.D. in clinical psychology and is an activist involved with Trikone and Glaad. He is a writer of fiction and editor of the anthology A Lotus of Another Color: An Unfolding of the South Asian Gay and Lesbian Experience *(Alyson, 1993).*

Where the Pain is Buried

by Richard Newman

I

The hands of the men who molested me. I remember the hair on the backs of their fingers, the skin of their palms and wrists. I remember their voices, one old and pleading, the other strong and demanding. I remember not knowing what to call what they were doing to me, thinking that I was not suffering, that adults did such things to little boys. That little boys had no choice but to take it.

II

My father's promise that he would come back. The fact that he never did.

III

Sitting with my brother at the kitchen table, watching whatever it is that is preparing our breakfast. It *looks* like my mother, *moves* like my mother, but its builders neglected to give it my mother's voice. Instead, the robot communicates in a tone so flat and unemotional, so lifeless, that hearing it gave me my first experience of fear as an emotion containing the end of my existence. "Your mother is gone. I am her replacement," are the first words out of its mouth, and each syllable is a dart that fills my arms and legs with numbing cold. Death itself, I think, is creeping into my body. I watch for a sign that this is my real mother playing a game, but find none. Either she is a perfect actress or this really is a near-perfect duplicate; I cannot tell for sure.

Pancakes slide from the frying pan onto the serving plate and the robot says exactly what my mother would say, "Eat, while I make some more." I realize I am glad for the obviousness of its inhumanity. Otherwise, I might have called it Mom for my whole life and never once suspected I was not addressing the flesh and blood from which my infant body had emerged four or five years earlier. I start to wonder what my mother could possibly have done to deserve being taken away like this, in secret, without even a chance to say good-bye to her children, and before me looms the random universe, time's complete indifference to what is or is not just. I see that I, too, could be taken away, replaced as easily as my mother, and unless the people who cared about me were very diligent, they might not even know I was gone. I swear to be vigilant, for their sake if not for my own, never to let one moment pass without the absolute certainty that I am who I think I am. I do not know it yet, but I am learning to live with chaos, to survive, if necessary, by the grip of one hand, never looking down as I dangle over the edge of my own annihilation.

IV

Getting ready to leave the beach with my father. We are in the locker room taking off our bathing suits and he is talking about something I don't really listen to because he is naked, big, and very hairy. My eyes wander among the whorls of black fur that run from the nape of his neck, along his shoulders and arms, down his back and into the dark cleft of his buttocks. He turns around and I can see where, at my eye level, the hair of his back meets the hair of his front in the bush between his legs. His penis hangs like a pendulum, its skin a slightly deeper hue than the rest of his body. When he walks, it swings slowly between his thighs, and I wonder if it gets hard like mine does, if he plays with it like I do. I want to run and throw my arms around him, to pass through his skin and know what it means to live with such size, but I content myself with the knowledge that his body will someday be mine, that my body is his in the making.

V

Playing doctor with the girl next door, touching her everywhere the doctor touches me. A cushion on the floor serves as my examination table, and after I have listened to her heart and lungs, hit her knees to check her reflexes, I have her lie down so I can probe her belly. The curve of her back, molded to the curve of the cushion, pushes her body into a pose that I will eventually come to know as seductive and inviting, but it is still eight or nine years before I discover the *Playboy* magazines hidden in the bookcase behind my grandfather's favorite chair. What I am interested in now is the way the chubby bulge of my friend's belly bounces back when I push on it and how she laughs when I run my fingers up the narrow flatness of her chest and into the hollows under her arms. I crouch between her legs and put my hands softly on the hairless lips I find there. She giggles and tells me that is where she pees from. When I look inside, the flesh is pink and red, wet and warm.

I do not remember my friend examining me.

VI

I am ten years old, getting changed to go swimming. I turn my back to the other boys because I have an erection and cannot get my penis to fit comfortably into my bathing suit. From behind me a voice calls out, "Look at that guy's boner!" Hands appear on my shoulders and I am turned around to face the middle of the locker room. I stand there unable to move, wishing I had the ability to vanish into thin air, that *it* would vanish into thin air, but, no matter how much I will it, the damned thing will not go down, will not even soften. In fact, the more attention the other boys pay to it, the more I can feel the blood pulse that keeps it stiff.

The group bully steps forward, eyes me with a mixture of contempt and envy and then thrusts his face into mine, shouting, "What are you, a homo?!" The other boys laugh, "Yeah, he must like to look at other dicks."

"Better stay away from him!"

"You mean, he'd better stay away from us!"

"Hey, faggot, wanna suck mine?" I only half understand what they are talking about. I know that a "homo" or a "faggot" is not something I should want to be, but I am not exactly sure what either of those things are or why they are so bad.

Then, the most popular boy in the group speaks up, "Listen, I'd give my left arm to have a dick that size." I have no idea why, but those few words manage to silence everybody else. He looks at me and says, "You've got something to be proud of there. It's just a shame you don't know how to use it yet."

Though I do not fully understand what he means either, I know he is trying to defend me. I hear, however, the envy in his voice as well, and so I don't trust him. Nonetheless, his short speech seems to have defused the other boys' enthusiasm for ridicule and I am left alone to finish getting ready for a swim. When the locker room is empty, and I am sure that no one will see, I stand before the full-length mirror at the entrance to the showers and tuck my penis between my legs. The sight of my sexless self gives me an awkward kind of hope. I do not want a body that causes envy in others, and if sexlessness is what it will take for me to be able to live my life beyond the reach of the shame wrapped around me today by the other boys, then at least I have a goal. I put my bathing suit on, go out by the pool, and find a corner where no one can see me cry for the part of myself I have today disowned.

VII

"Next time," my mother laughs, "tell him you don't have such problems. Tell him you wear a steel jock strap." I am drinking a cup of tea with the women of my family, and we all laugh with her. I have just told them about my father's first and only attempt to discuss sex with me. I am sixteen years old.

I had spent the weekend with him for the first time in a long time, and, big spender as always, my father took me to Burger King for lunch before I got on the train for the ride from Manhattan back to Queens. Over the years of his broken promises and less and less frequent visits, our conversational repertoire had dwindled, so since Friday and Saturday had already exhausted the range of topics we could discuss meaningfully with each other, there wasn't much left for us to say while we ate. As he walked me to the subway, however, my father suddenly asked me if I had a girlfriend. I don't remember why, but I lied and told him no.

"Well," he responded, "you will soon, and once you start dating, you're going to run into situations you won't know how to handle." There was a long pause while he looked at me to see if I knew what he was talking about, and then he said, "I just want you to know that you can call me."

No doubt this was a well-intentioned if half-assed, and, as usual, too-late attempt on my father's part to establish some common ground between us. Of course, I knew he was talking about sex, and maybe I wanted to punish him for all the years he hadn't been there for me by not allowing him to be there at a moment when I thought most fathers and sons would be drawn closer together, but I couldn't bring myself to tell him that I'd already lost my virginity, that I had no need of the help he was offering. I did, however, like the dutiful son I was, bring this story back to my mother as further proof that I was more her child than his.

During all the years of my growing up, one of the worst criticisms my mother could level at me was that I was behaving or thinking "just like my father." She put into those words all the anger, all the bitterness and frustration she felt for having married him in the first place, and, when I reached puberty, she encouraged me to grow a beard because the degree to which I resembled him made her so uncomfortable. I learned very early in my life, therefore, to win her approval by doing everything I could to distinguish myself from him in her eyes. Most effective was to commiserate with her about how stupid and immature, how ineffectual and emotionally manipulative my father was, and, in fact, he was all those things. The more distant I became from him, the closer I felt to my mother, the more reassured I was that I was becoming the kind of man my mother would like, that any woman would be satisfied with.

My mother's comment about the steel jock strap, however, permanently ruptured this image of myself as her ideal man. Rather than a dig at my father's sexuality, it was a dig at my own, an unconscious expression, I think, of her anger at the identity he and I shared by definition, of her desire to erase the manhood into which I was growing, that would make me, irrevocably, his son in a way that I could never be hers.

VIII

I was a bed-wetter. My stepfather's strategy for breaking me of this habit—the wisdom in my family held that it *was* a habit and so not worth a trip to the doctor—consisted of his checking my sheets every morning and spanking me for not knowing enough, or not being able to get up in the middle of the night and go to the bathroom. I remember waking to the smell of urine and my stepfather's face telling me to go wash myself while he changed the sheets. When I came back into the bedroom, he told me to take off my underpants and lie face down on the bed. Because I know that my stepfather hated crybabies and would "give me something to cry about" if I could not keep the tears in, I buried my head in a pillow so I could stifle my screams. I waited in the knowledge that I had failed again, that I deserved what was coming to me, but I do not today remember either the sound or the pain of his open palm on the naked skin of my behind.

IX

Sitting with my father in the front seat of his car. "Why," he is asking me, "can't you learn to keep your mouth shut?! How am I ever going to trust you after this?" I try to apologize, to explain that I hadn't meant to tell my mother about the stops he makes at OTB on Saturdays before he brings my brother and me home. I don't even know what OTB means, and he never told us why it was so important to keep it secret from my mother. Only years later will I find out about the unpaid child support, the alleged unemployment that kept him from earning enough money to send my mother forty dollars a week but allowed him to keep betting on the horses.

Nothing I say, however, makes a difference. My father looks at my brother, who is sitting in the back seat wearing a look of bemused satisfaction, "Why can't you be more like Paul? At least he knows when to keep things to himself." And then my father reaches over, smacks me on the back of the head—it is the only time I remember him hitting me—and says, "I guess it's not really your fault. You're just too much like your mother."

X

My mother, angry at me for something that I don't remember, calls me a bed-wetter, a baby. I am about twelve years old and she is screaming at me from across the room. Later, while she cleans house—she is uncharacteristically making my bed—she apologizes. I stand there like an idiot, barely able to mumble my response, "Don't worry; it's okay." But even as my mother insists that it's not okay, that she was wrong and that I deserve an apology, I realize I have no way of accepting it because I do not really know from whom it is coming or to whom it is being given.

XI

Some of these memories have accompanied me for almost the entire thirty years that I have been alive. Some of them have seen the light of day for the first time on these pages. Placing the memories here, one after the other, trying, with the imprecise tool of language, to render with fidelity the contours and contrasts of my experience, I find myself wishing I could have shown you pictures instead, hidden my self-revelation behind the wordless and immediate apprehension of my life that would then be available to you. Memory, after all, is an inexact science at best, and who knows how much of what I have reconstructed here is pure fabrication. I know that, on an emotional level, what "matters" most is not necessarily the objective truth. At the same time, however, when nothing objective presents itself as an anchor for one's feelings, when all one has is the shifting shape of memory, the experience of trying to construct a reality can be quite terrifying, and so I come to one picture in particular, a family photograph taken when my parents were still together—which makes me about two or three years old.

We are sitting on the floor. My brother has been placed on his stomach between my mother and myself, and my hand rests just above his rump, as if I were trying to keep him from crawling away. My mother's hand and forearm disappear behind my back, and my father, with his arm around my mother, is sitting behind the three of us. I am not looking at the camera. My eyes do not look boyish, have none of the sparkle and enthusiasm for life that I can see in other photographs of myself at the same age. Rather, my eyes look old, tired and empty, as if they had seen more than they were capable of handling. My adult self clenches, as a feeling I do not want to own rises from just below my lungs and clamps my upper arms to my torso, pinning them there so that I cannot defend myself, though I have no idea what I have to defend myself against. An image flashes through my mind of myself as a young boy being held down and my stomach muscles spasm, tighten in preparation for the pain—of what? The image disappears, though I can still feel the grip of someone's hands on my biceps.

I try to enter the memory again, but I can't. I force myself to look at the picture again. There are lines under my eyes, dark circles, as if I hadn't slept the night before. My lips are parted slightly, but contain not even a hint of a smile. Someone has stolen my joy from me, and I want to know who it was and how they did it. The rest of my life may depend on it.

Richard Newman was born in Queens on January 20, 1962, but spent most of his childhood and all of his adolescence in Floral Park, Long Island, New York. Currently, he teaches English as a Second Language and English Composition at Nassau Community College. He is at work on a book of personal essays dealing with male sexuality.

When Mommy Breaks Down

by B. Michael Hunter

when mommy breaks down
nervous
you scour the bathroom
scrub the floors
wash the windows
do the laundry
dust the living room
change the light bulbs
when they burn out
clean the kitchen
buy the food and cook
for yourself and mommy broken

you walk through the house
quietly
trying to be air
as if the floors were hot coals
broken glass
or a bed of needles

you speak at a volume just right
tone emotionless
watch the news
late-night talk shows
the late movie
listen to the radio
at a volume so low you could hear
mommy's breath in the next room
and you read about history
about triumph
about life

you go to school
on time
late or not at all
but you always do well enough
so mommy would not have
to leave the house
'cause you know mommy shouldn't leave the house
and when she does
you are always by her side
at the bank
(you wonderin' where
she got the check to cash
in the first place)
at the doctor's office
the pharmacy
some relative's house
by her side
always
she needing
to lean

when mommy breaks
you break
into fragments
but if you are to survive
your blood must become glue
'cause you must pull it together

you look into her eyes
around you and guess
guess
if she needs a blanket
something to eat
the tv channel or radio station changed
or it turned on or off
any sign of life
while all the plants in the house die
or try to
but you can't let them

so you take care of them too
you answer the phone
"oh she's not in"
or "oh she'll call you right back"
or "oh she's sleeping"
or "oh she's . . ."
you leave your friends
at the door
and it doesn't even matter
what you tell them
'cause teenage noise
would certainly disturb mommy
or you
or the stillness
and someone
something should explain
the quiet

"why is mommy . . ."
who cleaned the house
worked every day
raised four kids
single-handedly while going to college
bought food
gave you and every one
such good advice
"why is she so broken"
so you go through the house
looking for clues
you find papers
you read them all
between and behind every line
you uncover
pictures
books
pieces of the puzzle
secrets
skeletons
and lies

you ask questions
actually you only ask one
at a time
or maybe one a day
or week
or month
'cause you don't want to
wipe away her
surely-to-follow tears
you listen
she tells you everything
a burden lifted
she tells you
'cause you asked
'cause there is not noise in the house
'cause it seems that you and she are
the only living things
and you hear yourself repeating
"it's all right
everything will be all right"

you go to school
join a club
the track team
run in circles
for miles
a natural high
you are good
but you never excel
no
that might mean mommy
would have to talk to the coach
about allowing you to get out of town
to this meet or that meet
then he too might ask why
she doesn't come to a meet
to see how wonderful you are

"you explain things so well
you have so much insight
you're so mature

so thoughtful
so kind
so different" people tell
you thank them all
smile not too wide
'cause even the best glue
won't hold together
if you pull too hard
stretch emotions
too far

unknowingly
your vision becomes narrow
your horizon small
and all you remember is mommy
head bent
shoulders round
sitting in a chair
or on the side of a bed
still
alone
you remember your mother
without you
you think without you where would she be
what would happen

so you build a wall
a very tall wall
so impregnable
so high no one is able to climb
look over
or get through
it protects you
or traps you
or traps and protects you
it's in your face
your eyes
your mouth
your gait

B. Michael Hunter, a.k.a. Bert Hunter, was born in Hells Kitchen, NY, and raised in Spanish Harlem, NY. He is an educator, cultural activist and journal editor of Sojourner: Black Gay Voices in the Age of AIDS, *published by Other Countries: Black Gay Writers.*

Godly Flames

by Carlos Velazquez

As a child, if I closed my eyes and squeezed them hard enough a white light appeared giving me proof that there was a God. I used to squeeze my eyes shut and pray before going to bed. I would pray for my family, friends and, even at the age of twelve, I would beg for world peace. I was a pacifist at an early age although I didn't know it. I didn't understand that there was an ideology to my actions.

I remember one evening my mother hurrying to the living room and saying, "Mi hijito, call the fire department, we're in flames!"

She hurried down the hall and I followed. As she opened her closet door, I saw a flame emerge with smoke that seemed to soak into the ceiling. "Oh God!" I closed my eyes without much concentration. Nothing.

I ran down the hall and picked up the phone wanting an immediate response. I pressed the "0." My mom had limited English proficiency. In a time of panic she would be less proficient. So she depended on me to take care of this emergency without much consideration for my emotional response. I had every right to panic, but I didn't.

Hanging up the phone was a demand for a trust in others, an assurance that the firemen would find our house and save it without much damage to our belongings. Mom awakened everyone in the house and had them outside in their pajamas in minutes. Neighbors were beginning to gather near our home with looks of despair. I'm not sure if the looks were out of sympathy, pity, sorrow for us or a deep-felt concern for their own property.

I could hear the sirens in the distance. I could see the lights flashing, bringing a red to the tall trees that surrounded our neighborhood. The firemen couldn't figure out what street on which to turn. No other explanation could justify the lights stopping some feet away. Couldn't they see the smoke? The flames? Couldn't they hear four children crying from fright?

"What are we going to do?" my sister shouted as tears rolled down her face and saliva came off her quivering lips. There was no moon that night, nothing to lighten the darkness but smoke and flames shooting through the window panes.

What a sight we must have been to all who came out of curiosity: three children crying ever so helplessly stood still while one searched for the lights which didn't seem to come any closer. The assurance of help that was expected was being delayed. I ran toward the lights hoping to find some help. At this moment my mother looked at her children, standing sobbing and shiftless. I was missing. She panicked, questioning where I was—where I could be. Her immediate thought was that I was inside the house trapped in smoke and red flames.

She ran inside desperately searching for the one child whom she had trusted to call for help. Inside, she felt her breath surrender to the smoke. Her vision became blurred as she looked for her son. Outside, I ran barefoot down a dark street. Suddenly, I saw a white vehicle turn the corner and I started to scream with a boldness that surprised me, for I had never demanded as much energy from myself as I now displayed. The figure in the car spotted me and increased the pace of his approach. I turned around demanding to be followed. The assurance had come. But was it too late?

The day after, as we exchanged stories as to how we felt about the tragedy, my mother described her visions of finding me dead, scorched beyond recognition. She then sadly reported that we didn't have any insurance to cover the costs of our losses. She believed a divine spirit to be our insurance. I closed my eyes again. Nothing. How could an omnipotent God allow for children and a single mother to go without? The white light that I had grown accustomed to seeing for my evening prayers was gone. I'm not sure whether I no longer wanted to see the light as an act of self-revenge for the loss. However, I did know that the innocence of a child burned away like the flames growing to envelop all that had been mine. My bed, my books, my toys I had no more.

Years later, as the memories of the incident have become less important in the greater scheme of my ever-so-busy life, I can't help but wonder if the loss was really an awakening to an ability to question all the dogma that had been shoved into me in the name of religion and acceptance. The destructive flames and the suffocating smoke taught me to question before accepting and to accept the questioning. I question all the time.

J. Carlos Velazquez was reared in the deserts of Nevada by a single mother and supported by a family of four. Currently, he is a doctoral student at La Trobe University in Melbourne, Australia and leads an active political life in feminist and AIDS politics.

In Most Houses

by *Steven Riel*

"In most houses there is a room a child will not enter."
—Christopher Bursk

For us, it was the closet
between our twin beds, with its naked
lightbulb that peeled our eyes
as it revealed pink pimpled spackle
and the door to the attic.
Did my sister and I really believe
that ghosts kicked and bit back there,
that tornadoes of dust could drag chains?
We spun this woolly fear
into a blanket to pull over our father,
our eyes giggling into each other
as we plotted across permapress
continents divided by an abyss
yawning with alligators.
Our faces came so close once
we touched tongues, then squirmed back
in squeamish glee as that slipperiness
slid down our spines, getting a rise
down to the—*Quick! Shh, Daddy's coming!*
and there he was when we most
expected him. He always announced himself
by light, whether it was the lit tip
of his cigarette, or headlights
slicing through venetian blinds
as he turned into the driveway and dinner
popped out of the oven. We popped
under our covers and squealed *The ghost! The ghost!*
to get his mind off bedtime. Exasperated,
he'd trick us with a very short story
we knew by heart: *Once upon a time,*

there was a little boy with one hair
on his head, and he went
to the barber and had it cut off.
The End. He closed the closet door for us,
kissed us goodnight.

My sister's snores became thicker,
uninhibited. She had let me take her doll
to bed. Breathlessly, I inched my T-shirt up,
my pj's down. I scooped my arms under the rigid
doll and held her like ice cream to my lips.
She gave me goose bumps.
Without a sound, I turned the doorknob
to a room I had just discovered
where Superman rescued Lois Lane
from ravishing fires. I threw
a muscular life preserver
around her neck.
Real vinyl lashes fringed
her wide blue eyes
that stared with petrified awe
as we went up, up—but
then I stopped kissing her lips.
They were dead. I felt
under her black and blue plaid jumper.
There was nothing between her legs.
I slammed the door goodnight.

There was something puzzling between my sister's legs,
just like the inside of a green pepper.
I saw it when she pulled up her red
tights before catechism class.
There was something between Superman's legs
that protruded into my dreams. Sooner or later,
I peeked inside that door again,
leaving the doll on its shelf for
good. I brought a pillow with me
instead, kissed an S on its broad chest
over and over again (I hadn't yet
discovered the possibilities

between Batman and Robin).
The grey and silver shadow
on our black and white TV—
sometimes me, sometimes holding me—
paid out a string
of half-hearted excuses to Lois,
stripped down in the closet, slipped
off his glasses, then flew
to a secret mission
through silken sheers
that fluttered eerily.
He saved Metropolis
by undressing himself,
all along so afraid some thug
with krypton might find him out.
He was always homesick
for that planet where
one could be super
and not stick out.
In most houses,
there is a closet,
a Clark Kent.

Steven Riel was born in 1959 in Monson, Massachusetts, a small hill town in the western part of the state, and lived there until he left for college. He is currently a librarian at Amherst College and the poetry editor of RFD. *His first book of poems,* How to Dream, *was published by Amherst Writers & Artists Press in 1992.*

We Moved A Lot

by Neal King

When I was a boy, we moved a lot. I have somewhere, written in my dead mother's hand, a long list of the places and addresses she could remember from the various residences of my boyhood. They included the East Coast, the South and the West Coast. I don't remember the South at all; I was born in Florida, and my older brother in Georgia. I'm told we also lived awhile in Texas. I was too young, and we stayed too brief a time, for me to remember those places.

There are several places I do remember. Three in Connecticut stand out at the moment. One approaches the magical in my memory; it was rural, nearest to a town I remember being named Ledyard. Our closest neighbors were farmers, some distance down the road. I had a playmate there; we disturbed a bee or hornets' nest one day and I remember being very frightened. There were woods which seemed to go on forever behind our house; I was free to imagine them haunted or enchanted or inviting or forbidding, depending on my own state and need. I don't remember being old enough to freely explore them. I was old enough to take a pail across the road and pick berries, I guess with my parents and older brother. Were they blueberries or raspberries? They were delicious to eat while picking, turned hands and mouths delightfully amusing colors, and got cooked into pies and desserts. Those berries were great fun; the place and the time I remember as innocent, full of wonder, safe. I think we didn't stay there long, though I don't know why. It seemed pretty normal to pick up and move when I was a child, so I doubt I questioned it. I think New London was next, or maybe it was La Jolla and the birth of my sister and then back to Connecticut. I wish I could find that list!

I remember my sister being in both New London and Groton, and don't remember her at all in Ledyard, so maybe La Jolla was next. There, I remember an older woman who stayed with us a lot; she and I helped my sister take her first steps. I also remember setting fire to a neighbor's clothes closet with my older brother. Recently, my father, brother and I were in San Diego to celebrate my sister's fortieth birthday. With her, we drove past the La Jolla apartments where we

lived when she was born and where we set the fire. My father, seeming
to find humor in the recollection, asked if we remembered. My sister
didn't; my brother and I did. My own reconstruction from memory and
anecdotes is that we had been left with these neighbors shortly after my
sister's birth. My father was out of the country; my mother evidently
simply didn't come back for us. According to my father, the neighbors
eventually turned us over to juvenile authorities. He also says he was
called back to the States to find our mother, and eventually did, in a bar.
According to him, she'd been having an affair. I recall this as a time of
mixed emotions, bright with the arrival of my sister, dark with
abandonment and fear.

New London, then, had a shakier foundation than the brief time
in Ledyard; I guess there were no other innocent periods, let alone safe
ones. My folks had rented a large house near the beach. Several rooms
were closed off and I resented it, feeling shut out. I wondered what was
in those rooms, and felt that we were somehow lacking not to be able
to have the whole house. I learned to roller skate in New London; my
closest friends were two Jewish girls, sisters. We skated together, I with
a pillow fastened to my butt, an obvious commentary on my beginning
skating skills. My brother was in school; my sister and I weren't. He
was exposed to scarlet fever, but didn't contract it. My sister and I did.
I remember a sun porch where we convalesced; it became a pattern: my
sister and I together, sharing experience, our brother apart. Grandparents came to the New London house and I remember a Christmas
which in recollection feels warm and happy. I see a fire (in the fireplace)
and the glow feels warm, the people feel relaxed. I don't remember
other Christmases feeling like that.

The Atlantic Ocean was across and down the street. I loved, in
winter, standing against the seawall and feeling mesmerized by the dark
green waters and their sometimes soft, sometimes furious waves. I
loved the salt in the wind, the way it stayed in my hair and on my lips
after I was back snugly in the house. The Pacific Ocean is more blue,
but I suffer the same paralysis today, gladly, as I stand and let it take
me outside myself. I remember, too, an amusement park down the
street, but I think it was closed because of the season; it feels like the
rooms of the house, something there but not there, a tease, something
I didn't get to have.

Groton was less dramatic. My brother broke his leg one day as we
both were riding our bikes to school. I raced home on mine only to find
that someone had called my mother and she was on her way to him. He

recuperated on the front porch.

My sister and I had bunk beds in our shared bedroom. Once, from the top bunk, I leaned outside the open doorway and looked into the living room where my parents sat (talking? kissing? watching television?). My mother screamed at me to get back to bed with a tone which sent cold terror into my heart. It cemented a knowing I had already, from La Jolla, that she wasn't safe; I couldn't trust her and had to keep some part of me free and protected from her.

I remember school being closed due to snow, and sledding on the hills near the house. The neighbors had a boxer named Stormy, and we turned our needs to love and held onto him. I remember Stormy spending lots of time in the Groton house, and was happy he was there. From the classroom window I remember one day being able to watch the launching of the nuclear submarine *Nautilus*. I think Mamie Eisenhower broke a bottle of champagne over the bow. The adults were very excited about this event; the teacher said something about us witnessing history. I remember thinking it was odd to break a tiny bottle on a big ship; I wondered if everybody got splashed with champagne and whether glass cut people who stood nearby. One Fourth of July in Groton (we probably weren't there for two), Dad put some firecrackers under a tin can at the bottom of the steep stairs outside the kitchen. The can shot up into the air as the firecrackers went off; I was delighted! In Groton, too, Dad brought home the brand-new 1953 Ford, red and white, with overdrive. His parents were visiting from Iowa the Sunday my brother and I decided to take our little sister to the park. We couldn't understand why the police had been called and everyone was so upset when we returned hours later. She had, as we anticipated, enjoyed the park very much. Although I don't recall this one, I would guess my brother and I got spankings for that: over the knee, bare hand (Dad's) on bare bottom . . . a favorite form of discipline during the early years.

I attended three schools the year of second grade. My brother and I started in one, then changed to one with fewer stairs when he broke his leg. Then (surprise!) we moved, this time to Monterey, my first introduction to Northern California, which was to be my adult home. I finished second grade there before we moved to West Los Angeles, where I got to complete two full years of schooling in the same school! From Monterey, I remember chicken pox and the indelible first sight of the Big Sur coast, an enduring adult place of sanctuary and respite. Cookie, the mutt who was to be my companion and playmate for the next twelve years, joined the family in Monterey, after insistent lobbying on my part. I picked him out of the accidental litter which befell some neighbors and their fenced Scotch terrier; a local boy believed her lonely while in heat and shoved Cookie's father over the fence to keep her company. I'm grateful to him. Cookie was: a good friend, always happy to see me, "so ugly he was cute," smart enough to let us hide and then find us in hide-and-seek, the daily alarm clock, always there. When I was nineteen, visiting on spring break while a college student, my mother and I made the decision to put him to sleep. He'd suffered a hernia; surgery would have rendered him a partially immobile old dog. Until the day of his hernia, his "puppy energy" was intact. I still think we did the right thing with him.

West Los Angeles was: the Irish nuns at the Catholic school, my first big crush on a boy named Teddy, scares about my mom's health due to varicose veins and blood clots, first awareness of my father's touch being somehow not right (with suspicion now that the years of nocturnal fondling had their beginnings at this time or before), a pattern of stealing candy from the corner store, delight in flying kites across the street, neighborhood playmates, Allen next door, Larry up the street, Andrea down. In the back yard we had a huge fig tree which I loved to climb, and plum and apricot trees which bore voluminously. The neighbors gave us avocados from their trees. My brother grew pumpkins (and tomatoes?); I collaborated with Allen next door in planting a large succulent garden. We built forts with several rooms from large cardboard boxes. Allen and I discovered, and frequently enjoyed, secret pre-pubescent sex play; Andrea and I didn't. I remember fondling Larry in his sleep one night when we slept in the same bed at his house. My father and brother were often rageful during our West Los Angeles years; I received beatings from both, my father's both verbal and physical, justified as discipline. My brother was shy, withdrawn, very bright, large for his age. These years, I believe, were the beginnings of his jealousy at my relative social ease and popularity. My father and brother are very good with things, both engineers; I've always been better with people, though there's a paradox there as well.

In West L.A., I remember well-planned and well-cooked meals, playing croquet as a family in the back yard, a semblance of the "normal" family. We moved again when I was nine, to another part of Los Angeles. What was already in place simply grew. My mother's depression and drinking worsened; she increasingly abdicated her domestic responsibilities. My sister and I took on the shopping and the cooking. In high school (we stayed in the same house for ten years!), if I wanted ironed clothes, I ironed them. Recognition came in the form of being a good bartender (being able to make the perfect martini, and being shown off for this talent to neighbors and friends), while school achievements were pretty much ignored. My father's molestation of me, and I suspect (though he refuses to discuss the subject) my brother, became more overt. His drinking and rage increased. The house, the car, the draperies and the carpet were all gray; so were the moods and the souls of the occupants.

We moved a lot because my father was a military officer. Today, even though I've never been in the military, I still move often and have all my adult life. It's my experiential norm. Currently, I'm living in a place I love. I've been here less than a year, and wonder constantly where I'll go next. The pattern has receded in recent years, as I've made a commitment to my work and practice as a psychotherapist; I move now within Northern California. Previously, anywhere on the planet was fair game; I've lived and worked in several parts of the world.

I tire of the old and am fascinated by the new—new places, new people, new ways of living. Some part of me wants to see all there is to see. I'm terminally restless and curious. I'm more and more curious the older I get about the inner world, and my travels center more and more in that direction. Although at peace with my gay sexuality, and blessed with several deep, rich and long-enduring friendships, the abandoned and molested child inside me continues to fear: loss of control, surrendering power in trust, putting it all in one place. My own wounds, of which incest and abandonment are the deepest and the most insidious, enable and enrich my work in the lives of others. My work is my most powerful reminder and encouragement to continue to work on my own life.

The many worlds, geographic and experiential, which together comprised my boyhood, are today all part of me. They inform and challenge, motivate and stifle, accompany and remind the man I am today with every breath, every step and every hour.

Neal King (b. 1947) grew up as a Navy brat in Connecticut and California. He is now a psychologist and psychology professor in Berkeley. He says he is still a boy, just older.

Lela Mae

by David Harrington Campbell

I told her I was going to be a movie star. I was clipping the grass around
the white fence posts. She was raking the freshly cut grass into piles.

"You don't want to be a movie star," Lela Mae said. "There's no
money in it. And besides, it'll take you away from home."

"But you could have been a movie star," I said. "I saw that picture
of you leaning against that car. You looked beautiful."

There was a photograph I had seen that morning of my grandmother when she was near twenty, around the time she got married. She
looked like a movie star to me.

"Only girls want to be movie stars. It's as bad as wanting to be a
whore."

That shut me up. We went back to our clipping and raking. She was
paying me five cents an hour to clip her grass. We sang our song. It was
a song we had made up and always sang when I clipped and she raked.

"*Five cents an hour, Mr. Poole, Mr. Poole.*

"*Five cents an hour, Mr. Poole.*"

I left home at nineteen and moved to Hollywood to become a movie
star. My grandmother was a mountain woman, born and raised in
southwest Virginia. What did she know about becoming a movie star,
anyway?

I didn't become a movie star and Lela Mae didn't live forever. I was
by her side when she died in 1991, two days before her seventy-eighth
birthday. Not long before she died she teased me about John-Boy. She
said she was glad I had played him on television for so long. It had kept
her in touch with me, she said, during all those years when I was gone.

"I didn't play John-Boy," I said, teasing back.

"But you could have," Lela Mae said.

When I was twelve, I told Lela Mae I didn't believe in God. She
started to tremble and cry. She screamed at me that I was a heathen and
that I was going straight to Hell. Good, I told her, Hell had to beat earth
and my stepfather who hated me. I ran away from home right after
that, after seeing *Jesus Christ Superstar* in Roanoke, Virginia. Every-

one thought I was dead but I was in a Holiday Inn in Wytheville, Virginia, eating burgers and watching television until two a.m. My friend Sammy, who had a car and a driver's license, drove me around. We hid out for three days. He kissed my lips, like Jesus. When I returned to my mother's house, they were all there—mother and stepfather, father and stepmother, Lela Mae and my grandfather. Lela Mae grabbed me first and trailed me as I ran to my bedroom and slammed the door. I could hear her telling everyone to leave me alone, I'd be fine in a few days.

Two days before Lela Mae died, she told me she was scared. My sister, Susan, asked her if she wanted us to sing hymns. She said no. So Susan told her we would hold hands—Lela Mae, me, Susan, and Randy, my brother. She told her we would pray silently. I called to the spirit guides and angels and the visions Lela Mae had seen earlier of loved ones who had gone on before. I called to them to help her with her crossing. I whispered to her that God was in her, was in all of us. I was thirty-six years old. Lela Mae was leaving me, leaving us all.

"God is in all of us," I said.

My grandfather stabbed a cow to death with a pitchfork. He was drunk when he parked by the road. I could tell by the way his leg came out of the pickup truck. Lela Mae and I were milking in the barn. I ran to her to tell her he was drunk. Before I knew it she shoved me in a stall filled with cow shit and hay. I was seven years old, on my two-week vacation with my grandparents. The cow was trapped in the stanchion which was used to keep it still while the milking machine sucked its teats. When my grandfather crashed through the barn door it scared the cow. It kicked the milking machine away from its teats. Milk went flying. My grandfather grabbed a pitchfork and started stabbing the cow. I could hear flesh tearing and bones cracking. Lela Mae went after him. She was no match for his rage. He shoved her through the door of the stall where I sat hunched in a corner. She surrounded me with her body.

"He won't hurt us," she said. "I promise."

Through a crack in the door I watched. Blood was squirting out, all over the barn and all over my grandfather. The cow bellowed and moaned. The pitchfork went gliding into its neck. The cow slumped. It was dying. My grandfather beat it with the side of the pitchfork. It lay motionless on the barn floor, in its own shit.

Lela Mae picked me up and ran with me through the barn. We ran to my great-grandparents' house, my grandfather's parents, a quarter mile away. Before I knew it, I was snug beneath handmade quilts, Lela Mae beside me weeping, crying out that nothing like that would ever happen again.

But it did.

And now, one day after Lela Mae's funeral, with mounds of flowers on top of the fresh dirt of her grave, my grandfather, a man of eighty, cusses out my five-year-old nephew. We all flee into our cars, away from the man who made Lela Mae's life hell. But before we go, we all, in our own way, get in his old face and cuss him out. It doesn't take away my grief. It just makes me feel better.

When I was a little boy, I used to pray that my grandfather would die first so I could have some time with Lela Mae without him around. Today, he sits alone in their farmhouse.

After my mother remarried and my stepfather beat her head against the wall, blood sliding down the white walls of the living room, I told my grandmother I wanted to live with my father. She screamed, "No! Children belong with their mothers."

At age ten I made a decision to stay with my mother. Lela Mae was proud. I was not. Later I told her she had been wrong. She said, yes, she had. She was sorry. She had been afraid she'd never see me again.

When I was eleven, my stepfather gave me a BB gun at my grandparents' house. He told me to go outside and kill something. I told him I didn't know how to use a gun. He laughed at me and said I was a boy, I could figure it out. I looked around at my family for someone to rescue me but no one did. They all just stared. I put on my coat and went outside. I walked down the steps to the road. I was cold and the BB gun was cold. I stood under an electric wire that crossed the road. A redbird landed on the wire above my head. It was so close I could almost touch it. It started to sing. I felt my stepfather's eyes pinned on me, staring at me from a window in my grandparents' house. The bird hopped a few inches on the wire and fluttered its wings. A cold wind had just passed through us both. I lifted the BB gun and saw the redbird through the U-shaped thing on top of the barrel. I pulled the trigger. The redbird fell to the road. It was a few inches from my feet. Its head and neck were twisted around its shoulders. It was dead. I carried it inside and handed it to Lela Mae.

"Give this to Charles," I said.

There were tears in her eyes. "I wanted to do something," she said. Her voice was cracking. "But I have to live with your grandfather." There were more tears as she reached for me. "And your mother has to live with Charles."

I pulled away from her reach. I laid the BB gun on the kitchen table and went upstairs to bed. I could hear my stepfather and grandfather drinking and cussing in the living room.

I went to sleep wishing I was a redbird, with strong wings to carry me away.

My grandfather was pitching a fit on the back porch. An old, crumpled-up man, unable to tolerate the loss of a hammer. It was six months before Lela Mae died, two weeks after her cancer diagnosis. Lela Mae and I sat listening to him, side by side on the couch.

"Is it any wonder," she said, motioning toward the back porch and looking me in the eyes. "Is it any wonder," she said, "that I have cancer?"

Lela Mae came to visit me, on the island where I live, two years before she died. She had more energy than I did. One morning I awoke very early and saw her wandering around my decks and yard, looking at my flowers. I could picture her large, wraparound porch, filled with geraniums, petunias and pansies, flowers I had watched her raise and helped her water since I was old enough to walk. Every now and then she would stoop and snip a dead bloom off a plant. She thought she was alone. She thought I slept in until nine or ten like I used to. She didn't know that I couldn't sleep past six anymore, hadn't slept past six for years. She was inspecting my home, three thousand miles away from her own. I watched her poke around and lean forward around the corners. After a while I couldn't restrain myself. I walked toward her, the morning sun shining through the northwest evergreens to reach my flowers, to reach her face. She saw me and smiled.

"You grow flowers just like a woman," she said.

"A man can grow flowers, too," I said.

Lela Mae and I hooked arms and began walking.

"I just can't get over you and your flowers," Lela Mae said. We were passing by white geraniums and rose bushes thick with color. She couldn't take her eyes off them.

"And I can't get over you," I said to Lela Mae, her white hair shining in the morning sun like the blooms on my geraniums.

David Harrington Campbell was born in Galax, Virginia in 1955 and reared all over southwest Virginia, and southern California. He now lives on Vashon Island in Washington State where he has just completed work on a new novel.

Aunt Dot

by Cary Alan Johnson

I remember being young feeling grown
at seven among the feet of many mothers
impatient with wallpapered kitchen
conversations and hot combs.

Twice-a-year she came
with the harvested suns of a thousand
Dixie streets
a visitor to Troy
bearing pecans for the women of our clan
who killed chickens and cooked pork in offering.

Our tribe is matri-local endogamous complex.
We trace our history from a common female deity.

Twice-a-year she came
bringing news from home
South
our harvest home
our burial home
our home in times of war and famine
South
we sent our sisters
pregnant with shame in love
South.

Twice-a-year she came
elders delayed decisions to her arrival
marriages births lives hung pending
we were ellipses to her exclamation
she judged wisely
she was the ballast of our family ship.

She taught us
that there is no shame in being poor
nothing white about being smart
no hope without forgiveness.

And when at twenty-two I returned
to Rocky Mount
and found her babbling vacant
mind broken and scattered in flowerpots
that schoolteacher intellect
now lining the pockets
of a torn housedress
I pointed my car toward Washington
and escaped
before the sun could set
on the blue tips of rigid mountains.
Those selfsame mountains she had crossed
twice-a-year
Christmas to New Year's
moverin' moverin'
Memorial to Labor
moverin' moverin'
going north
going Greyhound
bearing pecans
bearing wisdom
bearing love.

Cary Alan Johnson is an author, Africanist and human rights activist.
Originally from Brooklyn, Cary has lived and traveled throughout
Africa, Europe and North America.

Family Ties: A Grandson's Remembrance

by Randy Hilfman

"I want to go right along with him!" Grandma Bertha cried the morning Grandpa Joe died. I was a naïve nineteen, ill-equipped to console her anguish that November morning. It was the day after Thanksgiving, 1969. In those confused and grief-stricken hours after his death, my family collectively tried to comfort and reassure her that life was indeed still worth living, that rich adventures lay ahead. Joe, who immigrated from Germany in 1906 at age fifteen, had lived in Washington, Iowa, the small community in which I grew up, for half a century, and was my first grandparent to die.

Grandpa's death is a vivid memory. Visiting him at the hospital the night before he died, I recall his ashen face and how tired and scared he looked. I think he feared his life was slipping away. Later, I remember his waxen countenance in the open casket at the funeral home and how bizarre it all seemed. It was only the second time I'd faced the death of a loved one.

I was fortunate to see my grandparents regularly in my youth. Joe and Bertha, my mother's parents, lived in the same town as my family; my father's parents, Ralph and Edith, had a house eighty minutes away in Bettendorf. Though I loved them and received their warm and loving support, I wonder now why I didn't ask more questions about their childhoods and their recollections of raising my parents. I suppose those questions didn't occur to me at the time, busy as I was trying to make sense of my own life, and I regret not discovering more about my grandparents' lives. At the time, I probably assumed they somehow would live forever.

After immigrating from Germany, Grandpa Joe made his way to Davenport, Iowa, where he worked with his uncle in the clothing business. In 1915, he moved to Washington and worked at Klein Klothing Kompany and in nearby Fairfield before establishing his own store in 1951. Joe returned to Germany for a visit in the 1920s, met Bertha, a romance developed and they decided to marry. Bertha followed Joe to the States soon after his return. Married in Chicago in 1924, they would live in Washington for the rest of their lives.

Their marriage was traditional. Joe was the sole breadwinner and ran his business (in later years) with my father. Bertha stayed home and was primarily responsible for raising daughters Helen, Franny, Babe and Marilyn. My mother remembers a warm, nurturing, and moderately permissive household, though undoubtedly each daughter's experience was different. As parents, their greatest satisfaction possibly lay in rearing healthy children and sending them to college.

Bertha and Joe were extremely close. My father characterizes their marriage as a "lifelong romance," a rarity in the divorce-torn late twentieth century. I never witnessed any serious squabbling. My mother only remembers one argument herself, when Joe chided Bertha (in pre–Imelda Marcos days) for taking too many shoes on a trip.

A stout, substantial man, with a shock of gray hair and bushy eyebrows, Joe's main focus was his clothing business which to this day bears his name, Joe Falk Co. An unfailingly generous, modest man, Joe was forthright and fair-minded. Active in community affairs, he cared deeply about his family and valued time with friends. Bridge and cribbage were favorite diversions. Quiet and stoical, he never complained about his heart condition or emphysema, neither of which robbed him of his vitality.

I can still picture Joe sitting comfortably in the living room, watching television. He would audibly sniff at semi-regular intervals, a sound my Uncle Don wished he could hear just one more time after Joe's death. I remember him walking arm-in-arm with Bertha across Central Park on the way to Winga's Café where he loved to watch me consume heaping mounds of mashed potatoes. I recall the day he presented me with a Rotary Club award when I was in high school. Shunning a sentimental introduction, Joe simply blurted, "Here, take it!" And, of course, I remember him puffing on cigars, which he smoked with regularity until his 60s, when the doctors insisted he quit.

He usually addressed Bertha as "Schatz," which means treasure in German. And treasure her he did. He would customarily say "wonderful meal, Schatz" after dining. Even if (on rare occasions) a particular dish was not a culinary triumph, he'd reassure Grandma, "That's just how I like it." When the oppressive Iowa heat and humidity prompted Bertha to grumble, Joe would respond to his daughters, "It doesn't hurt me at all and it does your mother so much good." Joe often removed his dentures and put them in his shirt pocket, causing Bertha to admonish him. His impish retort: "I'm saving them for your next husband."

Grandma Bertha was a short, sturdy, buxom woman with auburn hair. According to my neighborhood buddy, Richard, she never stopped sounding like she "just got off the boat." A big-hearted, cheerful, compassionate woman, Bertha was always a good listener. She volunteered as a Gray Lady at the local hospital for many years, enjoyed bridge games with Grandpa and socialized with local women at the Fortnightly Club.

Bertha loved to cook, and many of my fondest memories center on food. No wonder I'm an epicurean to this day. She baked mouth-watering rhubarb pies and unforgettable wafer-thin, cinnamon-coated cookies. She concocted a cottage cheese, cream cheese and sour cream dip my brother David was particularly addicted to. We could always count on finding oversized Hershey bars in her kitchen cabinet. Her succulent pot roast dinners with potatoes and green beans were incomparable. And, not surprisingly, she had a touch for *Kuchen,* a tasty plum cake.

Bertha, like most housewives of that era, focused on home and family, supporting Joe in every possible way. Sometimes that took the form of gift-wrapping packages at the store during the holidays. Mostly it meant devoting herself to maintaining the house, raising the children, and, in later years, doting on her grandchildren. She also coordinated the periodic visits of Hermina, Dave, Fritz, Bert, Ernie, Sara, Anna and Caroline—Joe's colorful siblings from Chicago. She appreciated the importance of schooling and always told us kids, "They can never take education away from you." I remember how radiant she looked in her blue chiffon dress at my wedding in 1980, when advancing years could not diminish her buoyancy.

I remember shopping for her at Swanson's Grocery—"the little store" on the corner—and picking her up, clutching her bags of groceries, at Fareway, a local supermarket. I recall her sitting on the living room couch, where she shared my appreciation of Tom Snyder and his offbeat parade of guests on the long-departed "Tomorrow" show. I remember driving my grandparents' long green Oldsmobile, a little shakily I guess. It was the only car I ever ran out of gas in, and I also managed to dent the driver's-side door while angle-parking on the town square. Bertha never learned to drive.

Bertha died on my mother's birthday in 1982, at eighty-five, while my parents were visiting me in Seattle. I remember hearing Aunt Marilyn's message on our answering machine, imploring my mother to call her "immediately." My mother sensed that it had something to do with Grandma, which was quickly confirmed. Bertha had died of a stroke while playing with my cousin's daughter. It was about the only time I remember my father shedding a tear, as he lamented, "She was such a great old gal." I still have the scrap of paper on which he wrote down emergency flight plans back to the Midwest.

I keenly remember the gaunt, stooped figure of my Grandfather Ralph. It was comforting to have your grandpa be your dentist and hear his reassuring "um-hm's" in the dental chair. Grandpa's dental techniques and philosophy were quite advanced for his time. He was the oldest licensed dentist in the state of Iowa when he died. He found a special joy in his work. He was a natural bending over patients or working in the tiny adjoining room of his office where he prepared fillings. I was so impressed with him as a boy of twelve that I wrote an essay about wanting to be a dentist when I grew up. It didn't happen.

One of my fondest memories is playing golf with him at Duck Creek, our favorite course. He usually hit the ball straight, but not far, and he always pulled his bag along, never riding in a cart. He savored the exercise and the opportunity to spend a few hours with his grandson. It was a special pursuit only he and I shared, never a "good walk ruined," as Mark Twain would have it. Grandpa loved his Iowa Hawkeye sports. As a University of Iowa graduate, I did too. He was so tickled when I wrote the football coach once, instructing him—as my father still does regularly from the sidelines—on the finer points of coaching.

He was an easy-going, occasionally playful man. I have so many different memories of him. Once when he was carrying Grandma Edith's purse briefly outside my parents' home, the curious sight sent my mother into absolute hysterics. I recall meat juices dripping from his mouth as he ate beef tenderloin at Slavens Manor in Bettendorf. I remember his standard, clipped retort—"Okay, all right"—when Edith would heckle him about his driving.

Voluble, silver-haired Edith was proper and reserved, a "lady of the first order." But she was a kind and loving, if nervous woman, extremely protective of her husband and children. A poem by her daughter, Louise, portrays her as a regal "dowager queen." Although Edith did have hobbies—she knitted afghans and typed Braille books —and was involved with community affairs, my basic memories of her, as with Bertha, concern the family where she concentrated most of her energies. She baked these incredible sour cream cookies and a mean *bundt Kuchen,* kept house, and helped organize Grandpa and structure their social life. Edith's unofficial marriage contract resembled Bertha's, as she was primarily responsible for raising her children, Louise and Leon. In later years, she savored time spent with her grandchildren. We could always count on Grandma to make a fuss over us.

She was a dedicated correspondent during my 1969 European vacation. I remember her having some sort of rash on her leg, and I wonder if there's a genetic link with the psoriasis that plagues me now. She was always boldly assertive at restaurants, never hesitating to complain if she deemed something amiss. She also became a more excitable and overcautious driver as she aged, honking indiscriminately at whomever she perceived to be in her way. In my family, these behaviors are the stuff of legend.

Married in 1923, Ralph and Edith always seemed happy and companionable to me. I never remember seeing them argue. Close and demonstrative in later life, they would hold hands in public. They enjoyed an excellent rapport over the bridge table, and it was a proud moment when they won a tournament at the Blackhawk Hotel.

I remember the High Holidays at Temple Emmanuel, especially the pleasingly sonorous notes of the choir, the foods and rituals of Passover seders at Aunt Louise's, excursions to the ritzy Outing Club. I salivate to this day when I recall the corned beef, lox, thick bricks of cream cheese, aromatic rye bread and Max's pickles we'd enjoy when Grandma and Grandpa brought their moveable feast from Rock Island to Washington. I still love deli food.

Despite family tragedies during her youth, Edith seemed mostly content with her life until later years, when several family crises surfaced which made her defensive and apprehensive. Her brother had been killed in a car accident when she was twenty years old. Her mother, never recovering from the loss, had committed suicide when Edith was twenty-nine, and Grandma couldn't bring herself to tell her children what had happened. This pattern of burying feelings and denial has occurred in my immediate family as well, concerning my career path and my divorce. My father suffered through a scary bout of depression himself a number of years ago, but fortunately faced up to and overcame it. Dealing with Ralph's Alzheimer's disease and its ramifications in later years took its toll on the whole family, though I was geographically removed from it and only saw him once after he was afflicted. Notwithstanding the sadness of the illness, I prefer to remember the more amusing aspects of Grandpa's behavior, personally observed or recounted: repetitive pontification about the virtues of stannous fluoride, mistaking my sister for my mother, reports of uncharacteristically cantankerous actions in the nursing home where he eventually died. Edith felt tremendous grief that Ralph was losing his faculties, and my father thinks it stole five to ten years of her life. Ralph died in 1985, at age eighty-six. Edith died ten months earlier, at eighty-four, the same day my nephew Abraham was born. The ironic rhythms of life and death, alpha and omega.

My grandparents' lives were far different from mine: Joe and Bertha were German immigrants who spent most of their lives in a small midwestern town. Ralph and Edith (born in New York and Illinois) lived in a medium-sized Iowa city. Born in Los Angeles, I grew up in a small town and attended college in Iowa, but have lived since in Ann Arbor, Los Angeles, and Seattle. So I've moved more as an adult and lived in larger cities, and though I haven't enjoyed the particular sense of community smaller towns afford, I've made friends wherever I've lived. I've also nurtured a nationwide network of friendships forged from my longtime involvement in the men's movement and through my contacts with writers, editors and publishers.

My grandparents' marriages were both traditional, embodying the classic support system: the husband was the exclusive wage-earner; the wife was the head of the household, chief child-rearer and helpmate. This arrangement seemed to flourish for my grandparents: One marriage endured forty-five years, the other sixty-one. Was either marriage oppressively male-dominated or exploitative? Not that I observed, but I can't really presume to know the inner lives of my grandmothers, who lived most of their days before the rebirth of the women's movement in the 1960s.

My marriage in the 1980s was more equitable. In terms of wage-earning, my ex-wife and I both worked after her undergraduate days, and we shared household responsibilities and child-rearing. So, unlike my grandmothers, my spouse worked outside the home. I was also more deeply involved than my grandfathers in the day-to-day life of my child. Notwithstanding the egalitarian ideals of my marriage, I still ended up divorced, though Clare and I agreed on joint custody of our son, an arrangement virtually unheard of a generation earlier.

Though dissolving my marriage was painful, I choose to emphasize its positive aspects. It's enabled me to take what I learned from married life—among other things, how communication and passion can wane and die—and accept the challenge of applying those understandings to my subsequent relationships with Rose and Wendy. New liaisons, though scary, can also be energizing and uplifting. It's frustrating to compare my struggle to create a mutually loving bond with a woman when I contemplate my grandparents' marriages, seemingly so solid and secure, though admittedly of a different era. I sometimes question my ability to love unselfishly, to overcome sexual fears, to devote myself to one woman as my grandfathers did for decades. I admire my grandparents' ability to sustain and support one another over the years, even through the roughest times. Because of them, I know it is possible.

Both my grandfathers seemed content and fulfilled, Ralph even joyful, in their professions. I've never achieved a comparable level of accomplishment in my career, but I have cultivated friendships and proven my skills while toiling in the peripheries of the legal profession. I've also derived pleasure from my freelance writing and editing, political work and teaching in the University of Washington Experimental College.

My grandparents' parenting styles were inevitably different from mine, considering the fact that the prevailing expectations of the time were that mothers, not fathers, raised children. A more egalitarian child-rearing approach existed in my marriage and current joint custody arrangement, where my son is with me during alternating two-week periods.

I'm a "new style" father compared to my father's generation, a more involved type of parenting increasingly mandated by contemporary societal expectations. I am certainly not a perfect father, but a father who witnessed my son Zack's birth, changed his diapers, gave him baths. I now comfort his tears, encourage him to play baseball or audition for the school play, wrestle with him, cook for him, argue with him and nurture him while trying to remain sensitive to his emotional life.

Though my father remembers fishing trips, hikes and Hawkeye games as activities that nourished his relationship with his father, I know he wishes he'd spent more time with him as a youth. This may be the lament of an entire generation, and I am mindful of its import.

As a part-time single father, I'm probably a more permissive parent than any of my grandparents. This is partly for reasons of personal style, partly because my nine-year-old is growing up in the era of Bart Simpson, and sometimes merely due to exhaustion. Joe and Bertha raised four children; Edith and Ralph two. With only one child, I haven't dealt with issues of sibling rivalry, but have faced the challenge of a lack of readily available playmates. Though I believe Joe and Ralph genuinely enjoyed being fathers, their self-worth may ultimately have derived more from their professional accomplishments than from how worthy they viewed themselves as parents. I'm sure they were proud of their children but, being products of their time, providing for them financially was inevitably a major concern.

Though Zack and I were always close and spent considerable time together while I was married, I naturally spend more time with him by myself as a joint custody father. Neither my parents nor my grandparents ever raised a child alone, so this is a new, exhilarating adventure for me. It's an uncharted journey, and I can draw only so much from past experience. As a single father, though, I think I view parenting as a career more in the sense that my grandmothers doubtless did. It's a challenging, consuming responsibility, but I relish the soaring pleasures that it provides. Sometimes it's extraordinary simply to ponder the bond of father and son.

In his memoir, *Half the Way Home*, Adam Hochschild speaks of possessing "your own past, which belongs to no one else, and whose power over you must be admitted, felt, before you can leave it behind and live the life before you." I've come to realize that it can be invaluable—and potentially profound—to ask our grandparents (and parents) about their lives while we have the chance. (Indeed, talking to my parents about their parents for this article was illuminating.) I believe it can make a difference in our lives: it can help us understand why they act the way they do, and aid us in piecing together patterns in their parenting that we may unwittingly be emulating. Not only can they share the amusing times, the joys and the delights, they can reveal trials faced in their youth and how they dealt with them—deaths of loved ones, squabbles with siblings, taunts from friends, moments of uncertainty, pain, anger, fear. I urge you to talk to them now. It's too late when they're gone.

Randy Hilfman was born in 1950 and spent his boyhood years in Washington, Iowa. He has written articles about sexuality, men's issues and fathering for Changing Men, Men and Intimacy *and* Nurturing News. *His erotic writings and crossword puzzles have appeared in* Libido *and* Sex and Sensibility. *A former editor of* Brother, *he lives in Seattle where he co-parents his son Zachary.*

Iyay

by John L. Silva

Family lore has it that I gave my nanny her name when I was three years old. I was obsessed with the song "Old MacDonald Had a Farm," and would listen to it endlessly on a wind-up phonograph in my bedroom. As the record slowed or ended, I would call out, like in the song, "Eeyay, Eeyay, Oh." My *yaya* (nanny) would stop whatever she was doing (usually reading her favorite *Bulaklak* magazine), run to the phonograph, and wind it up again. Other servants in the house, seeing her snap to my calling, thought I had given her a new name and began calling her Iyay. My parents continued to call her Sali, short for Rosalita, her real name. But whenever they referred to her while talking to me, they would say "Iyay mo" (your Iyay), not just as a recognition of my nickname for her, but because she was my very own nanny.

Iyay started work as a childservant for my grandparents. Her parents worked as field hands in my grandparents' sugar *hacienda*, San Vicente, on the island of Negros. Her grandparents were among the thousands of laborers brought to Negros from the neighboring island of Panay in the late nineteenth century to plant sugar cane when demand for sugar rose in the Americas and Europe. Negros, thickly forested, populated by aborigines and naturally fertilized with volcanic soil, was transformed in no time into one vast expanse of tall, swaying sugar cane fields. In 1925, when my newlywed grandparents moved into their two-story Caribbean-style mansion on the hacienda, with a retinue of house servants, gardeners, and livery boys, little Iyay was one of them.

When she was seven years old, her task was to remove the *arinolas* (piss pots) from under each bed, drain and wash them. Another chore was to attend at every family meal, holding one end of a long pole to which was attached at the other end a thin bamboo ring with long strands of colored paper glued to it. She would stand erect, a slight distance from the dining table, so as not to interfere with the servants scurrying about with the dishes. Iyay's eyes would be focused on the dishes and, if a fly tried an approach on the food, she would gently wave the pole with its dangling paper over the table and everyone's heads to frighten the fly. She would make sure she waved it just so discreetly as to shoo away the fly without disturbing the family.

Being a trusted and loyal servant, Iyay as a young woman became the *yaya* to my uncle, the sole and favored son of my grandparents. Inevitably, she was "passed on" to me when I was born, being the first male grandson.

My first recollection of Iyay is a sense of complete security. I was four years old. I was playing with the chauffeur's children on the open-air balcony at the top floor of our house, an art-deco-inspired three-story building resembling a landlocked ship complete with porthole windows. (From the balcony there was a grand view of the river, the church spires and the rooftops of the city of Iloilo.)

Suddenly the floor swayed, and the house began to creak loudly. It was an earthquake. For a moment, we all looked at each other in amazement, but when we were tossed around the room and could not stand up, we started crying. I heard Iyay scream from below, "Johnny Boy, Johnny Boy!" In an instant she rushed up the stairs to the balcony, dashed over to scoop me and another child and run down so many stairs, all the while crying, "Ay, ay, ay," half-reciting the Hail Mary in Ilonggo, clutching us tightly. Several times she nearly slipped on the shaking marble floor; her glasses flew off her face. Sweating profusely, her face was etched with terror. Yet, with my arms around her neck, cradled tightly in her powerful arms and hands, watching her face in total concentration, I felt a tremendous serenity and comfort. I laid my head gently on her wet shoulder, stroking the scapular that she kissed each night hanging from her neck. I was oblivious to the chaos as she cleared the stairs, zig-zagging through the moving furniture, dodging breaking glass and falling plaster, finally reaching the porch and the garden. I remember Iyay sprawled on the lawn, exhausted and in shock, and me bending over her soaked face, kissing it all over, each gentle kiss reviving her slowly. I knew then, in some vague way, that Iyay had just saved my life.

Iyay was a tall, bony woman who lorded it over the other servants. Her lengthy service to the family, along with being my nanny, made her the *mayordoma*, the head servant of the house. She had high cheekbones, full lips and deep-set eyes characteristic of Visayan peasant women. (My mother had initially thought of hiring a Chinese *amah* for me but was dissuaded after hearing some talk about certain *amahs* spiking their wards' milk with opium to keep them quiet.)

With her light blue uniform, Iyay wore wire-rimmed glasses that added to her authority, simple earrings, one ring with a plain gold band and a thin Bulova ladies' watch. She was not beautiful but she had a pleasant disposition, and her smiles, earthy laughter and generous smack-sounding kisses made her attractive to me.

Iyay was bent on protecting me from any unnecessary sadness. At the first sign of raised voices, shouting, and crying between my parents (usually emanating behind the closed doors of the library), Iyay would quickly lead me outside to play in the swing or the *nipa* hut playhouse, or take me to the servants' quarters where she would order a houseboy to strum "Old MacDonald" on the guitar. Other times, Geronimo, the driver, would recount his days as a *guerillero* fighting with the Americanos against the Japanese. There was also Muning, my sister's *yaya*, who had the most frightening *aswang* stories about half-bodied women who fly in the night and land on thatched rooftops, peering inside, looking for babies to steal.

Dad, a colonel in the U.S. Army, wanted me to follow in his footsteps. Literally. He once devoted an afternoon trying to teach me how to march! He had the furniture in the living room moved to the side to make one large space. He began by commanding me to attention as he stood erect. With eyes trained straight ahead, his left foot and right arm swung stiffly forward, parallel to each other, followed by his right leg and left arm. Reaching the other end of the room, he turned around to watch me repeat his steps.

I gently arched my left foot forward, toe first, as my sister's ballet teacher would do. My left arm ever so gracefully followed, and my right foot and right arm repeated the same movement. Iyay, who had watched me from the edge of the room, rushed up to my father, pleading to take me away, on the excuse that it was time for my *siesta*. Before my father could respond, Iyay led me by the hand up the stairs to my bedroom and into her enveloping arms.

Further defying my father's wish to make a man of me, Iyay often allowed me into my sister's bedroom where I would dress up her dolls and rearrange the dollhouse furniture. For every photograph dad took of me in little general uniforms, military cadet suits or cowboy clothes, Iyay took fuzzy ones of me in ballet poses, in my sister's dresses with a bandanna over my head, or as a gay little pansy.

Siesta time in the afternoon was the hottest time of the day, and I was always very uncomfortable. Iyay would splash powder on my front and back and put me to bed, using her lap as my pillow. Even with the large windows wide open, the heat was suffocating, and I usually whined about it. "All right," she would say as she stroked my hair, "I will call the wind."

Yes, that's it. That soft, sustained, pleading whistle ending with a high-pitched note. Whistle a few more times, Iyay, make sure the wind hears you. There, I can feel it! A breeze tickling my nose. Aaah, now there's a gust of wind hitting me with the scent of hibiscus and ocean spray.

With my eyes closed, I imagine the wind flying around the room, pushing creaking doors, making the curtains flutter, the bamboo chimes click away.

Hold me now, Iyay, while this breeze caresses me to sleep.

Years later, I asked her how she summoned the wind. She said she had learned it from the cane cutters who whistled to keep cool under the hot sun.

I started first grade in Manila and we lived with my *lolo* and *lola* (grandfather and grandmother) in their house fronting Manila Bay. Each morning, Iyay accompanied my older sister Marie and me to school in a chauffeured car. As the car neared the school entrance, I would always ask her to reassure me that she would fetch us in the afternoon. Yet, when the car stopped and the door opened, I would quickly dash out evading her goodbye kiss. (I was learning from other classmates that *yayas* were servants, and affection for, and from, them was discouraged. Each day, I saw classmates yell at their *yayas*, pinch them, kick them and throw their lunch boxes at them. I didn't follow their behavior, but neither could I reveal my love for Iyay.) When classes ended, I would rush out of the school gate, past cars with their waiting nannies, and into our car. As we drove off and reached a "safe" distance, only then would I climb to the front seat to embrace and kiss my waiting Iyay.

Sunday was Iyay's day off. She would wear her best clothes, dab on a bit of makeup and perfume, and go off to play mah-jongg with her friends. I would give her some of my allowance, which she considered good-luck money, and waited for her to come back before dinnertime, straining from a window that overlooked the steel gate entrance. Whether she won or lost, she always returned with sweets for me: Serg's chocolate bars, sugar-coated peanuts, drops of molasses in little wooden globules disparagingly called *pungit sang Igorot* (the snot of the Igorot), or Chinese dried plums called *champuy*.

On the off-days she didn't play mah-jongg. She would have the run of the house right after lunch when *Lola* was off to her high-stakes

game of *monte* and *Lolo* rendezvoused with his *querida*. Being the
mayordoma, she could do as she pleased. She would turn on the
overhead fan and the cabinet radio in the living room, while the other
servants sat on the polished wood floor or lay on the woven straw *banig*
mats they brought from their bedrooms. Iyay would slowly turn the
tuning knob until she found a soap opera, and they would all listen to
that. Later, there was "Dear Tia Dely," an on-air query and advice to
the lovelorn. These were restful, lounging afternoons, as one servant
would hold another's head on her lap, pulling white hairs or pinching
lice. Another would be reading a magazine full of hit-song lyrics. Our
cook, Tiya Soling, a chubby, stern-looking woman who constantly
wore the native plaid sarong called *patadyong*, would have a young
female servant snuggled up to her as they lay on a mat. Everyone
suspected that Tiya Soling possessed a love potion that made any
woman fall in love with her.

When "Hit Parade" came on, all languid feelings ceased in anticipation of Doris Day's hit song, "*Que Sera, Sera*." As in a Broadway
musical tableau, everyone shuffled about, readying themselves to sing
with Doris. One would be by the window, another would have her
cheek pressed to the radio speaker, while another would stand erect,
hand close to her mouth, clutching an imaginary microphone. For Iyay,
the song had tragic significance. Our family was moving in a few
months to the United States without her. My two younger sisters would
take a nanny with them, but by then I was six years old and deemed old
enough to take care of myself. Everyone followed along as Doris sang,
and Iyay sang the song with much resignation and tears.

Que sera, sera . . .
Whatever will be, will be.
The future's not ours to see.
Que sera, sera . . .

To prepare for the move, Dad ordered my sisters and me to speak
only English, and if he should hear us talk in our native Ilonggo, he
would deduct five centavos from our allowance. Furthermore, I was to
be weaned away from Iyay. No longer could she crack the top of my
soft-boiled egg, or peel my grapes and remove their seeds, or scoop the
mango from its skin, or open sunflower seeds with her teeth. When Dad
took us to the Army-Navy Club to swim and acquaint ourselves with
American children, Iyay now had to wait outside with the driver. I
would have to change by myself, comb my hair, and carry my wet towel
and bathing trunks. To Iyay, cut off from the routine of caring for me,

this new regime was distressing. And when I spoke to her in English, she kept silent, understanding little and unable to respond. She would often give me an angry smirk for making her feel stupid.

When Dad was not around, Iyay would reimpose her hold on me, and off we would go to see a Tagalog movie about a powerful wonderwoman named Darna, or the carnival in Intramuros, the old section of Manila, to ride the Ferris wheel or see the snakewoman, or play *Laro ng Daga*, betting on which house in a circular row of spinning houses the white mouse would enter. (As the mouse dizzily made up its mind, drag queens in cocktail dresses would cajole last-minute bettors, while lip-synching Patti Page songs.)

On one of my last outings with Iyay, we rode on the open-air top deck of a *motorco*, blue double-decker buses that slowly plied the length of Dewey Boulevard. As the sky turned crimson and the sun slowly sank into the bay, Iyay and I held each other tight. Over the noisy *motorco* and the mufflerless jeepneys, with the ocean breeze howling in our ears, she repeated to me loudly, over and over in Ilonggo, "*Indi mo gid ako palipaton.*" (Don't you ever forget me.)

Dad came from a poor Ilocano family and was never happy living the grand plantation life of my mother's family. In the 30s, Dad had gone to the States as a young man, worked in California as a field hand and later joined the Army at the start of World War II. He was a self-made man, and he didn't see the same traits in me; I was a delicate and tender lad, rich, pampered and served by an obliging nanny. Dad didn't realize that I, too, had yearnings and feelings quite different from his and the family's expectations. Ordered to sleep alone in my bed without Iyay as my *tanday* (a custom of straddling someone to sleep), I began embracing my pillows instead, imagining them to be Tab Hunter or Ricky Nelson, and all the other exciting men whose pictures I saw in Mom's Hollywood movie magazines. I rubbed my penis against the pillow, thinking of the naked Americanos and their big dicks, whom I saw showering at the Army-Navy Club. Each night I fantasized about meeting Elvis, bringing him back home, letting him ride in my grandfather's passenger ship, visiting one island after another. Iyay would scoop his mangoes for him and make sure his sequined shirts were washed and pressed. How could Elvis not love me? I was beginning to look forward to my American sojourn.

The day of our departure came. I wore an *Americana* suit with a little bow tie, wet with Iyay's tears from when she tied it on me that morning. She had not slept, having cried the whole night. Dad had warned me not to cry at the airport, since I was now the only other man in the group of three sisters, one nanny and Mom. My grandparents, with servants and drivers, were there to see us off. I was torn, excited about taking the trip on a plane much larger than the DC-3's I had been on, yet unwilling to let go of Iyay's hand. I didn't want to leave this woman whose salty body fragrance I had grown up on, whose dedication to me was total, and whose love was unceasing. But I was six years old, with no control over who was to love me and whom I should love. In the midst of this crowded airport full of tearful people embracing and saying farewells, with loudspeakers announcing departures, I had to try hard not to cry.

"Well, it's time to go," Dad finally announced in jaunty American fashion. Iyay knelt in front of me, and I whispered softly to her in English, "Will you be here when I return?" She didn't understand me. She began to cry and held me in her arms, saying over and over, "*Palangga ta gid ikaw, indi mo gid ako palipaton.*" (I love you very much, don't ever forget me.)

To forget, you see, was tantamount to ending one's love.

Iyay sobbed uncontrollably as Mom gently pulled me away from her. Kneeling on the floor, her face lifted toward the ceiling, she wailed, "*Ang bata ko, ang bata ko.*" (My child, my child.)

The servants tried lifting Iyay from the floor, while my grandmother ordered her to stop crying, reproaching her for such uncivilized behavior. As we slowly walked to the boarding gate, I could hear Iyay's wail echo throughout the ceiling of the tall terminal. I covered my ears and turned around to take one last look. The drivers were restraining her from lunging in my direction, while my grandmother rapped her fan on Iyay's dishevelled hair.

I started running ahead, past my parents, my sisters and their nanny, past the line of passengers, to make my way out of the terminal. I darted across the tarmac and up the plane stairs, finally entering the huge Pan American stratocruiser to be greeted by a tall blond stewardess sporting a huge smile. "Why, how are you, little fella?" she exclaimed. I was repelled and attracted by her bubbly exuberance.

I remember sitting on a couch four days later with Marie in our new house in San Francisco, eating a whole box of Sugar Pops. We had been watching TV for hours, seeing all sorts of smiling faces, hearing fast talk and even seeing people kiss. (Back in Manila, when we watched television, *Lola* would pace the floor nearby, praying the Rosary. Each time a kissing scene came on, *Lola* would shout, "Close your eyes!"

That was the signal for Iyay to run to the TV set, stand in front of the screen and remain there until the kissing was over.) Now, Marie and I counted over a dozen kissing scenes just that afternoon.

Beside me and all over the floor were my new Remco Bulldog Tank, my Lionel Train and pieces of an Erector set. Marie had her new dolls and dresses from a visit to the Emporium. Substituting shopping for a missing affection was a long-standing practice in my family.

On the couch, my sister and I cuddled together, waiting for yet another kissing scene, not talking much, bored with our toys, and slowly forgetting those we had left behind, so very far away.

It was a brief two-year interlude in the United States. There is a picture of me during my first communion at Star of the Sea School, posing in a crisp white extra-long-sleeve shirt, hands folded in prayer and smiling to the camera. But my hair is in absolute disarray, like one who just woke up. If Iyay had been around, it would have been plastered down with pomade and sharply parted.

I soon developed my first childhood crush on a classmate named Edward Konwinski, a bright-eyed, blond, freckle-faced boy. Dragging the phone into the hall closet, I called him every night, ending my goodbyes by boldly declaring my love for him. (He wouldn't respond, perhaps attributing my queer affection to my being a foreigner.)

I did meet Tab Hunter at a Cow Palace horse show to which my grandfather, on a U.S. visit, took me one day. After Tab rode his stallion to the delight of the audience, I stalked him throughout the building and found him standing in a passageway. I slowly approached him, trembling with excitement. In my head I rehearsed my introduction and vows of love; I would entice him to the Philippines with the promise to ride my grandfather's Arabian horses.

As I came within a few feet of him he suddenly sauntered toward me and, not noticing, knocked me to the floor. Bending down, he lifted me back to my feet, smiled apologetically and rushed off. I was embarrassed but swooning, having felt his hard thighs against my face. Iyay would have corralled and scolded him, and forced him back to me, even if she had to bribe him.

When we returned to the Philippines, there was Iyay, amidst hundreds of people at the Manila pier, as our ship, the *President Wilson,* slowly came to dock. It was not her uniform, but her height and her jumping up and down, that made me immediately notice her. She was deliriously happy and sobbing like a mother reunited with her kidnapped son. Dormant feelings came back to me when we embraced and kissed each other. She looked me over, astounded by how big I had grown but she had a harder time understanding my Ilonggo, since it had acquired an American accent.

When I reached the age of ten, Dad decided he had had enough of Iyay's powerful hold on me. To him, Iyay represented all the decadence and sloth of my mother's family. He was certain I would grow up totally incapable of taking care of myself. The final straw for him was discovering I still slept with a teddy bear I had played with since I was five. He took it away from me despite my protests and tearful entreaties. Later, Iyay recovered the bear from his closet and returned it to me. Dad found out, and she was summarily fired. My mother intervened, assuring me Iyay would be transferred to my *lola's* employ. I cried bitterly, promising myself that I would never allow anyone to choose whom or what I loved.

In a few years, my parents were divorced, and Dad left for the United States. We eventually moved in with *Lola*, and I was reunited with Iyay. By this time, I was a precocious teenager not seeking Iyay's constant affection. Her hair had grayed, her figure was portly. She had become an occasional cook who baked the afternoon *merienda* cakes and pastries. Semi-retired, she was doted on by the family for her years of service, but feared by the rest of the servants. On Sundays, I still slipped her some money before she headed off to mah-jongg. When she was feeling affectionate, I gave in to her surprise embraces and smacking kisses.

My devotion to Iyay shaped my teenage years in the late 60s. I had a penchant for noticing the treatment of servants. At my Junior-Senior prom in the Manila Hilton, it appalled me to see hundreds of servants and nannies, exhausted and nodding off to sleep outside the ballroom doors, waiting for their *señoritas* to finish partying. In friends' homes, I observed the cruelties they exacted on their servants. In our own house, I saw the hypocrisy of my grandmother, just returned from her daily church service, berating and slapping the servants while still wearing her veil and clutching her prayerbook. I couldn't and didn't want to play *señorito,* which would have allowed me to abuse the servants. I refused to be part of the meanness, because it invariably meant hurting people I loved, like Iyay. I often wondered, if my family and friends were so vicious to their help, how genuine could their affection be for me or anyone else?

The second time I left the Philippines for the United States, I had grown into an angry, twenty-one-year-old radical. It was another tearful goodbye with Iyay, but this time I was ideologically hardened. I promised her that the oppression she and her peasant class had faced for centuries would soon be over. Iyay was quizzical of my zeal. Her only response was that I should send for her once I was settled so she could continue serving me! Instead of departing imbued with her continued affection, I considered her offer an example of the servility in peasants that only prolonged their class suffering.

Iyay and I wrote to each other on birthdays and Christmases, with lengthy summaries of our lives. Our letters were a study in contrast, one visionary, the other poignant. I wrote her excitedly about my trip to Cuba, seeing sugar workers live in decent homes with good wages and receiving free medical care. Their children were in school becoming doctors, engineers and teachers. I told her about my Marxist professor's optimism regarding the struggles and eventual victory of the world's underclass. I recounted my "working-class summer" spent at Dad's fruit farm in Fresno, picking and packing peaches, side by side with Mexican workers. I ended my letters with a ray of proletarian hope. I predicted that the days of cruel sugar landlords were numbered. They would, I assured her, soon taste revolutionary justice, and be strung up or executed for all their past cruelties. A happy and contented retirement was coming her way.

I also shared with her the happy news about my true love named Jonathan. As a postscript, I usually enclosed a twenty- or fifty-dollar bill for her mah-jongg.

Iyay's letters, written in Ilonggo, always began with effusive thanks for the money, and gratitude that I remembered her. My remembering her, she would remind me, was proof that I still loved her. She then gave a strict accounting of how she would use the money, and groused about my uncle for not remembering her as I did.

None of my rhetorical prattle seemed to matter to her. Instead, she wrote how every night, before sleeping, she prayed to God (*Mahal nga Dios*), hoping (*cabay pa*) that no harm (*disgracia*) might come to me in my travels, that my body (*lawas*) might always be in a healthy state, that my friend (*amigo*) and I might always help and love each other. As if to tweak my radical posturing, she included handwritten recipes, with very detailed instructions, of my favorite cakes and pastries she once baked for me: *Sans Rival*, *Brazo de Mercedes* and mango tarts.

She wrote how she would kiss (*haloc*) every photograph (*ritrato*) I sent of myself, how it would make her cry (*hibi*), because she missed me very much (*hidlaw gid*). She would ask (*kumusta*) about my father, hoping he was well, sending her greetings with no recrimination. She ended her letters with apologies (*paciencia*) for her handwriting and reiterated her love for me (*palangga*) with offerings of many kisses.

I took Jonathan with me on my return trip to Manila after an absence of eight years. I had written ahead to Iyay letting her know when to expect us. She had retired, surviving on a small pension provided by my mother. She was back in Negros, living with a nephew in San Carlos, a town near the old *hacienda*.

It was late afternoon when Jonathan and I reached the section of town where she lived. There were no street signs and the small cinder-block houses were unnumbered. Having forgotten the nephew's name, I asked around for Iyay's address until I realized no one knew her by that name. I started asking for Sali.

"Ah, yes," someone finally answered, "Sali, the *mayordoma* of Don Juan Ledesma. She lives at the end of that *calle*, the house with bougainvillea on the gate."

As our van slowly neared the house, I recognized a face, waiting patiently inside the gate, framed in red bougainvillea flowers. I jumped out of the van and ran to it, calling out her name. Iyay opened the gate and I became little Johnny Boy again as we embraced and kissed each other, my face buried in the crook of her neck, inhaling her odor, recollecting childhood *siestas* on her bosom. Her relatives came out of the house and neighbors milled about the gate watching Iyay and myself crying softly to each other. I could hear murmuring voices repeatedly saying, "*Naka dumdum siya.*" He remembered.

So, this is Don Juan's grandson whom Sali raised and boasted of whenever letters from the United States came, or when family messengers from the provincial capital arrived with packages. So, this is the good boy who traveled from far away to reach this town, just to see this poor old woman who once bathed and toilet-trained him.

I invited Iyay to stay overnight at the *hacienda*. We arrived at the mansion just before dusk. Except for an old caretaker, no one had lived in it since the *hacienda* was sold, many years back, to my grandfather's sister.

The mansion looked worn, with a broken window here and there. The fountain in the front lawn was cracked, long overtaken by weeds. It was eerie seeing the surroundings so desolate, no people in sight.

When I was small, at around dusk, scores of barefoot cane-cutters in tattered clothes, dirty and sweaty with long bolos in their hands, would trudge on the dusty road fronting the mansion, heading to their row of huts a distance away. There would be women returning from a nearby river, with bundles of newly washed and sun-dried clothes balanced on their heads. Peasant children would be everywhere laughing, screaming and playing games of *patintero* or hit-the-can. Young men would be playing basketball on a court at the other side of the road, shouting and bantering as they ran about.

At six p.m., when the *hacienda* chaplain rang the bell in the chapel for the Angelus, all movement would stop. Hats were removed, everyone made the sign of the cross, and all heads would lower. When the bell rang again, everyone would say "Good evening" to one another and continue with their lives.

When the hacienda was sold, the workers were no longer needed and all were relocated, with their thatched huts, to a nearby seashore to begin a difficult livelihood as fisherfolk. Now, the huts, the chapel, the store, the basketball goals were gone. The only structures remaining were the mansion and the scaffolding of a watchtower built by my uncle to spy on the cane-cutters and to leer at the women peeing in the cane fields.

The old caretaker was once a muscular house guard who stood watch every night by the front gates. Often, my cousins and I got him drunk and bribed him with a few centavos to show us his dick that everyone in the hacienda swore was the biggest, earning him the name "Longlegs."

Longlegs turned on the generator, and all the lights in the mansion went on. Iyay proceeded to make dinner and set the dining table for two people. Despite her protests, I insisted she add two more settings, for herself and Longlegs.

Just as we were to start dinner, Iyay disappeared into the bathroom and emerged minutes later with her hair neatly combed, a pin to one side, wearing a touch of lipstick and smelling of perfume. I sat her at the *cabezera*, the front of the table where my *lola* always sat. Jonathan and I served her first. She daintily lifted her fork and spoon, and began to eat slowly, her back erect, her eyes looking straight across the table.

I began telling Jonathan many childhood stories about the mansion, pressing Iyay to recall her stories about living there. She spoke little, hardly looking at me, and I started to wonder why she was acting cold and distant. What happened to the Iyay from the old days when I ate with her and the servants in the kitchen and, over dried fish and rice, the servants would share and snicker over the latest household gossip? Like when my uncle crawled into the servants' bedroom to feel up the breasts of a new maid. Or when the police raided *Lola*'s home for illegal gambling. Or when Gorio, my aunt's driver, peed on a bush where fairies lived, and his dick swelled up for many days? There was also the time an old *herbolaria* cast a spell against a granduncle for forcing everyone in the *hacienda* to vote for his favorite candidate. He wound up in a fancy Manila hospital, strapped to a bed, spitting cockroaches. Another time, Iyay, exacting revenge on my father, announced to all the servants why my parents got divorced. What was my young mother to do? Being twenty years older than her, my father, she haughtily declared, was *"indi na manamit"* (No longer tasty!). Everyone howled with laughter, and lunged at more food.

I couldn't understand Iyay's coldness. Was it because she was thirty years removed from all that ribaldry? Was she uncomfortable with my egalitarian gesture of having her sit to dinner with us? Was it because she was shy and unable to speak to Jonathan in English? Was she ill?

Then it dawned on me as I recognized the perfume she was wearing. Chanel was *Lola*'s favorite. All those many years, all the way back to when she used to shoo away the flies. Iyay had watched not just the food on the table but *Lola*'s every move, ready to respond to all her wishes. Now she sat, for the first time, in *Lola*'s chair, eating at the very table she had waited on. She was replicating *Lola*'s actions, *Lola*'s indifference to eating and to everyone else at the table, her habit of looking straight ahead, disdainful of the dinner conversation. *Lola* was an unsmiling woman, unloved by *Lolo* and her children, and incapable of giving love. Iyay was miming *Lola*, painfully reminding me of the absence of love, closeness and laughter in my family.

After dinner, after everyone retired for the night, I left the mansion, taking a flashlight with me, and walked down a silent and dark path— surrounded on both sides by tall cane stalks that led to a cluster of thatched huts by the sea where the former *hacienda* workers now lived.

There was, inside some houses, that very faint glow of little kerosene lamps, but most were dark. Once my eyes grew accustomed to the night, I could see that the huts were dilapidated, with torn roofs. Shadows of emaciated stick figures moved about. I heard coughing and children's voices crying for food. A skinny dog growled at me and darted off. At a distance, I could see the outlines of several outriggers and a black ocean reflecting the moonlight. I turned around and walked back to the mansion, crying, with the flashlight off, hoping to blend into the darkness of the cane fields and disappear.

Early the next day, Iyay took us to the bus station. I was the last to board the bus as I clung to her, assuring her of another reunion. She waved goodbye and blew kisses in my direction. I watched her slowly board a tricycle, cupping her nose and mouth with a handkerchief against the exhaust and dust kicked up by my departing bus.

Jonathan and I returned to the Philippines two years later. Meanwhile I had received letters from Mom saying Iyay was hospitalized and receiving blood transfusions. The diagnoses varied from hypertension to cancer. I sent her money for the hospital bills and medicine, and she wrote back to me, in somewhat erratic handwriting, expressing her gratitude. A few months later, a second, more troubling letter arrived. It was written for her by her grandniece. She was still weak, but she hoped to be better when I returned. In closing, she urged me to teach Jonathan to speak Ilonggo so that they could understand each other, *mag-intindihanay*. She would also teach him how to take care of me.

Jonathan came down with typhoid when we reached Negros, and I rushed him to a hospital. The doctors assured me that he was all right but needed to be on dextrose for several days. I still wanted to go to San Carlos and visit Iyay, but I couldn't leave Jonathan alone in a provincial hospital. I decided to stay with him and had a messenger take a letter to Iyay, apologizing for not seeing her, hoping she was better, and enclosing money for her needs. Jonathan recovered several days later.

A week after returning to our apartment in Greenwich Village, I received a one-sentence telegram from Mom. Iyay had passed away. I called Marie, who lived in San Jose, and we cried to each other on the phone. Then, in a daze, I stumbled out of the apartment and wandered towards Little Italy. I found a Catholic church, entered its dark hallway and began to reenact the ritual Iyay used to do whenever she took me to church. I approached the candlestand and lit one for her. I searched for a statue of the Blessed Virgin (Iyay had been a devotee of Our Lady of Perpetual Help), knelt before it and kissed its chipped plaster feet.

Groping my way to a secluded pew, away from the few worshippers in the church, I knelt down and cried long and hard. I felt guilty for not being with her in her last days. Iyay was now so far away. All I could do was cry the cry of loss and regret.

There, I finished sweeping around your grave, Iyay; there were many leaves and spider webs. Do you like the kalachuchi *and the* gumamelas *in the vase?*

So many people in the cemetery today, All Souls' Day. I'll be with you today and through the night. Your tomb feels hot, but I don't know how to call the wind.

The world remains the same, Iyay, the same as when you left it ten years ago. The misery hasn't ended and I'm sorry I couldn't help change things.

Even if I did send for you, you wouldn't have been happy in the States. The pace would have been too fast and your Ilonggo wouldn't have gotten you far.

I'm old now and have many ailments to tell you about. I have the occasional gout, and my doctor treats me for hypertension. Look at your little boy now, with a double chin and a pot belly. In the morning when I look at myself in the mirror, I look like Dad.

Thank you for your love. It's allowed me to love others. Please watch over Jonathan and myself as I know you have, all these years.

Jonathan is here, too, Iyay. He has something to say. Did you hear it? "Palangga ta gid ikaw." He can speak some Ilonggo now. Finally, you two can understand each other.

John Silva grew up in the fifties in Iloilo, Philippines. He is currently executive director of the Gay Asian Pacific Alliance Community HIV Project (GCHP) in San Francisco and a contributor to Filipinas Magazine.

"All Clear!"

Dreamwork on the road to recovery
by John Mifsud

The Dream

The night the United States started bombing Baghdad, I dreamt my father was a huge stone statue on a pedestal in a dusky war museum. The air was stale. No one was around. I vividly recall looking up at Dad, who was stoic and heavily armored from head to toe. He resembled Darth Vader, the dark father from *Star Wars*. Although not evil, he was nonetheless distant, mysterious and poised for battle. I remember sadly asking him, "What turned you into stone?"

Adrenaline rushed through my veins when my father's opponent suddenly appeared to my left. My heart started pounding. My mind raced with questions. Who was this powerful young man with silvery skin? What was the meaning of his glowing blue aura? Why did he have wings on his feet? And why did he want to fight my father?

I was only five years old in this dream, so I knew I had to get out of the way. This was not my battle and my father needed no assistance. Still, the stress had me trembling. Dad was not at all threatened, although danger filled the air. He was confident he would be champion. I was not as sure.

In a heartbeat, I found myself in the distant bleachers of a large arena, watching the two gladiators about to do battle. Oddly enough, although I did not want my father hurt, I also felt compassion for the man of silver. It was dreadfully quiet and fear quickly shivered up my spine when I realized that someone was going to have to die.

The young soldier had a strong grip on a long, ominous spear. A fast band of bright light flashed along the steel. Slowly, he raised the weapon into the air. He was on the offensive and prepared to kill my father. But why?

Suddenly, a crashing drumroll caved in on the quiet. Aiming directly at my Dad's chest, the man with wings on his feet ritualistically hurled the spear. It sizzled through the air. In the next instant, without even flinching, using nothing but the sheer strength of his raging will, my father redirected the course of the flying steel. It immediately bent, looped, and doubled back.

As soon as the lance pierced the young man's silver skin, it gouged his heart and went straight through his back. He stumbled to the ground, spurting black blood. His eyes rolled to the back of his head. Clutching the spear impaled in his chest with both of his hands, the Man of Mercury slowly disappeared into a pool of gore. His faint, blue glow lingered after he died, transfixed, with a smile on his lips.

In a flash, his javelin and silver heart rocketed into the air like a shooting star and found its place next to the moon in the brilliant night sky.

I rushed back to my father, who, although victorious in battle, soon began to wither. Dad was feeble as we walked along a short ramp. A waist-high wall separated us. Food appeared and he was glad to eat, happy for the familiar thick-crusted bread, the ripe tomatoes and black olives. He smiled, cut the bottom off a large green pepper and popped it into his mouth. I was a little taken aback. I cannot eat green peppers raw. They turn my stomach.

He enjoyed it but it did no good. He grew weaker as we neared the end of the incline. Slowly, Dad reached over the wall to me, much like God reaches for Adam on the cupola of the Sistine Chapel. I took his hand. Until that point he had not spoken, but Dad finally broke his silence.

"I am dying, so now it is up to you. You are my youngest, my namesake. It is your turn. You must carry on as warrior."

I awoke from the dream, sweating and disturbed. I momentarily thought it was time to start reading the many writings about masculinity and manhood that seem so popular these days. I still have not. I did, however, march in every anti-war demonstration I heard about and sang songs for peace at several Gulf Relief fundraisers. I also bought a large green pepper. It sat in the vegetable drawer of my fridge for more than a week. Every day I would check on it. Eventually it began to wrinkle, so I swallowed my resistance, lit a candle and did something I never do: I cut off the bottom and ate it raw.

The News

On the day of my dream, I had received a newspaper clipping from my sister Rose, in Detroit. It was sent to her by an old family friend back home in Sliema, a large harbor city on the Mediterranean island of

Malta, where I was born (*Sliema* means peace).

The largest English-language newspaper on the island is the Malta Times which runs an infrequent feature section entitled, "Fifty Years Ago Today." This clipping talked about several events that were originally reported on March 16, 1941, reprinted on that same date, fifty years later. Included in the array of headlines were stories about Mussolini's vain attempt to claim the Albanian front as a fascist victory and Yugoslavia's defiant determination to remain neutral, standing steadfast against Nazi capitulation.

In Malta, Hitler's Luftwaffe had begun to bomb the island. As it turned out, the final news item on the page was headlined "Police on the Alert." The reporter wrote: I would like the general public to recognize the prompt and immediate work of the Sliema Police, especially that of Police Sergeant John Mifsud. Yesterday, although his own life was at great risk from falling masonry, he managed to save the lives of many people who would otherwise have suffocated in an entombed shelter. . . .

Although it was right in front of me in black and white, I still did not want to believe it happened. I was overwhelmed by a relentless, deep-seated grief when I kept conjuring the recurring image of my father wildly tearing away at toppled cinder blocks, desperately trying to exhume the men, women and children who had been buried alive.

The War

Unlike my fleeting dream, World War II was a living nightmare for my father and the rest of my family. The Axis dropped over seven million pounds—3500 tons—of bombs on the 200 square miles that make up the little island of my birth. That was 35,000 pounds of explosives per square mile.

During 1942 alone, there were over 2000 air raids, more than five per day. Hitler wanted to ransack Jerusalem. Malta, a tiny British naval colony at the time, stood right in his way. It is said he planned to wipe the island off the face of the earth. During the war, more bombs fell on Malta than anywhere else in the world.

My family had to live underground for over four years. During that time, they sometimes starved. One day, they came up during an infrequent "All clear!" only to find everything they owned, everything they held dear, demolished under a cloud of dust. A bomb landed right on our home, leaving my family with nothing but the clothes on their backs.

I am convinced that World War II severely crippled both of my parents psychologically. It is no wonder that to this day, Mom still tells stories with the same panic and terror in her voice that she and her four children must have known in their hearts at the time. Living underground for nearly five years takes its toll.

I know the trauma she had experienced deeply affected me when I was a kindergartner. She passed on her trauma in paralyzing detail. It was as if she demanded that the last of her six children understand exactly what she had been through, exactly how victimized and powerless she had felt. Many years had passed. Still, it continued to baffle her. Mom's flashbacks of air raids, deprivation and bomb shelters overwhelmed me, too. Although she was emotionally inconsolable, she forced me to try and help. Mom constantly appeared on the edge, and because I did not want to lose her, I vicariously absorbed her horror.

My mother was haunted by the war. She could not help but use my vulnerability and undying attention as a refuge for the devastation and grief she never learned to accept. She did not realize that I would still be trying to sort through it thirty-five years later. At the age of five, I thought it was my responsibility to keep her sane. I think I did.

Peace

One of my many cherished childhood memories was when Mom first told me the story of the victory bells. I will never forget the look of relief on her face when she talked about how the radio waves broadcast the final "All clear!" The war was over and all of the island churches responded by ringing their bells non-stop for twenty-four hours. The triumph in Mom's voice was so vivid when she told me, "Hitler was brought to his knees!" As a kid, I loved the image of all those bells ringing in the dawn of peace.

Not long ago, Mom was visiting from Detroit, and I had some friends over to meet her. They were curious and asked her about Malta. As if on cue, she started talking about the war. I was not surprised, but cringed nonetheless. She went on and on, the insurmountable panic resurfacing like it did when I was a child. But this time, because I saw my mother through the eyes of my friends, several important pieces to the elusive puzzle of my life fell into place. Finally, loud and clear, two realizations resounded in my head and in my heart.

First, in her own way, Mom is a veteran who suffers from post-traumatic stress disorder. At that precise moment, surrounded by friends, it was so obvious, and there was no denying that it had shaped who I am. The second thing I suddenly realized was that the German concentration camps and Hiroshima and Nagasaki were not the only places where innocent people endured the genocide and unspeakable suffering of fascism during the last World War. Like all of the other people recovering from the difficult histories of their parents, I am the Adult Child of a Survivor of the Nazi Siege of Malta. It was such a relief to name it. Knelling the dawn of my own personal peace, victory bells began to ring inside me.

The Stranger

In college, I was a Board of Regents scholar, but for some reason I just could not get through History of Civilization 102. I enrolled and dropped it five or six times and could not figure out why. Once I signed up, I wound up not showing for classes. It was a required course but I could not hack it.

Now I see that the last thing I needed was a review of the Nazi horror stories. I had had enough, not to mention that the history books failed to mention Malta. The island is tiny but its role during World War II was far from small.

Dad never spoke about the war. He kept it all inside. It was not until 1982 that, as an adult, I traveled back to Malta to research his part in the whole tragic scenario. I took a room at the Savoy Hotel, right across the street from the Prince of Wales Police Station where he used to work. Although I had heard bits and pieces of stories, I never really knew my father or what kind of person he really was. I also knew that as long as he remained a mystery to me, I would never really know myself.

One day, I was walking my father's beat when a kind, elderly gentleman I did not know recognized our resemblance and stopped me to timidly ask, "Are you Sergeant John's son?" Caught off guard, I was even more surprised to discover that this stranger knew all about my dad. Meeting him was exactly why I went back. We talked at length. I was deeply honored by the stories he told me, but they upset me all the same.

There we were, standing in the middle of a waterfront piazza where my father must have spent countless hours, and his close friend told me that Dad used to single-handedly clear out bars full of drunken, brawling British and American sailors who were making trouble for local proprietors. "Two at a time! He'd headlock one in each arm and toss them into the sea like apples."

Just like the report in my sister's letter, the stranger told me he saw my father exhume bodies from piles of rubble. Finally, I was completely devastated when he explained that Dad deactivated unexploded Nazi bombs by hand.

As he smiled and walked away, the last thing I heard him say was, "They just don't make men like your father anymore."

The Loss

Sorrow knocked on my family's front door again when, just as in my dream, I was five years old. About that time, my father contracted Alzheimer's disease. It was an unfair and sad fate for a truly heroic man. It hurt me deeply that during my later childhood and early adolescence, when I needed him most, Dad was lost and could not be there for me.

My mother was dedicated to my father during his illness, but she was emotionally crippled and did not have the wherewithal to deal with it every day. It took stamina and she needed support. Often, Mom relied on me and my brother Tony. We were the only ones left at home.

When I was seven, Dad's early symptoms set in. From there, his memory loss and disorientation worsened. The older I became, the more I had to take care of him. At thirteen, I was parenting them both. Mom was hysterical at the most inopportune times; Dad slowly grew more delirious day by day. My father died when I was nineteen. Right up to his death, I was sadly never proud of him.

I was not proud of the debilitated person who spent his days chain-smoking in the back bedroom, waiting for a Bobo Brazil fight to come on TV. I was not proud of the fact that he did not know a thing about baseball like all my friends' fathers on our block in Toronto. I was not proud of the man who eventually could not even sign my goddamn report cards.

I was young and did not have the capacity to separate him from the disease. As a child, his illness was all I ever knew of him. No one told me not to take it personally. No one told me I was not alone. My family was in shock. We denied our grief and anger. It seemed a betrayal to admit the frustration. Alzheimer's support groups were unheard of. At the time, the best neurologists our limited means could muster could not even diagnose it.

As an adult, I have had to summon my courage and go inside all of that pain in order to let it go and get beyond it. Just as I imagine my father faced those unexploded bombs, it is only since I went inside the sorrow that I was able to defuse it. Today, I can breathe a sigh of relief and truly see that both my father and I are heroes in our own right. Thank heaven, the war is finally over.

The Back Seat of My Brother's Car

There is no cure for Alzheimer's. Even the family members of the ailing loved one do not fully recover. It always has a hold on you and pulls at all aspects of your world until, with years of hard work, perseverance and love, you loosen its grip and get on with your life, grateful the past is behind you and eager for what lies ahead.

One thing is certain. After so much sadness, you learn how to have a good time. No matter how simple or small, I rarely take any joy for granted. A shiny shell on a beach, another postcard from Tokyo, ice-cold watermelon, or "Aretha's Greatest Hits"—I am always thankful for what I have. I am fortunate to have a wide circle of diverse friends, and I am glad for a chance to slow dance with any one of them. I am especially grateful for the times when we throw our heads back and really laugh.

Given the circumstances, my early childhood was not all that bad. I still had fun. Lots of it. Dad did not become really dependent until I was about ten. Before that, my family knew something was wrong but we could not name it. So I was pretty oblivious, pretty much a regular little kid. I was addicted to Grape Crush. I loved nature, had lots of buddies, sang in choirs and got a medal for running track. I loved jumping rope with my girlfriends. I was an altar boy for years until I missed one early morning mass and mean old Father O'Connor kicked me out.

Later, as Dad's disease progressed, I found that I loved to act. To become somebody else and receive applause for it was a survival technique for me. It started when, as a kid, I used to try to lift my family's spirits by tap dancing in front of the TV with the June Taylor Dancers on "The Jackie Gleason Show." At the time, I had no idea what I was trying to fix, but, as long as they applauded, I kept on performing.

Through the years, the excitement of the stage curtained my sadness, so I auditioned for every play I could. I was a good actor and was cast in a lot of plays without realizing I desperately wanted to immerse myself in someone else's life. The escapism helped me through my own life.

When I was twelve, my parents and I returned to Malta. My father did all right there. He had his friends, his father and sister, and a familiar environment. Unfortunately, we had to return to the United States in 1965 because my brother Tony was drafted for Vietnam.

My family had already survived one war, and we depended on my brother for financial support because my father could no longer provide for us. Anyhow, Alzheimer's was enough of a battle and, as sure as I was the black sheep of the family, Tony was the saint. None of us could bear the thought of him with a gun in his hand. We could not risk losing him, so we came back to Detroit, glad to support his pacifism. He claimed us as dependents and was granted a deferment.

Unfortunately, we saved the one and lost the other. Leaving his immediate family behind, plus the traveling and changing environments, drove my father over the edge. I was about fourteen when Dad began having regular tirades and we could not control him. Because we were poor and could not keep him at home, we had to surrender him to Eloise County Hospital in Wayne, Michigan. In retrospect, it had to be one of the worst mental institutions in the country.

Every Sunday, my mother, brother and I took the elevator to the fourth floor. I rang the bell for a nurse to open the solid steel door. He always made sure it locked behind us. The bang of its weight slamming against the frame echoed through the desolate corridor.

We always took that reluctant walk down the hall that smelled of rubbing alcohol and urine. It was swarming with older men, schizophrenics and catatonics, more than half of them dressed in armed forces uniforms. I heard somewhere that 67 percent of all the men in this country's mental institutions are veterans of foreign wars. Like my father, they served but did not really survive. They were shipped back in one piece, but they never really made it home. Their minds were forever shattered and scattered on the beachheads of Europe or in the steaming jungles of Southeast Asia.

I had such a hard time believing that my father was locked up with all of those lunatics. The staff would always ask us to wait until they cleaned him up before we were allowed to see him. Only God and those attendants knew what we did not see. How I hated that place.

Even though his room was way on the other side of the ward, we could always hear Dad screaming his head off as soon as we got through that fucking steel door. As a teenager, I always wondered how long he had been at it. What caused him to yell like that?

Eloise was such a sad place. In 1965, I am sure the staff was underpaid and the work must have been frustrating. Unfortunately, I saw them take it out on the patients. My mother never knew that my brother and I caught one attendant slapping Dad in the face while he was helplessly strapped to a chair. I was so shocked and wracked with shame that some part of me believed he must have deserved it.

"I'm sorry, Dad."

Even delirious, I know my father would have decked the jerk had it been a fair fight. Reporting the incident to the ward supervisor was a joke, but I will never forget my brother's mettle. I can still see Tony staring the head nurse right in the eye and telling her, "You'd be screaming your head off too!" Here my father was locked up, and an ignorant, sadistic attendant was free to walk the streets at will.

In the end, it was inevitable, but no one warned or prepared me for it. One day, after we had calmed him down, washed and fed him, Dad's eyes met mine and he looked right through me. Gone was the usual, dignified nod of recognition. I was a blank to him. What was a feeble connection had completely dissipated, and he could no longer recognize who I was.

Then it was my turn to scream and I ran from the ward, demanding to be let out. I made my way to the back seat of Tony's blue Pinto, where, week after week, I cried my adolescent heart out. Episodes like that were constant. I was traumatized again and again for years.

I remember that asylum and a lot of the men dressed in Army issue. One in particular sticks out in my mind. His name was Andy. His was a pleasant madness. He was not morose like most of the others, condemned to repeating a single gesture over and over for the rest of their lives. Andy was always happy to see people. He would always smile and salute "Hello!" even though you could see the empty abyss behind his distracted eyes.

Andy was covered with buttons: all kinds of political, commercial slogans in different-sized circles of tin and aluminum, in all colors of the rainbow. He wore hundreds of them. His chest was covered, as were his shirt lapels on down to his trouser pockets. In such a sad place, he was a warm soul with a harmless humor about him. Amid all that pain, he always made me smile.

It occurred to me only recently that Andy was probably never decorated for his part in whichever war it was he had fought, but he must have felt as if he deserved it. Were the buttons his medals of honor? Was the number of them perhaps his way of overcompensating for the pointlessness of it all? He had risked his life, sacrificed his sanity, and was destined to spend the rest of his days locked up without parole. Had he not earned those medals?

I remember when I gave Andy a Martin Luther King button. It was a simple gift, but the man's face lit up with appreciation for the gesture. He melted and his eyes swelled up with tears as he pushed his chest forward, encouraging me to pin it on him. Believe me, trying to find a place to pin it was no easy feat, but I did. After I added *I Have A Dream* to his collection, he saluted me formally and went up to all of his colleagues, one by one, showing them his new decoration.

I did not realize it at the time, but as I honored Andy, I was accepting him on his terms, in the context of his particular madness. In doing so, I was learning to cope with the madness around and inside of me. Certainly, everyone there was a veteran—the lost men, my father, my family and myself. Each one of us deserved and had earned our medals for bravery. In decorating Andy, I honored us all.

The Lesson

It is no wonder that in my dream, Dad was a statue. He was hardened by the war, and the Alzheimer's had made him impenetrable. As a kid, I could not get through to him. The last eight years of his life, he was without facial expression or animation, frozen in stone.

Only after he died could I finally have the relationship with him that I had always wanted. As an adult, I have found reasons to place my father on a pedestal, so that I can look up to him, as I always wished I could—like I did as a boy in my dream.

I Am the Messenger

My father's opponent was silver—precious, malleable, the coating on the back of a mirror. He was a reflection of us both.

His aura meant he had the blues. The wings on his feet made him a bearer of tidings. He appeared to my left, carrying a message from the intuitive, creative side of my brain. He arrived from a different way of thinking.

I Am the Spear

The steel weapon was a difficult message—a lesson that, had he taken it in, would have broken my father's heart. Feeling that pain was something Dad felt he could never do, so he kept it all inside. He had to kill the message with the messenger. Denial is often unhealthy, but sometimes we use it to survive.

A Broken Heart, a Shooting Star

Grief was the black blood in my dream. Letting it flow brought new life. The messenger died ecstatically because he allowed his pain to pass through, glad for the shining transformation that came with the death of his former self.

In this way, the emissary was a mirror of me. Feeling my pain has freed me. Like the man of silver, I am grateful I can grieve, release my sadness and reflect that with a smile.

Raw Green Peppers

My father traveled the road of the warrior. He tasted the bitter fruit. Still, as soon as he refused to feel his pain, as soon as he refused to learn the lesson behind the blues, he began to wither and die.

The incline was my upward climb, my constant struggle to relate to him and to follow in his footsteps. His Alzheimer's was the wall between us, fortified by his inability to express his sadness. Although I carry his name, we are separate, distinct. That the barrier in my dream was from the waist down implied that our minds and hearts were free to connect as we traveled in the same direction but on different paths.

I Am the Promise

As we clasped hands, I made a contract with my father and with myself. His touch was classic, offering the breath of life to carry on as a warrior. His gift was the hero's journey, to know all of my self.

We all choose our battles or they choose us. We all find ways to deal with the madness. In the past several years, aside from creating intimacy and learning how to really relax, I have been developing affordable housing and educating people about racism, teenage suicide and AIDS. I have worked hard on these present-day bombs that are ready to detonate, just like the ones my father dismantled.

Oddly enough, after all that I have been through, including another twenty-five years of community activism, I have never really thought of myself as a warrior. I fear I have done myself a serious injustice.

This is probably because I did not want to be in competition with my father, afraid that next to his fortitude and the challenges he faced, the battles I have waged and won would pale by comparison. Way back in those desolate corridors of Eloise, I internalized the depredating effects of war on the lives of men. I decided that wars were evil. Maybe, then, I unilaterally condemned all warriors along with their battles. That was short-sighted. Maybe I feared winding up like the soldiers in my father's ward. Still, my dream invites me to reconsider.

Certainly, my father and I have no contest. He did not start, nor did he gain anything from the war. Still, Dad had no choice but to fight. He risked his own life protecting the lives of those he held dear. My father was a guardian of the greater good and made a meaningful difference. I gladly follow in his footsteps. Although our avenues are our own, I am proud to say I am my father's son, defusing explosive situations just as he asked me to in my dream.

John Mifsud is the Producer/Director of Speaking For Ourselves: Portraits of Gay and Lesbian Youth, *a national award-winning PBS documentary that associates a name and face with the many challenging issues and the courageous self-determination many young people face in the United States today. John is also the Executive Director of Clean House Association, a not-for-profit organization in Yakima, Washington, providing quality, clean and sober housing to people in early sobriety.*

The Magic Whistle

by Arthur A. Levine

"Who in his job as master of the house
will have the final word at home?
The papa! The papa! TRADITION!"

With these words from *Fiddler on the Roof*—as I remember my father
singing them—you may think I am beginning an all too familiar story.
How many times has this tale been told? The weight of tradition, the
passing on of roles, the father's expectations inexorably forging a path
for the children to follow. Or not.

My parents had three children, all boys, a particularly folkloric
scenario. I was "the baby." So who would blame me for looking to the
wealth of archetypes available in literature and folklore to help me
describe the patterns of my childhood? Why not see myself as the
youngest child, striving to achieve as he struggles to distinguish himself
from his elder siblings. Such a common theme, the challenges of this
child, with a father who is blind or indifferent to his talents or truths.
Don't we see it repeated in the stories of so many different cultures?

Sometimes, as in Shakespeare's *King Lear*, the children are compelled to compete with expressions of love. Or they are sent on a quest
for a gift for the father—the perfect gift. In other variations there is a
competition to see which brother can follow the words of their father
most closely. In one German folktale recorded by the brothers Grimm,
entitled "The Three Brothers," the siblings want to inherit a farm. To
do so, they must each try to fill the family barn to its fullest over the
course of the day. The oldest brother gathers in all the animals—a fine
showing. The next brother stuffs the barn with hay—even better. It is
almost dark when the youngest has his turn, and with all hope
seemingly gone, he pulls out a candle, strikes a match and fills the barn
with light.

I, too, am the youngest of three brothers. But when I was growing
up, my father's kingdom was the magical world of medicine. And a
happier monarch no jeweled crown could have made. During the week,
my father would come home from the office just before dinnertime,
singing "Oh, what a beautiful moooooorning, oh what a beautiful day."
He'd say his hellos, check in with his answering service and retire
downstairs for a twenty-minute nap.

When dinner was ready, I would sometimes be the one to go down to his den and wake him. I can still picture the loud burnt orange and black carpeting in the basement, a mesmerizing tiger pattern that leapt down the steps and sprawled over the main expanse of floor.

The walls of the main room were covered with pine paneling and photographs—all taken by my father—of my brothers and me: time-lapse sequences of our childhood and adolescence. Against the left wall was the paper-strewn, brown, upright piano that my mother some-times played for my father so he could keep close to the key—if not on it. ("People, people who need people . . .") Above the piano, set into the wall, were twin fish tanks filled with plastic plants, guppies, goldfish, and algae-eaters who didn't do a very good job. But if you looked through the greenish water, you would see into the laundry room beyond, one wall sporting an oversized poster of the N.Y. Sets of World Team Tennis. On it Billie Jean King stretches for a volley. And next to the laundry room stood my father's den.

I remember the wall next to the den particularly well. It framed the door to the downstairs bathroom, but left just enough space for an arch of important documents. Mounted on wood, laminated and varnished to a high shine, they made for irresistible lingering material (as I procrastinated from practicing my clarinet, or resisted waking up Dad). Square one: Arista, the honor society of Tilden High School, signed by the principal himself as well as the president of the student body. Square two: a diploma from Columbia University, embossed with "Magna Cum Laude." And finally, the twin peaks of the monu-ment: *Universitatis Harvardianae*—Harvard Medical School. And below it a picture of the class of 1954: white, smiling. "If I can make it there, I'll make it anywhere." They have comforting faces—purpose-ful, proud and serene. Even the one woman amid the rows of men looks casually defiant, daring to be at ease.

These documents were balanced one on top of the other like alphabet blocks, and to somewhat the same purpose. They represented the basic, inevitable progression of achievement for a nice Jewish boy like my father, like my brothers, like me: good grades in elementary school, so that you are put on the honor track in high school; good grades in high school so that you get into a good college; do well in medical school so that you can graduate, proud and happy, looking secure in your achievement and sense of purpose.

Truly, my father was. He certainly slept the sleep of the untroubled, like an angel, like a log. Waking him up, I couldn't just kiss him on the cheek, or sing, "Diiinner." I had to tap him on the shoulder, roll him from side to side, sometimes slap his face.

Then he would wake with a started: "Wha? What's wrong!" But he didn't wake surly. He could fit forty minutes of R.E.M. sleep into a fifteen-minute nap, and once he was up, he was up.

In a rush we would all be gathered around the dinner table for our twenty-five minutes together: rib steak, frozen french fries, frozen string beans, Jell-O, and "The Case of the Night."

Some fathers told jokes at the dinner table; mine told case histories: "So this man walks in complaining of lower abdominal pain and diarrhea . . ."

We'd all listen, chewing our steak, thinking about homework. Sometimes we'd try to guess the diagnosis. It was like a game show, a sort of Medical Jeopardy: "What is . . . pancreatic cancer?" "I'll take temporary incontinence for four hundred." My mom was usually the winner. ("Okay, Jay, tell her what she's won . . . !")

While we were finishing up, my dad would down a quick cup of instant coffee, and then his secretary, Florence, would be honking out front, waiting to give him a ride. I can hear my mom asking, "What time do you think you'll be done, Milt?"

"Oh," he'd say, "about a quarter to nine." And though this would be approximately the right time, his precision was not for the sake of courtesy, or science, but rather, because it was a cue to one of his favorite songs, which he would then launch into as he went back to work for evening office hours: "The staaaaaars are gonna twinkle and shine, this evening around a quarter to nine . . ."

My dad loved his work.

And when he talked to me about my future, he'd often joke, "Artie, you can be anything you want when you grow up." As he spoke he would count off on his fingers, "A surgeon, an ophthalmologist, a hematologist." And he'd laugh.

Was this pressure? Maybe a track I should follow? Even my Dad's mother, Grandma Lilly, put in her two cents when she could. "Oooo-oooh!" she'd croon, shaking my chin in her hand, "You're gonna make me so proud. When you grow up you're gonna be a doctor just like your father. And cure cancer, right? And keep your Grandma Lilly alive forever!" That's right, Grandma, that's right.

But is that the whole picture? Is that why Dr. Levine's two older sons became Dr. Levine II and Dr. Levine III? What happened to the youngest son? The strongest temptation for me is to claim a failure of Plan A in the "taking hold" stage, and to look for the responsible influence, the deflecting role models. Which magician cast the spell that led me to a typewriter rather than a stethoscope, declaring that I would fall into a hundred-year sleep at the mere mention of blood?

Clearly the white-haired man that seems to fit the part is my Grandpa Myron, my mother's father. My strongest image of him is at the head of the Passover table, reciting the story of Exodus in both Hebrew and English with a cantorial authority in his deep baritone, sweetened by an unfailing sense of humility and humor. We listened for key phrases in the ritual story, key moments that would call for participation. We listened for the history, for the blessing; waited for the exalted moment in the monologue when Grandpa would announce in Hebrew, "*Shulchan Orech*!" (Dinner is served).

Sure, some of us got impatient and wished he'd hurry. Some thought mostly of matzoh ball soup and little of slavery in Egypt. But, to this day, though he has been gone ten years, there is a certain part in the Passover seder when we all say in union, without rehearsal, in the exact tone of voice that Grandpa Myron used, "And Pharaoh made the Jews' lives *very* bitter."

And Passover wasn't the only time he'd tell stories. Another holiday, Purim, stands out as well, this one more individually. I remember distinctly, sitting in the crook of Grandpa's shoulder, sunk into the overstuffed sofa, listening to the high drama of Queen Esther's espionage for the ancient Jews. I can still hear how she was selected by the King to be his wife, though he didn't know she was a Jew. And how she kept this fact to herself as the king's prime minister plotted the Jews' destruction; kept it to herself until one fateful moment when she risked her life, revealing the truth and counting on the love of the king to be stronger than the hate of his minister.

How could I forget the effect of his storytelling: year after year practically holding my breath, waiting to hear if Esther would survive. Of course she did—every year, on schedule.

And my grandfather told non-religious stories as well: stories of the Old Country, Russia. Or rather, "Russia, Poland, who knew, it was always changing hands." And he was always running. Running from the Russian soldiers. Running from the Polish soldiers. Hiding at the bottom of a potato cart while a pogrom raged in the streets of his shtetl. Fleeing the country as a teenager with his little brother Morris, who was hardly more than a baby, along with a group of other Jewish children, on their way to Palestine.

Yes, my grandfather told wonderful stories. And he told them with brio and enthusiasm. So did my mother, for that matter, though her stories tended to be read from books. She was a conduit for the likes of Babar and Paddington, of Curious George, and Frances the Badger, of Mike Mulligan, and Madeleine. It was my mother who taught me to read and to love reading and books. She was certainly instrumental in showing me what I loved, and thereby suggesting what I might become: a writer of books.

But a boy grows up thinking he will become his father. And if I stopped here, I would leave you with a form of the archetype that I started out to describe: The youngest son, not suited to the ways of the father, is taken up by the mother's side. It's the easy way to end this, the way psychotherapists love: Young Arthur, cast out, ready to blind himself and commit unspeakable acts with blood relatives. And I could probably exaggerate the facts to meet that myth, were it not for Henry and the Magic Whistle.

Henry was a little boy who week after week got into terrible trouble: he was abducted by spies; locked in a bank vault by robbers and left there to suffocate; tied and gagged in the path of an onrushing locomotive; dropped from a ship into shark-infested waters. *Oy*, did this boy get into it. But he always got out again.

How? With the help of his animal friends, called to his side at times of desperate need . . . by means of a magical whistle. Here is where words are inadequate; you had to be there—had to hear it. It was my father, of course, who invented Henry, and my father who invented his magic whistle. It was something like a cross between a doorbell and a bird song. Musically, it was the "NBC" triad and then a long repeated note with a warbling vibrato, starting loud and then trailing off into a soft decrescendo. In a flash, the whistle called forth some denizen of the animal kingdom to help Henry out of the fix.

Most of the animals even had their own introduction, like Superman's "Look! Up in the sky, it's a bird, it's a plane." The one I remember most clearly was a large bird who was often called in when Henry was trapped on a desolate perch that no human could reach. Out of options, Henry would whistle, and then we'd all call out, "And down from the sky came Baldy Eagle!"

Okay, I'm not saying our dad was Mozart. Or Sendak. But he did make those stories up, just for my brothers and me, and that, to us, was genius. In fact, long after the "big boys" were "too old" for Henry stories, they would crowd onto my bed, pretending to be helping to tuck me in. But really they were looking for an excuse to listen in on what would happen to poor Henry next. A stampede of bulls? A helicopter spinning out of control? Floodwaters rising to the third-story window?

So what's my point, that the "Henry and the Magic Whistle Stories" were the only moments of relief in an otherwise unrelenting campaign of pressure toward medical school carried out by my father? That my brothers dutifully followed in my father's footsteps while I was forced to find secondary role models and tertiary influences to salvage my ego?

Not hardly, though I think that's a story I told myself for a long, long time. And why not? It fits the archetypal model so well. It paints me as the brave martyr. And doesn't every artist want to lay claim to the loneliness of the misunderstood, the pain of being outside the family fold, and the powerful honor of forging one's own way?

I'm not denying that I felt these things. I don't claim not to feel it when in the midst of a family gathering the phone rings, someone calls out "Doctor Levine?" and I'm the only one who doesn't get up. I'm not saying that when my confidence lapses I don't want to run to the nearest university and get some letters to put after my name.

What I'm saying is that my father gave as strong a message to me by the way he lived his life, and the manner in which he said things, as by exactly what he *did* in life and the things he said.

My dad loved being a doctor. That's why he did it, not because someone told him a doctor is what he should be. And that's the message he wanted me to get: Choose something in life that will challenge you always, something that you find hard to stop thinking about—even at dinner. Find something to do that makes you sing at the end of the day.

When he suggested I become a doctor it was only because he knew medicine to be a career that could offer those things. What other career did he know? Perhaps I can criticize his lack of imagination in this regard, but not his motives, which were always to encourage my happiness.

And even as he joked with me, "Arthur, you can become anything you want...", he gave two messages at once: one through content and another through form. After all, his joke relied on word-play, humor, timing: a writer's tools of the trade. And while the pressure was there in the second part of the joke: ". . . a surgeon, an ophthalmologist, a hematologist," so too was the implication that all such pressure was absurd—something to be laughed at.

The case histories at dinner? A mystery writer's dream: situation, challenge, twists, suspects, red herrings, suspense and solution. All between the first sip of Kool-Aid and the last drop of Sanka. And if I ever doubted the effects of any of this, there was always Henry and his Magic Whistle.

The bottom line is that, tempting as it might be poetically, I can't truthfully claim tragedy as the genre to describe my childhood or my relationship with my father. Perhaps I'd use something closer to Grimm's "The Three Brothers." We, each of my brothers and I, listened carefully to what my father had to say. We each went out and got something into the barn. I just had to find my own way of doing it. And I did, with a little help from Baldy Eagle.

Arthur A. Levine was born in 1962 in a hospital not far from his boyhood home in Elmont, New York. In addition to poems and essays for grownups, he has written three books for children, including All the Lights in the Night *(nominated for a National Jewish Book Award),* Sheep Dreams, *and* The Boardwalk Princess. *He works as a book editor for a New York publishing house.*

When My Father Hit Me

by Bob Shelby

For decades I have been plagued with a certain tension in my gut, located between my navel and my ribs. At times the tension is fist-tight and at others it is spread out, like a strong hand resting on my belly and capable at any time of squeezing shut. Medical doctors sent me to psychologists, and psychologists told me it was anger. I have been living and working with that anger for a long time. I can now say that a more accurate description for that anger is "rage."

Rage is an expression of self-preservation, an instinctual response to a violation of one's boundaries. Most animals, except human beings, seem to understand this use of rage to protect boundaries. Humans are the only animals that, for the most part, fail to respond to each other's cries of rage and persist in violating the boundaries that the rage attempts to protect.

I, like any child, was angry at times. My anger, I think, went beyond the amount a child—limited in ability to influence adults—might have as a response to the normal frustrations of being dependent on them. The experience that formed the foundation for my anger occurred when I was seven months old and my mother had to have emergency surgery. I didn't see her for a month. While she was gone I protested, cried and raged until helplessness, sadness and depression covered the rage and buried it within me.

Later, when I was three and four, my anger would erupt at my mother. She was puzzled by my behavior and asked others for advice. My anger was attributed to my willfulness. She tolerated it, but my father saw it as unruliness that had to be tamed. He began spanking me, and out of self-preservation I again buried my anger.

By the time I was five, my father and mother began having arguments that escalated until my father would hit my mother. Often I had the impulse to confront my father with my own rage at him. But I was frightened by the possibility that he might hit me. Another layer of helplessness covered my rage.

The physical hitting stopped when both of my parents became frightened by its intensity. My mother tried to defuse my father's anger

142

by running away. She pushed her position only so far, and when he became angry she grabbed her purse and left. At first, she would say that she was leaving and never coming back. Then she would say that she was leaving and going to kill herself. After years of such threats, she began taking tranquilizers and took refuge in depression and weekly sessions at the psychiatrist.

My reactions varied. I was angry at both of them for arguing: at him for provoking her and hurting her to the point where she had to leave the house; at her, for terrifying me with her desertion and for leaving me with a man I hated, feared and loved. I felt confused by my feelings for my father and angry that, because of his actions, my feelings of intimacy and love toward him were changing to fear and hate.

No matter how much I loved my mother, I could do nothing to help her. At first, I took her threats of suicide seriously. Later, when I saw she always returned, I began wishing she would leave and never come back so I would not have to go through the gut-wrenching feelings I went through whenever the two of them fought and she left. I felt guilty for having those feelings. The result was a further repression of my rage.

I continued to show my anger in ways my parents found difficult to understand and tolerate. I began running away from home. My father responded by locking the gates. I learned to climb over them. Through ages five and six, when their arguments erupted after I had gone to bed, I began having violent fantasies and prayed to God that I would die in my sleep. I wished I had never been born and found consolation in the idea that I had been adopted and that my real parents would come and take me away.

By ages seven and eight, I began killing ants by scorching them with a magnifying glass or sizzling them with the glowing end of punk or string. I became fascinated by lighting matches and starting small fires. I would steal matches from home or search gutters for matchbooks. Then I would go to the empty lot and start a grass fire. I kept the fires small, contained and concealed.

Along with my love of fire grew my interest in guns. I would search at a quarry for live .22 ammunition that had fallen when target shooters were loading. One time I persuaded a friend to roast a live shell over a fire we built underneath my back porch. The shell exploded. The bullet flew past us. My friend's hand was cut by the jagged edge of the casing. Another time, a friend and I used our slingshots to shoot the live shells at rock outcroppings, causing them to explode. We felt the excitement of hearing the occasional bullet sing as it passed near us. Both of us escaped injury. His mother found out and gave us hell. I suspended my playing with bullets and urged my father to buy me a .22 rifle. He bought me a pellet rifle instead, and we set up a target range in the basement.

I played with fire for the last time when I was ten. A woman was burning small amounts of leaves and garden clippings in an enclosed trash burner. Her telephone rang and she went inside to answer it. I decided to help her burn the rest of the large pile which lay against the side of her garage. I took a burning stick from the trash burner, nursed a flame in the pile and blew on it until it became a good-sized fire. The woman came out of the house in time to see the flames three to four feet high, lapping at the wood siding of her garage. She was angry and I ran away. That was the only time my father caught me setting fires. He was furious when he found out. But he didn't spank me. By then he knew the spankings did no good.

I had worked hard to prove to him that his spanking me or hitting me was useless. Whenever my defiance became intolerable for my mother, she would call my father at work. When he came home, he would spank me. His spankings would hurt and I would cry. As this cycle repeated itself, he would become more frustrated and would hit me harder and longer. I began to feel that his spankings were excessive. My mother knew that, too. She would try to tell him afterward that he had gone too far, but he wouldn't listen. She began to think twice before telling him of my misdeeds; I took advantage of this and provoked her a little more. I soon became involved in a battle with my father through my mother. By defying her, I could tell my father that I was angry at him. He would spank me; I would become more angry and defiant. I had begun a covert war of passive resistance.

Much of the development of my personality had to do with the complex issue of how to express my anger, yet conform to the standards of behavior expected of me. I had to gain enough approval from adults to keep my waning sense of positive self-esteem intact. My anger generated aggressive actions and violent fantasies against my parents. This frightened me. I remember asking my fourth-grade teacher how we were to love, honor and obey our parents if we didn't like them. She told me that it was a child's duty to love his or her parents. The conclusion I came to was that I was bad because I hated my parents. I thought that my heart had turned hateful and was no longer capable of loving.

Yet I could not live with that as the only possibility. Out of duty, I learned to do the things a son is supposed to do to show that he loves his parents. I became a "good boy" who, on occasion, acted bad. I complied enough to prevent myself from getting into deep trouble and defied enough to give vent to my anger and preserve a sense of myself.

From these experiences with my father, I learned about the abuse of power. By physically hurting my mother and me, he effectively stopped us from reacting to his humiliation of us. We ceased to protest his violations of our boundaries and his ignoring our sense of being individuals with needs, demands and rights of our own. After demonstrating his ability to hurt us physically and to overcome any attempts we might make to hurt him in return, he was then able to use threats to accomplish the same ends.

I have no doubt that my father loved me, but his love became misdirected. He said he wanted to give me what he didn't have as a child. Yet he often lost sight of me as an individual separate from him. I became the vehicle through which he would live out the unlived parts of his childhood and life. He insisted that I learn to do things his way. Gradually, he shaped me with his drive to be perfect, his inability to love himself, his conditional love of me and his false pride. He demanded love and retaliated sharply when criticized.

What he most showed me, however, was his difficulty in being loved. All his life he had struggled with feeling unloved. In despair, he substituted promises. Upon marriage, the promise was to have a beautiful woman to adore and be the mother he never had. Upon the birth of his son, the promise was to be the father he had never had and to shape the man he wished to be. His profession, too, held promise of acceptance and self-worth, feelings which he never seemed to experience. He never acknowledged how he suffered from not feeling loved; he only showed the effects. I was nine or ten the last time he spanked me. Before he hit me, I remember saying to myself that he would never get the satisfaction of seeing me cry. I decided that he could do to me anything physically that he wanted, he would never reach my inside core. As the intensity of the pain of his hits increased, I felt the hurt in my heart. I realized what hurt me the most were my feelings of love for this man who was hitting me. I covered my love with a dark cloth of hate. I did not cry. I took the pain from each of his blows and wrapped the cloth turn after turn around my heart. I converted the pain into anger and added the anger to the deep rage that already existed like a tight, dense ball in my gut.

With each swat, he beat out of me love, trust and respect. He instilled in me not only rage, rebellion and disrespect, but hatred, fear and betrayal. I waited until he was finished. I got up. I turned my back to him. I refused to look him in the eye. I went to my room, aware that I had triumphed. I knew that from then on I was safe from the worst pain of all: I knew my father would never hurt my heart again.

A few months after I turned thirty-two, my father shot himself by sticking a .22 rifle in his mouth and pulling the trigger. He ended his struggle with despair. For three days, his body lay in the front seat of his car. The windows were rolled up. The temperature outside was in the high 90s. The mortician would not let me see the body. The casket was closed at the funeral. During the memorial service, I had the urge to take a sledge hammer and pound on that closed silver coffin, to pound on it until it was misshapen and lacerated and until the rage I felt inside was spent.

Still I tear at the shroud of hate and rage that protects the vulnerability of a trusting, loving heart.

Robert Shelby's growing up occurred in a quiet neighborhood in St. Louis and on the farms of his mother's relatives in Illinois. He is a co-director of The Men's Center Foundation, Berkeley, California, practices tai chi chuan, and writes.

Snow Geese

by Robert Bly

The dark geese treading blowing Dakota snows
Over the fence stairs of the small farms come,
Slipping through cries flung up into the night,
And settling, ah, between them, shifting wings,
Light down at last in bare and snowy fields.

The drunken father has pulled the boy inside.
The boy breaks free, turns, leaves the house.
He spends that night out eating with the geese
Where, alert and balancing on wide feet
Crossing rows, they walk through the broken stalks.

Until graduation from high school in 1944, Robert Bly lived on a farm in western Minnesota. It was a wheat, flax and corn farm with much community work that took place in threshing and so on in those days before the appearance of the solitary combine. Robert Bly's prose poems, many of them set in that area, were recently collected under the title What Have I Ever Lost by Dying? *In late '92 HarperCollins published* The Rag and Bone Shop of the Heart, *a collection of poems from many cultures and languages developed during the workshops with men, and edited by Robert Bly, James Hillman, and Michael Meade.*

BEING A BOY
IN THE WORLD

Peer relations and proficiency are two themes that recur throughout boyhood. The roles of school, church and extracurricular activities all stress Erik Erickson's developmental stage of industry vs. inferiority which all boys pass through. That is to say, boys are introduced to the rigors of accomplishment (industry) and failure (inferiority) through academic training, athletic training and a variety of other disciplines from scouting and 4-H to music, art and dance lessons in a world rife with conflict and controversy. Almost always, boys participate in these disciplines with each other. In most societies, boys' play and girls' play are segregated; boys play with boys.

In remembering boyhood, men recall less its structure and more its character. In the foreground, men remember the play with other boys, the desire to fit in, the ambivalence about competition, the distance from girls and the testing of adult limits. The background of learning and failing meets the foreground of belonging and loneliness. At the edge is the suppleness of the boy caught in the contradictions of what the world demands of him and what he can muster and master in the face of those demands.

From "Chicago"

by John Gill

I was probably digging to China and almost through
when somebody gave me the exciting news:
a naked woman and a naked man were on the roof
of the apartment house next door five flights up.
I dropped my shovel and scanned the brick horizon
squinting against the sun like Adam after creation
wonder filling every muscle, sac and pore
sprouting visionary senses:
a naked woman breasts swinging as she pranced
her blinding V and her fat bouncing buttocks
and a man his bushy crotch with his flag wagging semaphore
(I knew that they must be drunk)
up on top of the world on the hot tar roof
waving and looking down on the walking dummies below
sedately zipped in their skins flags and negatives furled.
Oh, it was wrong! It was wrong! I mean
to drink and not to be at work (or quiet) in the daytime
and to climb on the roof and prance and shock the neighborhood
to bring the cops to drag them off shouting obscenities!

I never did see them up there although I looked for weeks
scanning that brick horizon faithfully (better than saying prayers)
and entered without knowing it another of Adam's worlds.

John Gill, 1924–1995, grew up in Chicago in the thirties. He was co-publisher of The Crossing Press *and a poet. His last book of poems,* Between Worlds, *was published by Hanging Loose Press in 1993.*

Daycare

by Matthew C. Montgomery

I was certain that the way I felt, the day that my mother first took me to Ms. Jenny Brown's for daycare, was exactly the way my body and mind had felt when my umbilical cord was cut. Momma had dressed me in my favorite corduroy pants. They were my favorites because they had the same name as the bear who had spent the night in a department store in my favorite book.

As we drove, Momma didn't talk much. At least not the way she usually did—in her quick melodic blur of sounds, ending in a high chirp of laughter about things I had learned or things I should notice. "Now, Matthew," she'd usually say, although it sounded like "Mat-two" as she hadn't totally lost her accent from growing up in Hawaii with Japanese parents. "Now Mat-two, what color is this?" She'd point at my favorite corduroy pants which were a deep forest green. Or she'd just ramble on about who lived in the houses that we were passing or what a nice car she thought "So-and-so" had. Or she'd ask what we should cook for Michele and Daddy when they arrived home. Of course, I didn't help with the cooking at all and my answer was always "French fries" or "pizza."

But on this day she wasn't talking. I also sat silently. The color and feel of the car was magnified. How had I never noticed how the cold royal blue vinyl of the dashboard held onto dust? This was certainly intriguing at age four and a half. I was fascinated by the way dirt could transform little legs, arms, and faces. I would halt my frantic playing during the summer months and look down at my bare legs as I licked my fingers and made a mark with the spit to see how much of the red clay dust of the small country farmyard had coated my exposed limbs. In the tub, later in the evening, I would watch as the sudsy, bubbly water would wash away the crust of dirt. Sometimes I'd sit and bury my feet and legs in the ground and jump with a start and dash away before looking down at how I'd changed.

As my spit-covered finger made paths in the dust on the blue vinyl dashboard, I looked over at my mother. Her black straight hair swooped on the ends to softly rest on her shoulders. The wide lapels of her pants suit coat framed her face in orange polyester. Her eyes squinted and blinked quickly behind the thick glasses that seemed so out of place on her nose.

Since my sister Michele had started school, I'd learned to play by myself. She liked dressing up in ribbons and pretty dresses and going away for school. During that time my mother's attention was all mine, so I liked her dressing up and going away, too. I was outside most of the time and Momma was inside, but anytime I wanted I could look up and see her in the kitchen window over the sink or talking on the phone. She would always look back with an approving expression that said, "Mat-two, you are such a good boy." I would respond by pointing at my secret hideout or my mud cakes. This was my way of inviting her into my world. I knew that she understood that the squares that I'd drawn in the sand were the houses that I'd built, and the boards leaning against each other were my castles. I knew that if anyone could see the fantasy lands I had created, she could. She could see them and she understood what they meant to me. Sometimes I seemed to be playing only to have something to tell her.

At the end of the trip I finally noticed the bag of books next to me on the seat. When the car stopped and Momma opened my door and stood me up, she shut the door without taking out the bag. A woman came out to greet us. The brown geometric shapes on the woman's polyester pants told me they were housewife pants like the ones Momma wore when she was going to be on her knees cleaning. The woman had large pink beauty salon curlers held down by a scarf tied in the back.

My mother's bag in the car meant she was leaving. So what about me? Had the trip been for me? Had we gotten up and dressed before the sun had come up because *I* had somewhere to go? I had no special place to go like Michele. I had no special friends to play with. I hadn't picked out my favorite clothes. Momma had done that. And now she was leaving.

When I cried it was with only a whimpering sound and a tiny shake of my shoulders, hardly the dramatic fits that I'd seen other children perform. Ms. Jenny Brown noticed enough to look up at Momma who was getting back into the blue Chevrolet next to her bags and books. Momma left the car running and she came over to squat in front of me. Her words said, "I'll be back," but the car running and the smell of hairspray and the way Momma's hair curled up at the shoulders and the bag of books and the brown polyester pants said I was staying and she was leaving. That was all that I could understand.

Ms. Jenny Brown sat me on a couch in a room filled with other children—loud children. She left me there with children who gathered around me and bombarded me with questions. With each new inquisition my head hung lower and I became more a part of the fabric of the couch. In my mind, I was invisible. No one could see me or ask me questions.

Momma did come back. The whole trip home I talked. I told her of the fat boy at Ms. Jenny Brown's and the hot dog lunch and the "Scooby-Doo" cartoons that Ms. Jenny Brown let us watch. I told her of the day's adventures as if to say "I survived today but *please* never do that to me again."

I did go back to Ms. Jenny Brown's and I actually came to like her even though I never stopped feeling as if I was waiting. I was waiting for mother. I was waiting to breathe, laugh, talk, live.

When I finally pried myself free from my mother's leg and ventured beyond the reach of my mother's view from her kitchen window, something began to happen to me with the loss of security and safety. That free-floating feeling of being in the world solely defined by my actions, words, or lack of words and actions made me realize the power I possessed. I had the power to explore, discover, and grow in ways that my mother could not make happen for me. In my green corduroy pants I had stumbled upon the fragile power and control that we each have over our lives and sometimes the lives around us.

My mother has often told me that my childhood was really like that of an only child because of the individualized relationship between the two of us. I know she's right, and the day she pushed me from the blue vinyl seat of her Chevrolet into Ms. Jenny Brown's polyester pants, she may have pushed me forever from her shadow and straight into a reflection of myself.

Matthew C. Montgomery (b. 1967) spent the first eighteen years of his life in the small farming community of Reynolds, Georgia. He is presently assistant director of public relations at Armstrong State College in Savannah. Also a freelance writer, he is currently working on a novel about growing up Japanese-American in the deep South.

Reflections on a Cold War Boyhood

by Harvey L. Schwartz

I. Landscape

I was born during a lull in the international Cold War, the icy, divisive, and theoretically permanent impasse between the societies of the East and West. Two older brothers, who were to become my earliest mentors in the discipline of allies and enemies, were well into their boyhood indoctrinations when I appeared on the scene. During the fifties and early sixties "program" of sex-role polarization, our fathers, like so many men pursuing the "Great American Dream," were virtually absent from the child-rearing process.

In these "patriarchal father-absent families" described by Chodorow (1978) in *The Reproduction of Mothering*, the children identify with an image or abstraction rather than a real person. Deprived of a real relationship, male children must settle for "being like" father in lieu of experiences of "being with" father. Only a symbolic bond is formed. This, in turn, produces an identificatory relationship with the construct or category of "masculinity" rather than with the characteristics of a real human being (Goldner, 1991). This process leads to false, and often inflated, passionate identifications with the "phallic imagery of masculinity" which in turn often leads to "hyper-masculine" stances. This caricature of masculinity has been described by Ross (1986) as a sense of manhood that is nothing more than a "screen, a sheath, an artificially aggressivized brittle cardboard creation."

My older siblings and street brotherhoods provided surrogate fathering. Unfortunately, this often meant that the meanest and most narcissistic boys were my role models and power brokers (abusers/protectors). The boys at the top of the street hierarchy usually had abusive fathering in their own homes which they readily passed on to other boys in various forms of terrorism and domination. Power hierarchies formed around these hyper-aggressive, bullying males. Systems of protection and retaliation and rival subgroups with their own hierarchies emerged. Survival in this all-male world involved learning strategies of power manipulation, forming alliances for protection, and resorting to blackmail and psychological "payola."

In my boyhood, females were regarded as rather useless in the all-important establishing of a sense of masculinity. Women and girls could humiliate or adore, but it is the resonance with and recognition of more powerful males that was the Holy Grail of my boyhood journey. Fortunately, I was blessed with two rather large, athletic brothers, far older than I was. Whatever pains and tortures I had to endure at their hands (and there were many), they were otherwise buttons on my lapel, "givens" in the geometric equations of male identity. Their mere existence and fraternal relation to me served as a protection against my real and imagined enemies. Whatever bullying might take place, and regardless of how cowardly I would or would not be in response to it, any opponent had to reckon with this reserve arsenal. My brothers' relative absence from the street scene only served to amplify their potential for protection and retaliation in the minds of most boys I grew up with. Idealization and absence produced a psychological shield. I did not escape terrorism on my brothers' account, but the fraternal entourage set some limits on the extent of my torment at the hands of other boys.

During boyhood, males become driven to compete, insisting on rank orderings for almost every conceivable physical, behavioral and power comparison imaginable. Who had *the* most baseball cards, who could urinate the farthest, and of course, who was better at each of a dozen sports—these were our most meaningful and passionate concerns. The need to establish these hierarchies and to find one's place in them was an obsession for many boys, as struggles for security and power in concrete terms. The fervor and concretization also speaks to an urgency and rigidity in the process of masculine identity formation in this culture, with its constricted options and its traumatic origins.

My father's modest version of the American dream was rolling along on schedule during my first few years. I was to spend my entire boyhood and adolescence in an attached brick row-house in a relatively new section of an urbanized borough of New York City. Within one generation, my parents had left the ethnic ghettos of their own childhoods and passed through a long series of tenancies to eventually become homeowners in their late thirties. Hundreds of thousands, maybe millions, of postwar white families were doing this at the time all around the nation. Each family was a fortress-minded economic unit poised against all the others, competing for the material wealth that promised prestige, social status, power and self-esteem. Fathers worked long hours, were chronically too tired to relate to anyone, and mothers were confined to meaningless, repetitive drudgery punctuated by occasional card and bingo games with other isolated, depressed women, with enough alcohol and little yellow pills to soften the pain. This was the landscape in which the baby boom generation was spawned.

My street had a symbolic but clearly drawn line down the middle. The new housing section where I lived had been built next to an already existing development of unattached brick homes erected during the thirties. These older homes, whose bricks were blackened with age, were inhabited entirely by second- and third-generation Catholics of Irish and Italian descent. The newer section was populated entirely by first- and second-generation Jewish Americans who had recently left their "old neighborhoods"—ghettos of New York where they and their parents settled immediately following emigration from the ghettos of Eastern Europe. My own family's house was the first building over an invisible dividing line which at times came to have the potency of the Berlin Wall. Neighborhoods like mine were also shifting at the time I was growing up to accommodate the black population arriving from the southern states in search of work and social advancement. Not surprisingly, each minority group was poorly received by the prior inhabitants, and what was supposed to have been a melting pot was actually a cauldron of seething racial hatreds and petty ethnic antagonisms. Twenty-five to thirty years later, these tensions are still erupting.

In the area where I was raised, the neighborhood tensions were religious and ethnic in nature; the race war was still about a mile away. Conflicts pitted Jews against Catholics. For us Jews, the Catholics could be divided into major and minor foes: the Italians, less fierce and sometimes allies, and the Irish, dangerous enemies never to be trusted. At Christmas, the houses on one side of my street would be lit by colored lights and huge plastic Santas and statues of the Virgin Mary, with tableaux of the birth of Jesus on the front lawns. Our side of the street was shrouded in darkness. In those occasional years when Chanukah, the Jewish festival of lights, fell in late December, every front window on my side of the street sported a small, uniform menorah. During these winter nights, the spectacle created by the imaginary dividing line took on a particularly eerie quality.

Before the age of twelve I had no clear idea who Jesus Christ was. Nor did I have any understanding of what Catholicism—or for that matter Christianity—was all about, aside from a gut experience of "other." Critical thinking on this issue was not encouraged by my family, or by the orthodox Hebrew school I attended each day after public school for a full five years. I do remember being taught never to say the name "Jesus Christ" but to say instead "Jersey City" or "JC." Needless to say, this did little to help me negotiate my fear of the dominant, intimidating and mysterious Christian world. These fears were so powerful that when I took piano lessons at eight years of age and my teacher was teaching me to play "Silent Night," I made him cross out the word "Christ" in the last line of the song. I couldn't have that word staring at me and play the piece of music with any skill.

As I grew older I became increasingly aware of the domination of the majority culture that I was not a part of, and that essentially wanted no part of me. This was painful and depressing. As a young boy of four or five I had probably thought people were basically alike. As I learned of my supposed "differentness," I eventually stopped feeling as if I were a complete person. I came to believe that I belonged to some despised in-between race, not quite white, not quite black. The religious warring on my block brought this point home rather sharply. From the protective insulation of the family cocoon, I emerged to see that I was one of "the few," not part of "the many." The large number of Jewish people in New York and the concrete grandiose thinking of very early boyhood had allowed me to enjoy the fantasy of ethnic sovereignty and empowerment. When this construction collapsed, I became extremely curious about, almost obsessed with black people and their culture. At that time, blacks were an abstraction to me, as the schools in my area weren't integrated until my early adolescence in the sixth grade. In the meantime, I became confused about the relationship between blacks and Jews. My father, who was quite bigoted, laughed at my confusion and told me that a Jew was a black person turned inside out and vice versa. I thought about that for a long time.

But I've gotten a little ahead of my story, for there was a period of Eden-like innocence on the block where I grew up, before the later onset of the overt and relentless religious war. The neighborhood's thirty or forty Catholic families had at least twenty children within three years of my own age, and the same was true for the Jewish population of the street. There was some early sense of "variation" that spoke to me in obvious terms whose meaning I could not decipher, except in terms of "difference." The Catholics seemed to have larger numbers of children, they had statues of various people and angels on their lawns, there were distinctive Sunday rituals involving Church attendance, the Catholic mothers seemed more worn out and less concerned with their physical appearance than the Jewish mothers, and the fathers of the Catholic households seemed even more absent than ours. We Jewish children were almost never invited into Catholic houses, and the few times we were permitted access (when our friends' parents were gone), the presence of statues, crucifixes and other religious artifacts everywhere was quite frightening, even paralyzing. I also remember strange lighting and unfamiliar smells, a sense of darkness and gloom. Yet despite these disparate worlds, overt signs of difference did not seem to have the divisive power that was to develop rather quickly later on. In my earliest years, all the neighborhood kids played, laughed, explored and rough-and-tumbled together, relatively unaware of the pre-existing dichotomy waiting to claim us.

For a while the children in my neighborhood attended the same musty-smelling six-story brick elementary school that held about 2000 other children daily. Half of my classmates were kids from my street, a balanced mix of Catholics and Jews. This seemed almost like a natural extension of the world back home, and we all eagerly anticipated our pre-existing camaraderie carrying weight against the adult powers of the public school. Although somewhat aware of ethnic differences, the meaning of these differences had either escaped us or had yet to be imprinted. Then one day, for reasons unclear to us, almost all of the Catholic children were abruptly transferred by their parents to the Catholic School in a church several blocks away. This radical migration was completed before the end of the second week of first grade. I can remember feeling sad, confused and uneasy about this sudden separation and I do not recall any discussion or explanation about it from school officials or family members. The overt effect was a complete rearrangement of the class structure, new teachers, new combinations of students, and an erasing of the original circumstances of our arrival.

The mere name of this parochial school and church used to scare us, and before we Jews knew the meaning of the separate words involved, we used to say it as if it were one word, one mouthful of meaningless consonants and vowels: "MaryQueenofHeaven." Once the Catholic children were split off from us and sent to this school, the long years of turbulence began. However, even before the religious conflicts exploded, most of the Jewish children had a real fear of that old monolithic church building. We had never been taught about Christianity, not even that it existed. We were never exposed to the concept of Christ, or introduced to any of the nuns who shuttled around in their bizarre black clothing. In the religion we knew, women were assigned a rather hidden, subordinate role. At MaryQueen-ofHeaven, there seemed to be an endless parade of these shrouded, mysterious and, to me, seemingly unhappy-looking women. We Jewish children began to hear rumors that the nuns used physical force as an educative technique. Stories of rulers and yardsticks smashing knuckles and buttocks circulated like wildfire, and this served to fire our curiosity, confusion and envy.

The very large crosses on the outside walls and roof of the church made us Jewish children feel quite anxious. Ubiquitous gruesome crucifixes, popular at the time, depicting a man whose identity was unclear to us, dressed in a loincloth with blood dripping from numerous wounds, were terrifying, and yet we did not understand the source of our terror beyond the obvious horror evoked by the image itself. It took me many years before I would consider entering *any* Christian religious institution. Even as a nineteen-year-old, I recall some hesitation about walking into Notre Dame Cathedral in Paris. As a boy I imagined all sorts of strange brainwashing schemes were taking place in the hidden chambers of the fortress-like houses of Christian worship. We avoided the building the way we would avoid snakes, spiders, or a haunted house. This meant taking a more circuitous route between the public school and our homes. In fact, for the six years that I attended this school I never once walked down any of the streets encircling MaryQueenofHeaven Church. Later on, in the upper grades, this circumnavigation was also a maneuver to avoid violent encounters with angry Catholic boys.

Our fears suppressed any childlike curiosity that might have led to investigatory behavior. Within the Jewish child peer culture, such inquiry was sharply discouraged. When I was seven or eight, well after the time when the religious war had begun, a rumor broke out among the Jewish children that Roseanne, aged five, and the younger sister of one of my boyhood pals, wanted to become a Catholic. She was attempting a pre-grade-school best-friendship with an Irish-Catholic girl who lived two houses away. This rumor of Roseanne's potential conversion spread with a vengeance throughout our child-community, and nothing short of utter disgrace can characterize the verbal and nonverbal attitude we displayed toward her, and to some degree toward her siblings as well. For years after, this rather innocent experiment of Roseanne's stuck to her like an invisible "scarlet letter."

Inevitably, two street cultures developed, based on attendance at public versus parochial school—which was of course itself based on religious and ethnic differences. Within a few months of attending MaryQueenofHeaven, the Catholic boys became increasingly hostile towards the Jewish boys. The emergence of this hostility felt sudden and drastic. I can remember groups of seven- and eight-year-old boys shouting angry words at groups of my little Jewish friends. Although some of the words had recognizable features, the real meaning of the litany eluded us for some time. The typical epithet: "You . . . christkillerredcommieniggerlovingkikesheenie–jew bastards."

I knew I was being hated (sibling life had informed me early on of such emotions), but I had to ask many questions of the older boys to fully understand what I was being hated for. The business about killing Christ, which seemed to be the pivotal point of all verbal tirades, was most perplexing to us six- and seven-year-olds. We were being told that we had murdered their God, and, as I interpreted this literally, this accusation disturbed me greatly. The force with which they would hurl the charge sounded to us as if we had just killed a family member that very day. The fact that their God could *be* murdered was an assault on my whole early boyhood construct of an all-powerful God. I also wondered if the Catholics were planning to murder *my* God in retaliation. I was also agitated about what would happen to people (to me!) if someone had, in fact, killed their God. Mostly I wondered where dead Gods went to and if their God was angry at me and other Jewish people for murdering him. For years I felt I was part of some terrible group who did awful things. Or, that the Christ-killing claims were false teachings of the Catholic School, as the Jewish adults tried to cajole us into believing.

The insults began to be accompanied by rocks, "dirt bombs," sticks, and "itchy balls" (hard seeds with little spikes that fell from the tall trees that lined our block). Often, Catholic boys would ambush a group of Jewish kids walking home from school, often with older boys directing the younger boys in how to manage the assault. Always fewer in number than our assailants, we would turn a corner and there they would be, waiting to lunge and shout insults, throw things and attempt to provoke a physical confrontation. Being outnumbered, we were doomed to lose. From time to time, there were physical fights, but this was more the exception than the rule, for it was the terror that seemed to be the objective in these ambushes. After some experience of these terrorist actions, we hardly responded at all except to steel ourselves, and remain calm and unprovocative, until the ambush was over. Sometimes we would try and reason, talk, or bargain our way out of the situation. After seeing us suffer for a few minutes, and after the thrill of the surprise element of the ambush had subsided, the Catholic gang would retreat, often spitting at us upon departure with verbal threats of more to come. These ambushes occurred weekly; during escalations in personal rivalries or current events, they could happen daily.

We Jewish boys almost never fought back with our fists. Instead, we used our ingenuity to avoid, to outsmart, to outmaneuver, to master the defensive position. I still feel ashamed to acknowledge that I was scared to walk down my own middle-class street every single day of my boyhood. We did, however, make war on each other, that is, on other subgroups of Jewish boys from neighboring streets. To my knowledge, none of the groups of Jewish boys we warred with, who also came from religiously divided blocks, and who were also terrorized, ever formed alliances against the Catholics. When I first began to learn about the history of Eastern European Jewry, I believed that millions of my people had walked into the gas chambers without protesting. This image of hordes of passive, compliant Jewish people walking willingly to their deaths was a piece of Nazi propaganda that found its way into my brain and into my dreams. The vision of mass passivity would circle around in my mind with agitating pressure. I felt deeply ashamed to be a part of this cowardly group. As a boy, I spent hours trying to figure out what this meant and who was really to blame. As a man I have spent part of my life and career, in one way or another, trying to understand human evil. There exists a personal and archetypal protest cry—and a retaliation impulse—that is so deep and powerful that I dare not get too close to it.

In any case, by the time I was eight years old, I had a lot of enemies. There were the Russians, the Cubans, the North Koreans and Viet-cong—all the "commies" in fact—the kids from other neighborhoods, the Gentiles, rival groups of boys, sometimes one or both of my older brothers. My most formidable enemies were the Irish and Italian Catholics from the other end of the block. I now despised them and their icons and feared them even more passionately.

A single ray of light interrupted all those years of religious hatred, and even that didn't last. A new Italian-Catholic family moved onto the block. Their children were unusually friendly and they attended public school. One of their parents was from "the Old Country." They must not have come from a similar neighborhood, or perhaps they had not been exposed to Jews in such close proximity, because we were easily welcomed into their home, and the eldest son, Marty, became a friend. Each time Marty would return to his home on his side of the block after playing with the Jewish kids, he would be verbally berated by his neighbors. His siblings would also be made to pay for his crimes of association. The message was perpetrated by each successive peer-age group in the Catholic subculture, which meant that the seven brothers and sisters he was obligated to protect were all under constant attack.

Marty and his family didn't seem to understand the block rules, and he had no apparent intrinsic familial anti-Semitism to rely on. By the middle of Marty's first year on the block, the Catholic boys, his closest neighbors, were beating him up regularly, terrorizing his younger siblings and generally making his life miserable. When the Jewish boys attempted to rise to his defense, he would end up doubly punished when he found himself alone again in the Catholic world. Thus a terrible bind developed in which we could not exercise our loyalty and gratitude to Marty without it backfiring and revictimizing him. As usual we stopped protesting. In the dead of winter that same year, on a particularly freezing cold night, a group of the most vicious Irish Catholics came out armed with water balloons and totally soaked Marty. Then they beat him up and held him down on the freezing ground. The next day, a group of Jewish boys went over to investigate the spot where the assault had supposedly taken place. Sure enough we found bunches of broken water balloons and the stale smell of urine. Evidently, this "baptism" was not by fire nor by water alone.

I didn't see Marty for a few weeks after that. At the start of the midwinter school year, he had been transferred to the same parochial school as the other Catholics on the street. He never played with the Jews again after that assault, and he was taken in by the Catholic gang as a junior member, treated as their flunkey in a sort of permanent pledgeship. By the beginning of the next school year, Marty had learned his anti-Semitism lessons well and was a full-fledged participant in the street war. More than a full participant, he became an activist for their cause. One of his last comments during a particularly dreadful ambush was, "Why didn't Hitler make lampshades out of all of you?"

Toward the end of my boyhood, the religious separation of the neighborhood completely rigidified. Each group of children played on their own side of the street, and there was a period of mutual, hateful avoidance that replaced the previous era of frequent confrontations.

Alliances were formed with similar groups on other streets and a
network of gang-like organizations developed. The Jewish boys played
street football, stickball, punchball and various running games on the
left side of the dividing line. The Catholics played some games, but
mostly "hung out" on the right half of the block. Adolescence was
dawning and everyone's energies and interests were shifting. The
taunting and provocative behavior gave way to a cold and sterile
silence—our own "Cold War."

I remember, however, one final encounter of this period. A large
group of Catholics, including Marty, was playing touch football in
front of their houses. At the same time, a relatively large group of
Jewish boys and early adolescents was playing stickball on the other
side. The Catholics sent an emissary, Marty, to challenge us to a game
of football. This would be the first time we would have all played
together in six or seven years, since our separation in first grade. Some
of the Catholics had already gotten into trouble with the law for petty
crimes, but they regarded the disapproval of the adults as a badge of
honor. They flaunted their "JD" cards, a police record indicating
juvenile delinquency. They had flaunted these cards during several of
the ambushes the prior year. Some of the meanest boys were out on the
street that day. Marty approached us in good spirits and we Jews found
his offer reasonable since we stood a good chance of beating them. A
victory would have provided us with an opportunity for some long
overdue retaliation and a chance to regain some pride. In any case, we
couldn't refuse because it would appear too cowardly and might have
re-ignited more primitive forms of conflict.

As the Catholics came over to our side of the street to play, they
seemed unusually unmenacing. Before the first throw, there was a
huddle of sorts. The Catholics took an unusually long time in their
huddle, but there were a good number of them and we didn't think
much about it. They threw the ball to our team and advanced upon us.
The receiver on our team made some sort of disgusted yelp as he made
his catch, and we all ran over to see that the football was completely
covered in spit. Laughing, the Catholics sauntered off to their side of
the block, jostling each other and boasting of their humiliating
conquest. We just stood there.

II. Rules of the Game

The local religious skirmishes of my later boyhood days were marked by a series of profound political events. The Cuban Missile Crisis was followed by the steady amplification of the Vietnam War; the boys of my generation endured the shocks of politically and racially motivated assassinations; we were subjected to the relentless, ubiquitous and very heated anti-communist cultural indoctrination program. We grew up during the era of the first James Bond films. Themes of espionage, double agents, and conspiracies filled the media air waves and settled deep into the imaginations of countless boys across the United States. Feeding these popular cultural fantasies were specialty toys and games developed to exploit the "Us vs. Them" mentality. The full combat apparel and military accessories of GI Joe, including his jeep, became more popular than the Barbie-like Ken doll and his T-Bird convertible because they offered parents the opportunity to de-feminize the doll play prevalent among their latency-age boys. Military board games like "Risk," "Stratego," and "Battleship" were also successfully marketed during this time period. Themes of conquest and world domination were blatantly celebrated in these games. The goals of the players were as simplistic as those of American politicians and their military-industrial complex: annihilate the enemy, take over the globe, *win* by any means necessary and at whatever costs.

Toy spy paraphernalia also appeared on the market to help young boys cultivate expertise in tracking and exposing "The Enemy." I remember one particularly ingenious device called "Secret Sam." This was essentially a toy attaché case containing, among other devices, an actual and well-camouflaged camera. Another memorable toy from that era was a huge plastic gun called "Johnny Seven," a rifle/bazooka with seven concurrent shooting elements of varying sizes and shapes. The proud owner of a Johnny Seven could instantly convert it from pistol to machine gun and spit out plastic bullets at the enemy of his choice. As boys across the nation were encouraged to play with devices like these in their leisure time, many of their parents were joining the growing ranks of the National Rifle Association.

Having older brothers meant inheriting their games as well as their clothes and protective potential. I was doubly blessed to have access not only to the war games of my own era, but to the war games belonging to my older brothers' boyhoods as well. When they reached adolescence, I inherited three elaborate military setups in boxes about three feet long and two feet wide. Each box contained a complete military installation of a different sort: the first was a medieval scene, with an entire castle, vassals with armor and weaponry, horses, and catapults. In another box was "Fort Apache," a cowboys-and-Indians set with dozens of soldiers for each side, horses with war paint, tepees, and cannons. The third box contained an all-green World War II setup with all the accoutrements of what was then considered modern warfare. In particularly aggressive orgies of retaliatory violence, one of my brothers and I would combine these sets of figures for our own version of "World War III." The possibility of an actual war preoccupied me greatly, as the media made frequent references to its apparent inevitability. From the first grade on, the excessive amount of speculating on television and radio and in the newspaper about who did or did not possess nuclear weapons, the recurrent images of missiles from Cuba aimed at northeastern cities (including my own), and frequent "shelter drills" at school in combination with other propaganda transmitted there daily—all these things served to alert my suggestible young imagination to the imminent danger of a sudden, violent, and overwhelming Russian invasion.

At home, I managed my apocalyptic anxieties by playing desperate games. My brother and I shared a room with only a small space separating our twin beds. We would take hold of every military set of toys we owned and add to them hundreds of little plastic animals, dinosaurs, stray soldiers and other figures from sets no longer intact. In the narrow corridor between our beds we would easily spend an hour or more carefully creating a make-believe plastic world, placing every item in some overall realistic scene. Finally, after pausing for a ritual moment of silence, we would take model airplanes, marbles, Popsicle sticks (sometimes even rocks), and vigorously demolish the entire complex. We bombed continuously until no "living thing" was left standing, and until we had completely released our aggressive energy. Screaming "Takka, takka!" we would laugh uproariously as we annihilated our little world. Although actually a Yiddish expression we'd heard our parents and grandparents use, "Takka" sounded to us like the thing a kamikaze pilot might yell as he dove toward the target of his suicidal destruction.

At school we had help in managing our war-related anxieties. The adults "comforted" us with shelter drills, civic assemblies, patriotic sing-alongs, and flag-worshipping services. Every school day began with a standing ovation to a flag of our nation-state: this mass recital of the Pledge of Allegiance was mouthed with our right hands positioned somberly over our hearts. (My right had was so reflexively trained to cross my heart at the sound of the Pledge that I learned to master the left-right distinction this way, by rapidly saying the first three words of the Pledge under my breath.) The words of the Pledge never made any sense to most of us, even though almost everyone could probably have recited them in their sleep. In fact, schoolyard debates took place over the identity of the mysterious man in the Pledge named "Richard Stands." We couldn't figure out why we hadn't been taught about this great figure in our nation's history.

School assemblies were even more blatant exercises in mind control. Everyone was expected to attend them in red, white and blue clothing: those who did not were punished by officially sanctioned ostracism, humiliation, and, of course, detention. During these mass gatherings, we would not only be led in mouthing the Pledge, but were forced to sing patriotic songs. For some reason and somewhat ironically, "God Save Our Gracious Queen" was occasionally added to our renditions of "God Bless America," the National Anthem and the "Battle Hymn of the Republic." Consistent with other versions of mass indoctrination, we had to sing these songs while standing for long periods of time.

The school's "color guard" provided glitz for these rallies. This elite corps consisted of a group of youngsters who would march into the room after everyone else had arrived. With great fanfare, the guard brought in three huge flags: the flag of the City of New York, followed by the flag of the State of New York, and finally (least exciting of all) the Stars and Stripes. Following several moments of orchestrated and perfunctory awe, the verbal part of the political service would begin. This would include, in addition to the singing, speeches by various authority figures and/or role models who exhibited the virtues of the school, the government and "Our Way of Life" (which, of course, was extolled as the "One Best Way").

Only male students were allowed to carry the flags. The readily accepted rationale of this fact had to do with the considerable size and weight of these giant icons and the superior physical strength of males. No one protested this division of labor and honor. Selected females—obviously chosen on the basis of their attractiveness as well as their good citizenship—were permitted by the adults in charge of the school to wear red, white and blue scarves and march alongside each flag-holding male.

While school assemblies were rather theatrical, the shelter drills were unnerving. Other disruptions in the school routine were eagerly welcomed by the understimulated students. Fire drills, for example, were very popular as they resulted in a momentary escape from the crowded indoor classrooms. Shelter drills, on the other hand, were conducted in a more somber and tense manner, and never involved going outside—after all, Russian bombers might easily sight you outdoors. A shelter drill was never initiated by loudly clanging bells like fire drills were. Instead, some unfamiliar adult would enter the classroom and whisper something in our teacher's ear. The stranger would then leave as abruptly as she had appeared and our teacher would become very stern, and immediately put aside her teaching implements. She would then begin to give a series of terse orders. The seriousness of the whole rehearsal ignited all sorts of fears and fantasies in us schoolchildren.

There were two forms of shelter drill, and I often wondered whether the difference in them had to do with the relative severity of the anticipated attack or to some whim of the school principal. In the first and more frequent form of the drill, we were taught to turn away from the wall of huge barred windows and to hide under the wooden benches attached to our desks. We were expected to stay absolutely silent and still under our desks for quite a while; even anxious rustling sounds were not tolerated. Some secret series of signals would then take place between the teachers who were keeping each other abreast of various developments throughout the make-believe crisis. I remember wondering if the Russian planes could fly through our classroom windows, and why the enemy would want to attack schoolchildren in particular. Then I would flash on the stories told by the older boys in the school yard about the sadistic Russkies. I wondered if our "camouflage" was effective or if the pilots could see us hiding under our desks. I wondered if children in Russia were hiding from *our* bombers, and if American pilots would ever be so cruel as to bomb schools with children hiding inside them. I comforted myself with the notion that the Russians were meaner than Americans, which also helped explain why we had to "beat" them, and, by implication, why war with them (or anyone) was necessary.

In the other version of the shelter drill, we were told to silently line up according to (for some reason) how tall we were. We were then commanded to "buddy-up" for protection and quickly shuttled out of the classroom into the school's windowless hallways. The simultaneous emptying of numerous classrooms of thirty-five to forty children each created a rather panic-filled scene. Once positioned in the hallway, the adults instructed us in firm whispers to crouch down, protect our eyes, hold on to our buddies and listen for further instructions. The seemingly interminable period of silence that ensued was soon accompanied by the pain of our aching knees.

When we finally completed our maneuvers, we would march back to our classrooms or come out from under our desks and resume classwork as if nothing at all bizarre—or disturbing—had taken place. Some days I remember going home from school and wondering if my parents were secretly Russian spies, and if I would someday, when they were discovered, be forced to go back to Russia with them to live, or if I would have to decide whether or not to turn them in to the FBI or CIA.

Given our actual, imagined, and official enemies, the boys on my block had a lot of paranoia to contend with. In retrospect, it appears that a good deal of our boyhood was spent preparing for one sort of battle or another. In fact, building forts and fortresses was for a long time a veritable obsession for the boys in my neighborhood. We constructed these forts from old refrigerator boxes or scraps of wood and metal from our fathers' garages. Mounds of dirt in vacant lots became castles to be defended with one's life. Every variation possible on "King-of-the-Hill" was played on these dirt mounds.

In the winter, however, the problem of finding building materials was solved by the abundant snowfalls. More than any other variety, our snow forts took on the aura of real military installations. The whole neighborhood would become virtually riddled with snow forts representing rival factions, each one trying to defend its territory with snowball artillery. We reinforced the forts with ice bricks made by freezing water in plastic and paper cups. To guarantee a sturdy and stable structure, we all loaded up our mothers' freezers night after night. As our forts were frequently under attack from either the Catholics or rival Jewish "gangs," it became important to develop offensive weapons as well as defensive fortifications.

I remember one military strategy we thought particularly clever. Out of sight of our marauding enemies, we drilled a hole about the size of a softball into the side of the snow fort. We then constructed an iced chute from the hole into the coldest section of the igloo/fort. In this hidden chamber we stored an ever-growing arsenal of well-formed snowballs. In very serious war situations we resorted to the secret weapon known as ice-balls—snowballs centered around a piece of hard ice made from cups of water in our mothers' refrigerators. These "ultimate" weapons were used (purely defensively, of course) against particularly vicious boys who had attacked us with their own ice-balls. As our allies outside the fort could mass-produce snowballs and quickly roll them down into the arsenal, we always had more ice-weaponry at our disposal than any invader could possibly carry with him to attack us. The entire process was exhilarating.

On some mornings we would wake to find our forts destroyed during the night by the older neighborhood boys. One time the fort itself was left standing but its arsenal had been selectively demolished. Clearly, this was a statement about the local "balance of power." The repeated destruction of our forts did not impede our efforts to rebuild them for as long as the snow would last. It seems ironic that at this same time, and before I had conscious knowledge of the war in Vietnam, the Vietcong were continuously rebuilding their hand-dug tunnels and other ingenious underground defensive structures following week after week of brutal bombing raids, much to the amazement and chagrin of the American military-industrial complex.

Aggression *within* friendship groups did occur in some instances, but with so many enemies to manage from the outside, boys of a given identity cluster tended to stick together, channeling most of their hostility to the outside. There were two games that stand out, however, that did seem to operate in a fashion to contain and ventilate tensions within a peer group; these were games that were never played with one's enemies, but could be extended to acquaintances or newcomers. Both games tested the limits of sadism and trust, dynamics that seemed essential for male bonding.

The first of these games was a card game called "Knucks." The technical goal of the game was to have the fewest number of cards left in your hand at the end. The winner would give "knucks" to each of the losers according to a specific ritual. Knucks are whacks or blows of the deck of cards in various formations across the opponent's knuckles. Each loser would count his cards and then close his eyes and pick a card from the deck. If the card was black, the knucks delivered would be soft. This was almost like winning for it guaranteed a ritualized hitting just to remind the loser of his defeat. In metaphoric terms, this also guaranteed us all a ringside seat for "the real thing." A red card stood for blood and this meant that the winner could be violent in delivering the blows to the opponent's knuckles. There were a variety of ways to receive the punishment. One could accept, for example, ten hard smacks against the hand, one after the other. Drawing blood and peeling skin was often the goal. There were "combination knucks," developed as ways to get the pain over with more quickly and developed to add variety to the sadistic offerings of the game itself. For five knucks you could "guillotine" the opponent. This involved taking the middle section of a deck of cards in one hand and raising it above the two side sections held by the other hand. The victim's knuckles were placed under this arrangement and the winner would slam the mid-section of the deck, in guillotine fashion, giving a sharper, more knife-like sensation. For ten knucks, you could do a "knucks-sandwich" where the loser's hand is placed between the two halves of the deck of cards and then smashed by the fist of the victor. Worst of all was a super sandwich, worth about twenty or twenty-five knucks (points). In this variation, a shoe would come down on the sandwiched hand instead of the winner's fist.

The more subtle aspects of the game involved covert agreements and communications based on mutual, prior understandings between pairs of boys not to hurt each other too badly. It was difficult to achieve the delicate balance between saving face for self and others and creating a convincing illusion of pain. These nonverbal covenants could also be broken or misunderstood, so that a boy who thought he had a deal going not to be hurt too badly by a would-be ally might be taken by surprise, and then retaliate. That is when the game became most outrageous and, of course, most bloody.

The other game with the more overt castration themes was called "Chicken." This game involved throwing a pocket knife between each other's legs, spread apart in the dirt or grass. The goal was two-fold: not to flinch when the knife was being thrown at you, and secondly, not to hit your opponent's body with the knife. An experienced player could really come close to the leg without hitting it and could also conceal any fear of being cut. Subtle communication always took place concerning the degree of dangerousness one was willing or desiring to entertain against the opponent. Trust, sadism and shame were juggled to master boyhood injunctions about fear, pain, and manliness.

Perhaps the most heartless versions of boyhood aggression were our cruelties to the insect world. Our collective violence knew no bounds when it came to our wars with the arthropods. Although my friends and I loved animals fiercely, we somehow managed to separate out this subgroup of the animal kingdom as an acceptable target of our childhood fears and traumas. In small groups of two or three, we would periodically venture into gardens, yards and vacant lots in search of conquest experiences. We armed ourselves against our doomed enemies with firecrackers, matches, sticks for digging, morsels of food for lures and sticks of scentless incense that remained lit for long periods of time that we called "punk-sticks," or "punks." An aura of exhilaration and secrecy was involved in these outings. Usually we got up very early in the morning to conduct our raids, so as not to be seen or questioned by adults. We planned our forays at least a few days in advance; they were rarely spontaneous excursions. Armed with our fire-weapons, and all the unspent retaliatory psychic rage energy amassed from our own recent subjugations at the hands of more powerful beings, we set out to decimate the insects. We lured them out slowly with bits of food, stalked them as they emerged, then pounced upon our helpless victims with our burning punk-sticks. In more impatient moments, we lit firecrackers and placed them into the tunnels connecting their nests and watched gleefully as all hell broke loose. In some sort of killing frenzy we engineered the obliteration of entire ecosystems. And we were not merciful either: usually we would not rest until there were no signs of life left in the tract of land we were "clearing." Even today, I can still recall the smell of burning ants in the early morning air.

By the age of eight or so we had discontinued these acts of aggression against the hapless innocents of the insect societies. Later one, we heard rumors that the older Catholic boys had taken street cats, dipped them in gasoline and set them on fire. When I first heard this I became immediately sick to my stomach and I couldn't stop thinking about the image for weeks. Even later, the image of a gang deliberately setting fire to an animal haunted my suggestible boyhood mind. I identified completely with the cat and it was easy then for the Catholic boys to hold all of my "shadow" (i.e., personal and collective) projections. Eventually I came to know, with great consternation, that I was not only the cat and its futile screams of agony, but the violent killer of the cat as well as the horrified, helpless witness to this act of cruelty.

III. Influence

As an adult, during my inquiry into the origins of male aggression, I learned that by late boyhood (around ten or twelve years of age), most boys are quite confirmed in their interest in violence and show clear signs of preferring one-upmanship, separateness, and rigid patterns of defensive autonomy instead of behaviors organized around cooperation and affiliation. The pattern of "acting upon" rather than "relating to" people, things, and events clearly drives the attitudes and behavior of pre-adolescent boys, "men-in-training." Identity and mastery revolve around conquest and possession. This is the aftermath of collective traumatic influence that is mastered, in general, by the psychological process often referred to as identification with the aggressor. This is more often than not a power-based (as opposed to love-based) identification aimed at mastering helplessness and extreme vulnerability.

Dis-identifying and dissociating the victim-position, the man-boy takes on the attributes of the aggressors around him. This inevitably leads to treating others the way he has been treated. In most cases, this means a lifestyle of turning aggression on others as a means of avoiding the experiences of powerlessness, loss and vulnerability to injury, and as a means of avoiding the memory and re-experience of his own emotional scarring. The masking of these primitive feeling states, and the dissociation of horror and dread associated with our own abuse and emotional wounding, are often maintained by cycles of addiction to violence, a need for a constant supply of reality and fantasy-based violent stimulation. Media models for boys' play and fantasy worlds include very aggressive sports, war toys, explosively aggressive and vindictive war films and games of domination. The cycle is self-reinforcing and is clearly perpetuated and celebrated by the dominant culture. The political machinery of warfare has at its disposal mass child-rearing practices capable of producing a large volunteer army and an even larger male culture tacitly supporting aggressive intervention and violent solutions to conflict.

In his insightful book *Fire In The Belly*, Sam Keen clarifies the relationship between masculinity and pain. The process of boyhood initiation into manliness involves hazing, humiliation, physical tortures, and mutilations of every sort. As a general rule, he says, the more a tribe or nation practices warfare, the harsher are the rites of initiation for boys into manhood. Painful ordeals inevitably accompany and dramatize the separation from the world of women. These dramatizations serve to set up profound, hazardous boundaries between boys and girls—and for males, major "no trespassing" signs on female aspects of themselves. In preparation for manhood, boys are taught to disdain women's ways, to reject the "sensuous knowledge" they learned kinesthetically from their mothers. All that is soft and feminine in themselves must be disavowed. More often than not, the price for manhood is the toleration and eventual practice of cruelty.

Having been conditioned as boys to value aggression above all other emotions, and having the expectation of being a battlefield sacrifice indelibly stamped into their developing psyches, most adult men have an aspect of self that is actually a hypnotized agent of the state waiting to be called into "active" service. Warfare has been romanticized and idealized for this warboy-self who has been exposed to years of mystification and glorification of male violence, plus a culture obsessed with manliness. The violence and trauma associated with this aspect of boy-self must be endured with pride, for the development of socially sanctioned masculinity requires a wounding of the body, the dissociation of pain and a renunciation of the world of tenderness. To be a warrior, one must be able to bear and inflict suffering without complaint. The older men of the society pass this form of personal and cultural organization down through the generations. Manhood is thus established and fortified by the willingness to bear the physical and psychological mutilation imposed by the ruling elders.

Men have been fighting wars for millennia. Perhaps the underlying problem is not so much men as a "sex." Certainly women have both conscious and unconscious layers of complicity in the evolution of male violence. The root of the problem lies in a social system that idealizes what Riane Eisler (*The Chalice and the Blade*, 1987) calls the "power of the blade." Both men and women are taught to equate true masculinity with violence and dominance, and to see men who do not conform to this ideal as too soft, weak or feminine. The teachings of the male elders cultivate glorification and righteousness in violence. Wrathful male deities, warriors, generals and famous conquerors become pivotal in the organization of history and religion. The central religious image of our culture revolves around a man dying on a cross, not a woman giving birth or breast-feeding. Most leaders of modern nations have been military men and "intelligence" experts, not poets and farmers.

The male-dominated economic sector is rewarded by money, status and power. It eats, it devours, it covets. The system of male domination where property is transferred from father to son, where benefits of women's and children's labor are accrued to the ruling males, where the drive to conquer and dominate other human beings is revered, will eventually cannibalize all existing social and ecological systems. The men with the greatest capacity for destruction have taken and been given the most power. The power that takes life is idealized over the power that gives life. In this cultural context, the boy, to save himself, must abandon and betray his mother and the world of women, and join the ranks of their oppressors; the rage at his own premature weaning and abandonment (perhaps part of the mother's unconscious participation in the conspiracy of male violence) may fuel this transition, but it is still a shift that occurs at a great cost to the developing man-child. Through internalizing the culturally sanctioned wisdom and knowledge base of the ruling fathers, he must prepare and practice for the eventuality of body-, self-, and other-sacrifices. This distorted base of knowledge, corrupted by power, is flamboyant even in the Bible, a central locus of law and belief in our culture, where horrific violent crimes are condoned. Killing in war, razing entire cities, destroying and appropriating property including women and children, and enslaving other human beings are divinely sanctioned. The most serious offense of all in this "Good Book" is to defy "divine authority." The most serious offense of all in the boyhood-manhood cults of our modern age is the defiance of masculine privilege. These are the lessons of boyhood in the cradle of modern democracy.

The social construction of masculinity during the boyhood era is marked by learning of stereotyping, ostracism and disparagement as tools of social control and as methods of establishing self-esteem. The exaggeration of gender differences as a badge of identity among boys, along with the fortification of masculinity based on repudiation of the "maternal" and the "feminine" elements, have severe psychic and cultural consequences. Boyhood, then, is not a time of transcendence. It is a time of influence. And even if the effects of that influence are to be overthrown someday, or deconstructed and reassembled, the effects on personality development remain. At the very least, this influence remains in the form of character crevices, marking the places where ancient waters of innocence have freely flowed.

References

Chodorow, Nancy. *The Reproduction of Mothering*. Berkeley: University of California Press, 1978.

Eisler, Riane. *The Chalice And The Blade: Our History, Our Future*. San Francisco: Harper and Row, 1987.

Goldner, Virginia. "Toward a critical theory of gender." *Psychoanalytical Dialogues*, 1991, 1(3), 249–272.

Keen, Sam. *Fire in the Belly (On Being a Man)*. New York: Bantam Books, 1991.

Ross, J. "Beyond the phallic illusion: Notes on man's heterosexuality." *The Psychology of Men*, ed. G. Fogel, F. Lane & R. Liebert. New York: Bantam Books, 1986.

Harvey L. Schwartz (b. 1955) spent the first seventeen years of his life in Brooklyn, New York and attended public schools there. He is a clinical psychologist with a private practice specializing in chronic trauma disorder and multiple personality disorder. He is an assistant clinical professor of psychology at the University of California in San Francisco.

From Banana to Third-World Marxist

by Fred Wei-han Ho

My early childhood memories begin at around the age of three. The second experience in life that I can remember was my first pain with white racism. At a preschool program, I remember my sandbox being segregated, how the white schoolteacher (at that time, white, black or Asian/yellow had no meaning) deliberately told the other kids (all white) not to play with me. But the feeling of isolation and avoidance by the other kids, and the pain I felt from this one particular teacher for singling me out, would remain with me for the rest of my life.

Around the time I started elementary school/first grade, I became aware that I was Chinese. Again, racism provoked a self-awareness of difference when the other schoolkids (except for the one other Chinese boy) made fun of and laughed at me for eating at lunch a Chinese *bao* (or steamed flower-shaped bun). The kids pointed at my favorite snack and ridiculed me/it: "Yecch, he's eating playdough!" From then on, a feeling of shame for being Chinese would take hold, even though I loved the foods my mom prepared. The *char sui* (Chinese roast pork), *lop cheong* (Chinese sausage), *bing bing* and various *baos* (fried and steamed buns) were my favorites, more so than American spaghetti or hamburgers (which I blamed my mom for not knowing how to make authentically). My mother tells me that before entering public school I spoke and understood more Chinese than English, but that after a few months of first grade, and the painful feeling of being different, I actively tried to give up everything to do with being Chinese. I wanted to be liked, to be accepted, to do well and be respected.

"White got the might/White is right/Might as well be White . . ." It wasn't until years later that I became clear about the pressures of white assimilation, self-denial and self-hatred. By turning away from my Chinese-American identity, I became a banana (yellow on the outside, white on the inside): actively disavowing my heritage and people and identifying with the oppressor *in toto* (physical appearance, politics, values, etc.).

My parents didn't want me to lose my Chinese heritage and pride. They never understood what they termed "Americanization," or what

I now call "whitification." They were immigrants. My father, a university professor, was seemingly bicultural: he was fluent in both Chinese and English (although he always had an accent), a tenured professor who taught Chinese political science. But he was actually culturally schizophrenic: he self-identified as a Confucian scholar who had to lower himself to function in the white academia, frustrated by the professional/career politics required to advance. While he was the most published of all the senior faculty members in his department, he was the least paid. He would take out his frustration with the job (which included his white students making fun of him for his accent), and be a Chinese feudal patriarch at home. We—my mom, myself and my two sisters—were the victims of his fulminations and violent domination. He battered my mom for her inability to speak English, for her wanting the independence that she perceived white middle-class wives possessed. One of my first revolutionary insurrections was when at the age of seventeen, I opposed my father's physical abuse of my mother. To get him to stop hitting her, I fist-fought him, giving him two black eyes. I remember the next day he went into work wearing dark sunglasses, not wanting to miss giving a lecture as the dutiful teacher.

Because my home life was so awful, it was very important to be accepted at school by my peers in a white college town. I parted my hair, tried to put in a wave. I tried to become a fan of white popular music. Strangely, when "Star Trek" had come on network TV in the mid-to-late 1960s, I came to identify with Mr. Spock, the half-Vulcan, half-human first officer—the "alien." Spock was good in math and science; so was I. Spock tended to suppress his emotions (his human side), and so did I. And Vulcans and Asians bore a similar physical resemblance. For two or three Halloweens, I just wore a blue turtle neck shirt bearing a Starfleet insignia I had made with crayons and cardboard. When the other kids shouted "trick or treat," I gave a Vulcan hand salute and stoically proclaimed, "Live long and prosper." Only a few white neighbors asked me, "What are you supposed to be?" (Interestingly, I never identified with Sulu, the Asian on the show; I think because he was so token, his Asian-ness completely peripheral or nonexistent, unlike Chekov or Scotty who spoke with accents to identify their cultural/national heritages, or Uhura who occasionally dressed in African garb or who viewers knew spoke Swahili. Sulu was completely culturally de-ethnicized.)

All the other Asian males on TV were pathetic stereotypes: comic-relief servant/sidekick types like Fuji and Hop Sing, or evil inscrutables like Hawaii Five-O's nemesis, the red commie Wo Fat (never played by an Asian). I tried to like David Carradine as Swai Chang Caine in "Kung Fu," but the fake martial arts couldn't make up for the even more fake slant eyes and yellow skin makeup (the racist Hollywood/ American entertainment tradition of yellow-face).

The one exception on TV while growing up was Bruce Lee as Kato on "The Green Hornet." Kato had a thick Cantonese accent, even in his common one-liner: "Whele to, Boss?" (Chinese make "r" sounds come out like "l"). Raised in the boys-will-be-boys heterosexual socialization of male aggressiveness and heroism, I craved an action-adventure character like Kato, who could really kick ass. I always secretly wondered why Kato wasn't the boss instead of the Green Hornet. But after all, I still hadn't begun to question the notion of the white man's world.

My sexual awareness started to take off at age eight when my family drove cross-country from Massachusetts to California. Bored from hours of simply seeing highway, when we stopped at stores to get supplies, I took off for the magazine stands. At first I was simply looking for new comics, but I quickly noticed "girlie" magazines. Of course, all the sexy women were white, busty, mostly blonde. After we got to California and had stayed in the Bay Area for a year, I noticed there were many more Asians, that Safeway supermarkets sold tofu, and of course, the openly run ads for topless bars in newspapers. Chinatown was next to the topless red-light district of North Beach in San Francisco. There was a lot for an eight-year-old to ogle.

I didn't like Asian girls. I was deeply entrenched in my banana-ness. My dad kept trying to match me up with this Chinese-American girl my age who lived right across the street. I had always lived and gone to school in overwhelmingly white communities where there were only a handful of Asian girls; your sisters and the others, who were like cousins because our parents socialized together. Romance couldn't be racially anonymous when it came to Asian girls. And besides, all that society upheld and promoted as desirable and attractive were white images.

Two significant factors worked to rid me of the white/banana syndrome: first, no matter how hard I tried to be racially effacing, I couldn't escape from racism at all levels: from jeers and taunting to outright restrictions—starting with the segregated sandbox. Secondly, the social changes of the late 1960s brought the first African-American teacher to my junior high. She wore a big Afro, projected militant black pride, and brought about the first "Black Experience" class that exposed me to African-American literature, including *The Autobiography of Malcolm X*. It was Malcolm X's life and ideas that awakened my political consciousness: that I/we are victims of a system of white supremacy and racism. For the first time, I began to theorize my personal experience to the level of social analysis and radical political concepts; it never could remain at the level of feel-good politics or "identity politics." More and more as I struggled to change myself through changing the social environment around me, I came to understand the structural and systematic roots of the oppression of "people of color," but also of the world's majority: the oppression of women, workers of all nationalities, entire peoples. The high level of political debate and struggle in the "movement" of the U.S. at this period eventually brought me into Marxism as I discarded my anti-white nationalism or "Third-World consciousness" for a more dialectical and thus scientific analysis. I am not anti-white, but anti–white supremacy. I am pro-liberation for women, gays, oppressed nationalities (what I prefer to call "people of color" as it specifically locates our political condition as oppressed, thus belying notions of "reverse discrimination," etc.), and I'm for socialism. I reject the homophobia, racism and sexism that also has infected parts of the American Left and the socialist movements around the world. While I believe that ultimately our struggle is for political and economic structural or systemic changes, I also uphold the critical importance of cultural change: creating new values and human relations and expressions. In my present profession as composer/baritone saxophonist and band leader of the Afro-Asian Music Ensemble, I insist upon and work toward an audience that is *not* majority white. This is integral to revolutionary change.

While I think it's possible to love anyone, as an oppressed nationality leader in the political and cultural liberation struggle, my sexual/intimate preferences are for oppressed nationality women (I choose to personally be heterosexual). But more importantly, such a lover and intimate partner must also possess radical political consciousness, be committed to the struggle, be personally intelligent, passionate, generous and mature, and strive to uphold the highest standards of excellence and responsibility.

The struggle for all of us who are serious about changing the world is to unite our personal, political and professional lives toward this work/goal.

Fred Wei-han Ho was born in 1957 in Palo Alto, California and spent the next five years in Michigan and Nebraska while his father searched for a full-time teaching job. From the ages of six to seventeen he lived in Amherst, Massachusetts. He is currently a professional baritone saxophonist, composer/arranger, leader of the Afro-Asian Music Ensemble in New York City and the Journey Beyond the West Orchestra in San Francisco.

My Other Life in Serendipity

by Bhante Wimala

(As told to Adam Rostoker)

I am Bhante Wimala and, as far as I know, I am the only Buddhist monk in the world who lives as I do. Unlike most monks who wander in their homelands or live ascetically in monasteries, I spend my life traveling over the world to teach and to heal and to bring peace to the people of our planet. I have been traveling now for ten years and have forged friendships across the globe. I like to think that there is a friend of mine who is just waking from a good sleep at every hour of my day.

As I think about this life that I live, and the string of circumstances that have led me to travel the world as a holy man among secularists, I can't help but smile when I remember that the name for my homeland, Sri Lanka, means serendipity. Perhaps it all makes sense when you think of Serendipity as your starting point.

I was born in Sri Lanka early in the summer of 1958 and spent the first twenty-one years of my life during my country's hopeful and prosperous era between our peaceful independence from Britain and the bloody internal conflicts that one hears about today. My lifetime coincided with the greatest period of change ever to happen on this small, tropical island. Mine was a time of naïveté and savvy, of respect for tradition and an ache for newness, an era of rich details and unstoppable change. Indeed, it was the most serendipitous time for an island called Serendipity.

As I write this, I am thirty-two years old and have spent more than half of my life as a monk. Like many monastic candidates in Sri Lanka, I was sent from my home to live in the temple at the age of thirteen. At fourteen, I took my vows as a novice into the order of monks in the Buddhist temple, and, at twenty-two, I was fully ordained as a monk. I remember that even before I was sent to the temple like other boys of my caste, to fulfill the family's obligation to our faith, I was a very independent and lucky boy. I had known a home. I had a life, a wonderful, magical childhood in the heart of this land called Serendipity. In this world, I knew my place and my future—the last thing I expected was to be selected as a monk.

Once I arrived at the temple, of course, the experience of my life became quite different from that of other Sri Lankan children. These changes comprise one of my strongest memories and mark my greatest transition besides birth. My life as a young boy before coming to the temple became the "other life" that I knew in this incarnation. With the passage from lay life to monkhood everything changed. I had to take vows. I had to shave my beautifully combed hair and wear a long saffron robe instead of shirts and pants. My family was replaced by my teacher and brother monks. Different rules, different values, different family, a different name, and a new home.

My temple had no female monks and existed as an exclusively male environment. All of my intimate friendships and interactions were with males. Although there would be some female family members and friends with whom I would enjoy close relationships, there was always—and still remains—a limit of distance that dates from that time. My "other life," my childhood, on the other hand, was typified by women, especially by interactions with my much-beloved mother, her sisters and her daughters.

I grew up in a family of nine children. I am the second youngest and have a younger sister, two older brothers and five older sisters. According to the standard of my village, I could say that I came from a middle-class family. My father was a respected man in the village; as a *gurunance* (an esoteric healer and astrologer), he helped many people. He was a farmer, ran a small restaurant with the help of my mother, and managed government contracts for road sand as a sideline. If he was an industrious man, my mother was an industrial complex. She was a miracle of a housewife and kept herself enormously busy, between fourteen and sixteen hours every day, providing love and care for her nine children, husband, friends, neighbors, and miscellaneous pets and livestock.

I grew up in the small village of Yatiravana, which means the "lower" Ravana. The village was surrounded by several green moun-tains, which made us in the valley feel particularly self-contained. All of our lives were held in this emerald navel of the world and I felt at home within those colossal, ancient walls. Growing up, our lives were filled with chores, school, play and worship. Everything we needed or wanted was within our reach. As I consider how snugly the whole universe fit me back then, I can't help but feel sad for the large and confusing world that most children know. We never had the knowledge that something was missing. Everything was at hand. We were content.

Most children that I meet today don't have this sense of fullness.

Our family had two small houses. The larger one, a four-room residence of painted brick and tarred tin, stood in a bamboo grove at the foot of the hill where most of the villagers had their homes. My brothers and sisters lived there with my mother. We had a large kitchen that was the pulse point of our family. Unless we were sleeping, there was always some cooking or craft going on in the kitchen. It was the stage for most of our daily dramas. We had a small porch which witnessed our kinetic comings and goings but was peaceful at evening time when we would worship or sit together. We drew our water from a well just outside the door and it was a short walk—even with my little-boy legs—from there to any spot in the village. The second house was much smaller. It was a white, thatch-roofed adobe cabin which stood with the home of my delightfully eccentric Aunt Tilaka by the river a few minutes walk from the village. It was more private and less frenzied. My father lived there and it was close to the family farm. It held my father's tools and clothes and the family's second kitchen. Just outside was the main family business, a small wooden luncheon counter where the villagers would come to drink tea, have light lunches and gossip together. The second house was my father's domain, although all of us slept there at one time or another, and it was here that my parents could be alone.

The Ravana River flowed through our village and provided water for all our local needs. It was also a fun place to be. People swam, bathed, and washed clothes in the river. On some days after school, we would go to the river, leap into the water, and play there for hours. Generally the weather was between 85 and 90 degrees and the Ravana was a fine place to cool off. We would gather small rocks and make dams, build sand canals, observe the movement of fish and track them through the currents. There were a few places where we would climb ten feet up onto a rock and jump into the water. Our river was one of my favorite playthings and one of my best friends.

My sisters used to wake me up early in the morning and drag me to the river with them. I would perch on a rock while they dipped into the water to bathe in their bathing clothes. After this they would wash their clothes and towel dry their long, long hair. Then we would walk home together through the quiet and the mist.

The girls would never go to the river alone after dark, of course, or early in the morning, even when two sisters got together. The presence of a male, even a little boy like me, was considered an important tradition. Quite often my sister would bribe me or my brother Siri with sweets, money or sewing to go with them if they had a social call after dark. I have always had a strong fear of the darkness, and I remember balancing my fear against the thrill of being needed by my sisters and the pleasure of family duty. Like many gender-oriented traditions in Sri Lanka, this has changed now, and women are often about in the night. Still, I remember many nights as a boy when Siri and I would summon up our courage against the darkness of night and execute our traditional duty as our sisters' little guardians.

My childhood in Yatiravana was shared very much with Siri. Ours was a special friendship. Although he was eighteen months older than me, it was my role to be the older brother. Siri was a twin to my older sister who had died as a child, and he was always small for his age. He was, and is, more a follower than a leader. I always seemed stronger, braver and more capable than him. I was the captain of our adventures and the financier. From the time I was ten years old, I managed to earn money from my labor to buy my own clothes and pay my way to social events. I have always been independent. My family always remembers me as being the least burdensome. I simply always had enough. And enough to share with Siri.

And yet, for all this independence, I don't remember having any goals in my life. Having no goals, however, didn't mean there was nothing I wanted to do. If anything there was always too much to do, especially for a pair of curious boys. Siri and I would often pack a lunch and travel to the woods for a picnic in the forest. We'd sun ourselves on rocks, drink stream water, and eat berries from the vine. We loved to notice nature, and nature, it seems, loved to notice us. I remember one time we were chased by a wild water buffalo and, in my haste to leave the forest, I ran through a barbed wire fence and got a fine set of scars for my trouble.

We had many adventures like this. Once, as a child, I wanted to have a pet goat. After what seemed like an eternity of begging, my father bought me a nanny goat. I loved caring for the goat and made it special leaf baskets so it could eat all night. Often I led the goat to the woods for even finer dining among the vines and creepers. One day, after returning from school, I found my goat was missing. It had somehow wrenched its peg free and gone off in search of greener pastures.

Fearing the worst, my brother and I split up to rescue the nanny goat. I scoured the countryside between sobs of loss. Eventually I jumped the fence of a neighbor's garden to see if my pet had decided to preempt their harvest. Suddenly the neighbor's dog came rushing toward me, barking like a thousand wolves and baring its long teeth. The dog sank its teeth into me and stripped the flesh from my skinny leg. There was no one around but me and the dog, and I guess both us became a bit overwhelmed by how fast everything had happened. We both looked at each other, shocked and frightened by what we had managed to do to my leg in such a brief time, then we both took off running in different directions. I hardly remember scurrying home holding my bleeding leg to fall into my mother's arms.

My strongest memory of the whole incident was my mother's calm patience when I returned all gory from my goat rescue mission. Mine was a serious injury, but we decided against a hospital. My mother laid me down, applied herbal remedies and soothed me with her calmness. The wounds scarred me, of course, but they always reminded me more of my mother's calmness and love than the dog's fangs.

As it turns out, Siri found the goat grazing illicitly in the woods and brought her home. It seems that the dog and the goat both got special meals that day for all my trouble.

Siri was the co-star of many of my childhood games in Yatiravana. We were always close friends. We played together, went to school together and, once in a while, skipped school to have secret adventures together in the countryside. We were inseparable, held no secrets and shared our boyhood. One thing that we never did was to fight with one another. In thirteen years of growing together, we never had a physical fight, not once. Even a verbal argument was rare.

When I recalled this with Siri, who also became a monk for a time, and who now studies English in Canada, I mentioned jokingly that I didn't fight with him because I had no energy left after fighting with so many of my classmates. I was quite a scrapper as a child, fighting several times a week. I defended my brother and my friends against bullies, and, as a result, somehow ended up with a reputation as a bully myself. It's funny how that happens. As a man who tries to devote his life to the promotion of peace, I have often thought about the many fights I had as a boy. My name at birth was Amarasinagha which means "the eternal [or] deathless lion," so perhaps I had been given the early suggestion of physical courage. As I remember, all of those fights involved my protection of a friend or family member against some injustice. One incident I remember well was fighting with the biggest kid in my class, a huge bully of a girl with the ironic name of Shanti, which means "peace" in Hindi. A head taller than me and a full two years older than any of my classmates, she had come from what we would now call a dysfunctional family and had been held back twice for bad grades. She was known to be particularly aggressive in school, and sadistic to the weaker children. She was as fearsome a threat as any dragon.

Shanti used to leave me alone, perhaps because of my own reputation, but would torment my friend Dasanayaka without mercy. One time she tortured him by slashing her ink pen at his back causing indelible stains on his white shirt. This was particularly cruel since it provoked teasing from his other classmates and punishment from his parents for soiling his clothing with such a strong stain. Her marking of him caused much nervous tittering in the classroom, for the children were frightened of Shanti; there was no humor in it. When the noise had subsided, I told her I would take my revenge if she ever did anything like that to one of my friends again.

As I think about this now, I can see that I helped to create a situation very much like the now defunct Cold War. Shanti lived in fear of me and I lived in fear of her. Both of us lost face because of our fear, and other people, like poor Dasanayaka, proved to be the battleground on which we fought our smaller battles. As ugly as this seems in children, I have come to find this thinking is even fouler when practiced by adults, and deadly when practiced by nations.

The next day, however, our childish Cold War broke. Again, she and two of her friends marked Dasanayaka's shirt and tormented him because of his hot tears of frustration, embarrassment and anger. I remember my fury so well. Something snapped in me and, in a flash, I ran up to the three girls, slapped their faces, called them names, then ran away from the school and into my mother's arms. Oh, how I remember running into her arms.

I told her I had left my books in the school and never wanted to return: an impossible choice. The world seemed so unjust. I had done a noble thing to protect my friend, I thought. I stood up to a bully. And yet, I knew that if I returned to school I would be punished for hitting the girls and, no matter what happened, I still had my father's wrath to look forward to. Was there ever so miserable and so righteous a martyr as this child just years shy of the monastery?

As it happened, my aunt was a teacher at the school and had monitored my Cold War with Shanti. Despite my crusade against bullies everywhere, I was a good student and, I think, a good kid. She asked the principal not to punish me and to ask me to return to school, which he did. After a few false starts, I even found my "shanti" with Shanti.

As I consider this violent story from my childhood, and compare it to the monk I see in the mirror, there are several thoughts I have. One interesting thought is that my boyhood name was, as you remember, Amarasinagha which meant "the deathless lion." Later, when I was ordained, I was given the name Wimala which means "without stain"—or more colloquially "pure one." Perhaps a person's name contributes to a cycle of self-fulfilling prophecy; certainly I remember all the adults in my boyhood telling me how brave and independent I was. Perhaps my violent behavior, however nobly intended, was, at least in part, an effort to live up to their expectations of me.

I was very close to my mother and this is another point I share with Siri. It still pains us beyond description that she passed on due to heart failure in the spring of 1984, while caring for my little sister's newborn. We remember her as a loving, caring and trustworthy woman. She was graceful and wise, her wit warmed our home, and this earth has seemed a drearier place since her passing.

My brother was so attached to her that he reacted to her death in 1984 by leaving his worldly life and becoming a monk. On his birthday, a few months after her death, he lit candles on her grave and slept all night on it. When I heard of my mother's death, I repeatedly fainted where I was teaching in Canada. I required medical care to overcome and heal just the shock of the pain. Even these examples cannot communicate the closeness and love we knew with our mother and our grief at her loss. The most powerful and beautiful memory I have of my childhood—indeed, of my entire life—is the power of my mother's love.

Perhaps because of her love for us, we always felt that it was a mutual exchange—that she genuinely loved us for ourselves, not merely as her children—and this is why the feelings remain so alive with me even today. She was, and is, a living goddess to us.

One of the strongest early memories I have of my mother concerns breast feeding. In Sri Lanka, a mother will often nurse her children much longer than Western mothers. I was an extreme case in that I nursed until I was six years old and still have conscious memories of breast feeding. I understand that I was aggressive in seeking out my mother for breast feeding and she didn't have the heart to turn me away, even when I began taking milk that should have gone to my younger sister. Eventually, my mother put a bitter herb on her nipples to keep me away from her milk. I guess it worked, but it reminds me of how close I was to her.

This does not mean I was not in a hurry to grow up. I remember that on the first day of school, I was very excited to go. I had always wanted to go to school and thought it was high adventure. All the other children were experiencing their first separation from their mothers and were sobbing uncontrollably. I remember myself as a very small island of calm in a very large classroom of tears. It was a strange memory, but reminds me how, even then, I was interested in new experiences. Perhaps because my mother had been so near to me for so long, I had all the strength I needed to face my newest adventure. I often think of my mother as being near me now. I know that I would welcome her always.

I had a different feeling for my father. It was not a love that we had for him as children, but rather a respectful sort of fear. We remember him as the most powerful person in the family. After him came a gap. My mother was the second most powerful and my older sister after her. While I always enjoyed my relationship with my mother, brothers and sisters, I *maintained a relationship* with my father. Even today it is difficult for me to separate my fear of my father from my love of him. Although I spent much time with my father, working and learning, it was always spent in at least a little fear. My father, however, always liked me better than the other children. I was a courageous, energetic and curious child, never lazy. When my father or mother needed a hand, they could always count on me—unlike my brothers. After school, since the age of seven or eight, I used to help my father on his farm. My father used to go around the vegetable beds making holes with his fingers and I would follow him, dropping seeds in those tiny holes and covering them with earth—I always loved getting good and grimy. I woke up at 5 A.M. with my father to water and tend the vegetable beds. I also used to work in the rice fields with him. I loved being useful, and often stretched my limits in this regard. Many times, my mother would warn me not to lift such heavy loads or work so hard, but it was a great source of pride and identity for me. "I am the strong, courageous, hardworking son," I thought. In particular, I was very good at climbing trees, and sometimes I would climb the neighbors' trees and pick coconuts for them for pocket money.

My father didn't actually approve of me climbing trees for money. It wasn't seemly for me to act like the child of a poorer family. I remember one time I was in the top of a tree and my father stood beneath it for a long time, waiting for me to come down to my punishment. After what seemed like an eternity of nervous standoff—it may have been an hour—my mother came out and rescued me by luring my father inside the house. When I timidly returned home later, she had lessened his rage such that all he did to me was to bellow.

Of course, I was lucky that time. While I do not remember my mother ever hitting me or even speaking a harsh word, my father was a cruel and frequent punisher. One of my strongest memories of him involves my fear of his cane. Like many Asians at the time, he considered physical punishment the ideal method of disciplining children. When I went to school nearly all of the teachers had canes for hitting children—especially the principal, who had extra canes in his office. When my mother prevented my father from punishing us, my father accused my mother of interfering with the correct discipline of the children. Sometimes her interference worked; sometimes it didn't, and we could all be beaten very severely. While I recall the beatings as extreme, the sins which earned them seem so innocent to me now. Skipping school, scrapping with other children, and climbing coconut trees were just a few of the many things I remember having done to earn a dose of his civilized punishment.

By civilized punishment, I refer to a standard procedure of punishment with a cane. There are two places in the body which can be struck—the palm or the buttocks. The child is commanded to stretch the hands forward and hold the palms up to receive the whipping. Even now when I think of flashing colored lights, blinking stars, and electric shocks, they remind me of those pains. Although the canes were only as thin as pencils, and just a yard long, when the teachers or parents would take out their canes, only the bravest wouldn't shiver, and even they would still perspire.

Of course, it is no longer as acceptable to whip children as it was in my childhood, and I think this is better. Most of the difficult memories of my childhood, and many of the fears I carry as an adult, stem from this ancient and stupid practice. And it makes me wonder, even today, when I recall my memories of fear and pain as a boy, exactly what is meant by the word "civilized."

And this brings me to an interesting point. One of the most difficult memories for me was my boyhood fear of my father, and the sure knowledge that I could never tell him the truth if it was something different from what he expected. His immediate reaction to any behavior beyond his expectation or outside of the social rules he had always known, was to punish quickly and severely. And so, when I hit Shanti and ran from the school, my greatest fear by far was of his retribution. And, when I fell out of a tree while playing with some friends after school and sustained some serious internal bleeding and bruises, I would not tell my father what had happened, eventually concocting a story about falling off a rock. My mother, too, was worried about my father's punishment of me and often tried to protect me by begging him not to hit me, or warning me to lie about the circumstances. And yet, the man I knew as my father was a man who told me he loved truth.

There were other reasons to fear my father. He was the village *gurunance,* a combination of shaman and astrologer. Astrology plays an important part in Sri Lankan culture and it is traditional to consult an astrologer for many reasons. The day after a child is born, a horoscope is cast and astrologers are then consulted on every stage of development. Auspicious times are chosen for the first eating of solid food, the first haircut, the first reading of a book. Parents often take extreme precautions to avoid premature occurrences of these events.

My father was such an astrologer, but unlike most astrologers, my father was also a healer, medium and a psychic for the village. He performed exorcisms, banished curses, and advised people on spiritual, romantic and financial affairs.

One of the most frightening incidents of my life was when I went to see my father at one of his shamanic ceremonies. As I mentioned, I had a strong fear of darkness and this rite took place on a moonless night, lit only by dimly flickering torches and the dull red coals of hot incense. Many villagers I knew were there, but they were dressed strangely in bizarre masks and unfamiliar costumes. All around me was the constant din of drums and horns. Of course, I had often heard the drums and horns at night in the distance and knew something of my cultural heritage, but to be there in the wildly leaping shadows, with masked demons dancing and wailing around me, the reek of incense in my nose, the throbbing of drums and the cacophony of horns—it was almost too much for a little boy to bear.

The rite was an exorcism. They usually were. When demons plague a man or woman they exhibit certain well-known signs. The afflicted person becomes physically ill, shows bad luck or has nightmares. Sometimes there will be signs of dizziness or fainting. At these signs, people become suspicious: it is the nature of demons to conceal themselves as long as possible to avoid the travail of exorcism. As time goes on, people begin to suspect possession. Everything about the person begins to be interpreted in these terms. After a while my father is called in to investigate and, if need be, to begin the rite of exorcism. The purpose of the exorcism is to drive the demon to the surface of the patient so that all persons can see it, then to confront the demon and force it to leave and never return.

The first step is to build a small shrine stocked with food, coconut flowers, incense, certain powerful artifacts, and blood drawn from a living chicken. After a time, lured by the food and the smell of blood, the demon is drawn to the surface. During this time, the participants dance and chant to energize the shrine. Once the demon presents itself, which is normally a horrifying moment, the tests and tortures of exorcism can begin.

My father was the leader in all this. He blew on a conch shell and wore a costume of pure white with a red turban. He directed the building of the shrine, the costuming of the dancers, and led the chanting—some of which came from scriptures that were written in languages that ordinary people never knew. Some chants were fast and would serve to energize the shrine. Other chants were harsh and forceful, calling out the demons and issuing challenges.

When the demon surfaces, the features of the possessed victim seem to change. The demon cries out in unnatural ways and causes the victim to be seized by twitches and convulsions. It is impossible for the victim to resist the energy of the spirit. Now, my father's real work began. Armed with the knowledge and will to force the demon to leave, he would confront the demon and begin the exorcism. Sometimes these negotiations were done symbolically or magically; sometimes they involved physical ordeals. My father would yell or threaten a demon, force the victim over hot coals, or slice a melon on the victim's belly. Sometimes my father would beat the victim until the demon would leave.

If this sounds simple, it wasn't. The rite could last for hours and there were complications. For example, my father could not accept it when a demon at last offered to leave. You can't go around trusting a demon at its word. My father would ask for a sign, like causing a limb or fruit to fall from a tree with no apparent cause. Only then would he know the demon was sincere about leaving and not returning— although there were times when the sign was left incomplete and the rite had to be done over. And the demon didn't want to leave either. It had come for a reason and it intended to stay for a while. A demon's resistance is fairly potent and it has considerable resources as well. A possessed man is endowed with enormous strength and feral cunning. Once, as a child, I saw a possessed man break free of the half dozen men holding him, charge past me, and grab the chicken that had been bled. Although the chicken squawked, shrieked and flapped about, the crazed demon began gnawing off the poor bird's neck and sucking its blood. There were screams of fear all around me. People ran into the darkness—there was an enraged demon among us! Finally my father and a few stout men used magic and force to beat down the demon and bind him again at the shrine. The next day, my father explained that such strong outbursts are quite rare. This did very little to make me happier.

As bizarre as this may seem to some, my father was deemed quite capable in this work and it gained him much respect. The injuries he inflicted were considered par for the course and it was allowed that, after possession, the victims become healed and transcend the pain of the wound. The renewed energy in their lives is considered ample reward for any lingering aches and pains.

It is interesting that my father's respect for propriety and shaman- ism led him to a disappointment involving me. In Sri Lanka, as in many countries, there is a tradition of sending one child from each family to the temple. In this way, the family's piety is demonstrated and their community position is stabilized. At first my brother was chosen for the clergy, as he was deemed quieter and more peaceful than I was as a child. But after one year of training, I went to visit my brother and the high priest determined—through horoscopy and palmistry—that I was the family member destined to be a monk, not my brother.

My father was not pleased with the high priest's decision to retain me for the clergy since he had assumed that I would carry on his work as a shaman. As things happened, my brother drifted around law enforcement before eventually becoming a monk, and my father's work ended when he became too ill to continue. Still, it is interesting to think of how I turned out. Had things been just a bit different, I would be leading exorcisms in a red turban and beating the devils out of my neighbors like my father before me. He was, and is, a complex and forceful man.

And yet, there was another side to my father that I saw only rarely, and which surprised me—a part of him that was filled with love. I still remember how my father held me with great tenderness and wept on the day before my ordination. Like most men at that time, he usually did not show his personal emotions beyond anger, so I was quite surprised at his affection. I remember this well because it was one of the few times he ever hugged me.

Also, my father was an honorable man. In Asia, the practice of wife-beating was so common that my father was a notable rarity because he never hit my mother. I was very fortunate not to witness any physical fights between my parents. My father greatly enjoyed the role of family man, provider and protector. He took seriously his responsibilities of feeding, clothing and housing the family.

He was also the spiritual leader of our family and he led a prayer meeting before every evening meal we had at our home. At 7 p.m. every evening, just before dinner, everybody had to stop what they were doing and gather on the front porch of the big house. Attendance was compulsory, and absence without a strong reason resulted in punishment. A few flowers, incense, and a small oil lamp were placed on the altar in front of the picture of Buddha. We sat in a row starting with my father, then my mother and then the children in order of age. Since I had been old enough to sit I had been joining them. We would chant for about ten minutes, meditate for about five minutes, and then worship first the father, then the mother, then all the older brothers and sisters. I thought it must have been terrible to have been the youngest in the family, and I was glad to have had at least my younger sister to worship me. All things considered, however, these prayer meetings were some of the most important and pleasant times in my childhood.

I have considered that these kinds of prayer meetings were a very helpful tradition and had a considerable positive impact on everyone in the family. After this small ritual and meditation, we all felt calmer and more respectful to each other. This created a fine atmosphere for a quiet family dinner, and did much to smooth relations among my eleven family members. I always knew that, no matter the reason, the family would gather for prayer before meals. Perhaps this first taught me the benefits of self-discipline and continuity.

And then again, part of my childhood was filled with the knowledge that I lived in an ever-changing universe. Not only did the universe have cycles, like planting and harvest. Not only was there an end to school when a child became an adult. Not only did all things that were born come to die. More than this, I lived in a time when many, many things were changing in Sri Lanka.

There were so many changes from then to now it is difficult to think of them all. Yatiravana of the 1960s had neither electricity nor indoor plumbing. It was quite primitive. We used kerosene oil lamps and my mother cooked with firewood. In fact, we greatly enjoyed joining her for firewood expeditions in the forest. We had no refrigeration and so our food was very fresh. Vegetables were bought every few days or harvested just before dinner. The milkman came every day to supplement the produce of our cows and goats, all of which had to be used before the day's end to prevent spoilage. Of course, rice was stored for a long time in a large box on the kitchen floor. We also stored spices like chili peppers, coriander and black pepper seeds, and a special kind of dried fish which I never ate. Nothing in the kitchen was ready-made or instant. Everything was hard work for my mother. She did an extraordinary amount of work and spent most of her time cooking. Likewise, my sisters were taught from a young age to be very efficient in the kitchen.

But the lack of modern contraptions had its good points as well. One of these was the tremendous peace that came over the land at evening time. I miss this peace very much. It is difficult to describe the depth of quiet without resorting to the descriptions of technology. I must say: there was an absence of television, an absence of radio, an absence of recorded music. There was only the quiet music of the night. And, without television or modern conveniences, we were a considerably more social people. Without banks, labor exchanges were common, especially during harvest time or time of need, like convalescence. My neighbors' harvests felt like a continuation of our own. Our lives, in general, were more closely joined.

Cricket was a boyhood passion of mine and I remember being honored when, at twelve, I was invited to play with the adults on the village team. I don't remember any other boys that young being asked to join the teenagers and older men that comprised our team. I was so proud even to be asked. The memory is somewhat marred when I think of how nervous I was to play in front of my mildly disapproving father. I didn't score that game, but I was a valuable scorer in many others.

Tropical weather in Sri Lanka made it possible for us to play outside all year round, except during monsoons. Non-stop monsoon rains can make children feel quite miserable in Sri Lanka—they simply aren't used to being crammed indoors for long times. This is also the time when all the crawling, creeping things start to multiply. The most common are the leeches, of course; but also common are snakes, cobras, and scorpions. When it rains, every time you return home, you open the door, shake out the umbrella, place it in its stand and undergo a proper inspection for leeches. There was always a pretty good chance that we would find a leech sucking blood between the toes or on an ankle. To Westerners, this seems shocking or revolting, but as a boy, I remember that looking for and finding leeches was just another part of life.

I was always taking in animals. Whether it was a squirrel who dropped from a nut tree or a puppy whose mother had died of an accident, I was the one-boy disaster relief team for all of Yatiravana, and my hospital often seemed to have a helpless resident or two. I loved caring for hurt little animals and was fascinated by the study of them. This occupied quite a bit of my time and occasionally earned my parents' frustration. I regret that sometimes, in my desire to help, I'd harm these poor creatures or cause death through ignorance, but in my heart I was sincerely trying to realize my daily meditation which, when I was seven, included the passage, "May all living beings be well and happy." And, after all, most animals survived my treatment and went on to live productive lives in their respective societies.

In Yatiravana, there was life all around me. We had hens and roosters and we gathered our own eggs. When a hen succeeds in laying an egg, she often starts cackling loudly. As a boy, when I heard this sound, I would run in to find the hen clucking proudly around the hot new egg, freshly laid and waiting in its basket.

My mother would never boil eggs because she thought she killed life by boiling eggs. Instead, my sisters had to cook the eggs and I don't recall my mother protesting their involvement. Likewise, she would never cook meat. Among Buddhists in Sri Lanka it is considered bad karma to kill an animal, even for food. There is no such thing as a Buddhist-owned butcher shop. At home, we would hire an Islamic, Tamil, or Christian to come and, for a small sum, kill, clean and prepare the meat for our family dinners. Of course, some Buddhists slaughtered their own chickens or rabbits—never their own cows or goats, perhaps because they were so much bigger—but the "good" Buddhists didn't take life at all.

In my mother's case, this reverence for life was extreme. I never recall her hurting or killing any living thing. She wouldn't even kill mosquitos when they bit her; she'd gently brush them away. My brother tells a story of a time when she found ants infesting the coconut she had planned to fix for the family dinner. She had had a hard day, he says, and she angrily threw the insects into the cooking fire. So far as we can remember, it was the only time she ever did anything immoral.

Throughout my childhood there was the understanding that life was sacred. This did not mean that life was not common or that it could not end; it meant that life was a miracle, just for being, and it required reverence. This reverence for life is part of my inheritance and was often manifested in my early childhood. When, for example, my childhood friends went fishing at the river, I would only watch. Never would I kill a fish or even touch one when it was dead. I remember being particularly horrified when they used firecrackers to cause explosions underwater, causing the dead or stunned fish to rise to the surface as easy pickings. Of course, these young fishermen were the children of the lower caste families and their irreverent behavior was expected and tolerated, if not endorsed.

And so I think that reverence for life is the most important quality I inherited from my mother. This was reinforced since Sri Lanka is an agricultural country and we grew up around farms. The farms of American standards are hundreds of acres of land, thousands of cows, and row after row of grain or fruit. In Sri Lanka, family farms were small: an acre or so of rice, an acre of vegetables and a few cows or chickens, maybe a pig. I grew up in close relationships with the land and the animals as well as with my family and the people of Yatiravana. My friends and teachers included the milk cows, the chickens, the goats, the cats. They were all around us and we had daily encounters with them. I saw cows being born and dying right at our back door, even when I was very young. Later, in the monastery, all this would change and I would become insulated from the cycles of life, death and rebirth.

One of my fondest memories of farm life was the harvest time. Our family would call the neighbors and sharpen their harvesting knives. Everyone would meet and line up on one end of the field. Then they would harvest the rice by cutting the stalks, which looked much like wheat stalks, advancing through the field. While cutting, the men would chant special poems about the harvest. Sometimes people would play drums to keep the enthusiasm high. Often neighbors and passers-by would stop to help, even for short times. The rice stalks were tied in bundles and carried on the women's heads to a large pile in the middle of a field. This takes most of a day. Then, at twilight, a process began which separated the rice grains from the stalks. Large buffalo were yoked together three and four across and driven through the piles to trample the stalks. After a time, the rice separated from the stalks and then the stalks were removed with a long pitchfork, leaving mounds of fresh rice. We harvested not only our own crops, but helped the neighbors with their crops—and celebration dinners—as well.

For the most part, I feel very lucky to have been raised as I was in the safe valley of Yatiravana, surrounded by ancient farms, caring neighbors, and a closely knit family during the last days before Sri Lanka's technological revolution. I befriended animals, both wild and tame, ran through jungles and plunged into rivers. I learned my voice, listened to others, and celebrated a lifestyle that is now quickly vanishing. I felt needed and loved, and I learned to need and love other people. I consider myself very lucky and filled with gratitude for the joy I knew in my first life in Serendipity. I have found still more happiness as I remember my days there. It was a great and fanciful life. I only wish that every child born could somehow know as fine a childhood.

Bhante Wimala was born in 1958 in Kandy, Sri Lanka. At thirteen, he became a novice and, at fourteen, became an ordained Buddhist monk. He directs the Center for Conscious Evolution in Cambridge, Massachusetts and has traveled the world for the past twelve years teaching meditation and peace.

Bottom Land

by Don Carroll

The soft green pasture field was
    a boyhood place
with the large oak tree
    standing king
    on the hill
boughs outspread like giant
    muscled arms
acorns scattered extravagantly
    about

The field surrounded by blunt
    wire
drawn around the minds of cows
    and boyhood play
keeping out, and keeping in

I would usually walk alone each day
    to the pasture
    to see: had a cow tried to get out?
    or fallen hurt?

when I got to the field
    my thin body slipped beneath
    the blunt wire
    in a quick head bowing move

Often I climbed the bulging
    oak tree limbs
to where I could see to the
    tree lined river bank

at the edge of the pasture bottom
          to watch the late afternoon sun
turn the river into
          shiny roof tin

Sometimes I saw ducks come to the river:
          mallards, wood or maybe teal
sail in and anchor the sky to the
          water
and float like punctuation
          on the river's shining body
          of unspoken knowledge

Sometimes I went with my father
          at dusk in the old pick-up
we approached through an aged cattle guard
          a place the blunt line was magically
          erased
driving across in a bone shaking
initiation
that reorganized our thoughts
          so we were different inside

Either way the field was
          sacred for me
          and my father

The two of us didn't talk much
          when we were there together
we watched the cows gradually
          disappear into their own shadows
as gray light turned black

my father seeming to count
          his lips moving slowly
with unspoken words tied
          together like a string of beads

When night and cold finally held us
in a firm embrace
he touched me lightly on the shoulder
we moved back across the field

Behind us, like we were pulling it,
came the river mist
settling like a quilt
on bottom land.

Don Carroll's boyhood rose in sight of the Virginia Blue Ridge Mountains and was a steady tributary into the James River near Scottsville, Virginia in the 1950s. He has published two books of poetry: Midlife: Through the Eye of a Needle *and* Poetry Among Men. *He lives in Davidson, North Carolina, and is co-authoring a book about archetypal empowerment that springs from the workshops and training in archetypal empowerment he co-leads. He also earns a living as an attorney and counselor at law.*

Slowly Becoming

by Malidoma P. Somé

Two people fascinated me in my family: my mother and my grandfather. I loved my mother because she loved me. Although she would, at times, storm at me for my insatiable greed for everything, she provided me with anything I asked for. Every three days, when she went to the village market to sell her grains, I knew she would come home with some treats such as cakes, European bread, or even a worn-out T-shirt for me.

Every three days came a new day for me, a day of excitement and expectation. Up until I was three years old, my mother would carry me on her back, tying me with a solid piece of cloth whenever she would go out in search of wood or grain or simply to farm. I loved to be knitted so closely to her. I loved to see her collect wood with me on her back, carry this wood on her head, and walk home singing. Although her songs were sweet, her tremulous voice made me wonder sometimes if she was not mourning something or someone.

It felt good to be suspended there behind her, but one thing I did not like was my not being able to see where we were going until we got there. Being too small, I could not see over her shoulders, and mostly she would cover up my head with an extra piece of cloth to make me sleep. Consequently, the journeys to the savanna were least enjoyable. However, once at the wood spot, she would untie me and set me free. I would then go wild, running at random as if to recuperate from the immobility of the trip, as long as she did not yell at me to come back near her.

One day, a strange thing happened after which my Mother never took me to the bush again. As I was running around, I stepped on a rabbit which, as one may guess, dashed out of its hiding place. A wild race ensued. The rabbit was running straight toward a bush in which I used to feed myself with fruits of all sorts. I knew the rabbit wanted to get in there to hide, and I rejoiced at the idea of catching it because I knew every corner of that little bush. So I ran faster and we almost arrived at the bush together. I slowed down to avoid crashing into a tree, whereas the little rabbit, having no such fear, disappeared into it like an arrow shot into a pot of butter.

I followed with caution, guessing where it was likely to be hiding. I turned over the first set of grass; the rabbit was not there. I checked another thick part of the bush where there was a huge anthill, behind which there was a nest for animals. One could tell by the fresh marks of their little paws. I removed the grass, ready to fall headlong onto the miserable rabbit. But I never completed my gesture. All my movement was suspended, as if by electric shock.

Where I had thought there would be a rabbit, there was none. Instead, there was a tiny old man as small as the rabbit itself, sitting on an almost invisible chair, and holding in his right hand a minuscule cane no bigger than a finger. His head was covered with hair so white and shiny that it seemed unnatural. His beard was long and white, too, reaching almost to his chest. He wore a traditional Dagara mantle, also white.

All around him there was a glow, a shiny rainbow ring. Inside and beyond the circle there was an immense world, and although he was hiding most of its panorama, I could still see much of it. The circle looked like a window to that world behind the old man.

But what surprised me most was that nature in that world was unlike anything I had ever seen before. Planted on a sloping, oblique land, normally the man could not possibly sit like that without falling into it. But I noticed that something like a thin wall sustained him. So he was not leaning against the chair he was sitting on, but against that thin wall.

When my eyes moved from that wall and world back to the man, I saw that his thin legs had nothing to cover them. His legs were bare, with toes so small I could barely see them. Petrified by something that was neither fear nor mirth, but something like a tickling all over my body, I forgot to scream as the man said, "I have been watching you for a long time, ever since your mother started bringing you here. Why do you want to hurt your little brother? What did he do to you, little one?" His tiny mouth was barely moving as he spoke, and his voice was very thin. Confused, I tried to reply.

"I . . . I . . . don't know," I finally heard myself say.

"Then be friendly to him from now on. He, too, likes the fresh air of this place. He, too, has a mother who cares for him. What will his mother say if you hurt him? Now go, because your mother is worried." While the little man was speaking, I saw the little rabbit who was hidden behind him in the magic circle move backward, further down the steep marvelous place, and disappear behind a tree. Meanwhile, the earth seemed to open, for there was something like a cracking where the old man was sitting. He disappeared into the opening, leaving a halo of fresh breeze in his place. At the same time, I heard my mother's faint voice calling me. "Mado, please answer me, where are you?"

Still in the fervor of the experience, I opened my mouth to answer but no sound came out of my throat. She called again and again, and finally I screamed back at her. I heard my mother give a yell and accelerate toward me, still unseen. When she finally got to me, she lifted me up in the air and ran out of the bush as quickly as she could.

"I have been looking for you since noontime," she said between breaths. "It's now almost dark. What have you been doing all this time?"

"I saw a man in the bush. He said I should be friends with rabbits."

"What man, what rabbit? What are you talking about?" She looked panicked, and without waiting for an answer, she began talking to herself: "Oh poor child. Some witch must have taken his soul away. Please, spirits of nature, help me get him home alive." She went on and on with something that sounded like nothing more than gibberish to me, until I felt like speaking again. "The man is very small and very old, Mama," I said. "He lives there, but he just left."

"Oh dear ancestors. My child has seen a *kontomble,* what else can it be? Do not talk anymore. Let's get out of here. I'll never take you out again." Saying this, she loaded me onto her back, tied me with the same piece of cloth she had kept with her all day long, and walked panting to her basket, now full with heavy pieces of wood. She then lifted the whole thing on her head and proceeded toward home. She was not singing anymore. As we neared the house, she spoke again: "You will say nothing to anybody or I will never take you with me again. Do you hear me?"

"Yes," I replied. And that was all she ever said during the six-mile walk back home.

My grandfather was my confident interlocutor, ever since I was able to move on my feet unaided. For fifty full years, this man had been the priest, the leader, the counselor of a family of nearly one hundred souls. Faced with domestic problems of all kinds, he had had to be tough. Judging from his physical appearance, one could say that he had been a robust young man, capable of sustaining long hours of demanding physical labor.

But Grandfather was mostly known in the village as the "upside-down arrow shooter," one of the people in the tribe whose names make people shudder, for they shoot at targets from the quiet of their chambers, putting the arrow upside down. The arrow kills whoever or whatever is named to be killed, then re-materializes in the chamber, ready for its next assignment. Grandfather had made himself famous in local wars, when the tribe was under attack by the white man coming from the Gold Coast. Other tribes dared not go into conflict with the Dagara because they did not possess the secret of the upside-down arrow. Consequently, and for lack of opportunity to demonstrate the power of the tribe, Grandfather used it to defend his own family farm against nocturnal ravage by wild beasts. He also displayed it as a dissuasive weapon to ward evildoers away from his family, the Birifor.

Grandfather's permanence at home made him a fit companion. I loved his company and he loved having me next to him. He used to call me his brother when he had something serious to tell me. Otherwise, he would call me by my tribal name. I asked him once why he called me Brother and he said: "You are ancestrally my brother because you are a reincarnation of someone in the family I used to like very much. His name is the name that is carried now by the entire family. This means that you are Birifor and a Birifor. He was the elder son of my parents. Our father, Sabare, was the owner of the spirit and a hunter. When you grow up and become big, you'll learn about the secrets of the Birifor Magic. Do you want to know them?"

"Yes," I said. "I want to know all about the upside-down arrow. I want to be a hunter like Sabare and fly in the sky. But, Grandfather, you have not told me why you call me Brother yet."

"You are my brother because after the death of my brother and the ceremony of investiture that brought me up to the leadership of this family, your father came back from the Gold Coast and took a wife, your mother. After the birth of your sister, I was told that my brother Birifor had been ordered to return to the family. It was an agreement between him and Sabare. A year later your mother was pregnant, and the baby inside her, whenever he would speak to me, would begin by calling me brother. I knew it was Birifor about to be born again, and that you would be a boy. So I waited until your birth. And since that night when you came to life at dawn near the river, it has been my turn to call you Brother. Now do you understand?"

"No," I said. "If I am Birifor, why do you call me Mado? And if I am Mado after all, why do my father and other people call me Patrice? Now tell me this: between Mado, Brother, and Patrice, which is my true name?"

"None of them is true. However, there is one that is almost true. It is the one your ancestors know about. The one by which they call you. It is Mado. Your true name is Mado. This is what your ancestors know about. The rest are things like tools that will get you out of trouble later. Patrice was given to you shortly after your birth. Your parents, as you know, are friends with that white-bearded man up there on the hill. They seem to like his *titiulu* (shamanism or the art of divination), that is why he comes here so often. Long ago he changed their names so they would come see him often. They go there once a week. I do not know what they do there, and I don't think I want to know, either.

"But to make a long story short, Patrice was handed to you up there on the hill. Use it whenever you are out of the tribal boundaries. Brother is mine. Nobody else has claim to it. Birifor . . . well, nobody will ever call you that. Mado is something you will start hearing a lot when you become big. So be alert and prompt to answer. You never know what name the other will use. This is something you'll have to live with. That's enough for today."

It was dark already, and the farmers were returning from their day's work. My mother was the first to come into the compound, loaded with a pack of dry wood on her head. She dropped her load carelessly and went into the *zangala* in search of food. Shortly after, my father arrived. My father had a bicycle which he had brought back from the Gold Coast, where he had spent three years and six months in the gold mines of Takouradi. It was a huge English bicycle. He used to call it *gawule,* the ga-tree branch. Ga is a fruit tree popular in arbustive savanna, notorious for its long branches.

The bicycle was a blessing to my father. Thanks to it, he could afford to be the first at the farm, the last to leave it, and among the first to get home. With my father's arrival at home, everybody was supposed to be back. His task was to check everywhere in the seventeen compounds of the house to make sure that everybody was in.

My father was a quiet man, rather gloomy. His calmness had increased since he became a follower of the priest on the hill. His dreamy and taciturn air came from the multiple trips outside the limits of the Dagara tribe which he had made early in his youth. Grandfather told me that my father started traveling when he was fifteen, and never stopped until he was thirty. He also said that father had had some tremendous emotional problems which contributed to his gloominess. He said that father had married after returning from his first trip somewhere in the Ivory Coast, where he had served as a soldier in the colonial army. From this first marriage, twin daughters were born. He was asked to perform the ceremony proper for the twins, but his adherence to the new Christian faith kept him unsure about the validity of such rites.

On a number of occasions, Grandfather had warned him about the urgency of the ceremony. But each time, he had played deaf, neither refusing nor accepting the responsibility. The white missionaries had told him that this ceremony constituted a sin because it meant adoration of the devil.

My father did not like the idea of going to hell, but at the same time, he understood the validity of a simple ceremonial act destined to save the lives of his children. But somehow, the missionaries in the nascent parish of Dano convinced him that he had nothing to fear. They had told him that the Almighty God was taking good care of his newborn, and that he would do it better than the ancestors. These ancestors, they said, had been condemned to eternal hell, and, busy burning, they needed more than ever the prayers of their saved grandchild. So they had no time to enjoy sacrifices.

The years passed. The twin girls Elizabeth and Marguerite grew without problem, and father was convinced that the priests were right. But Grandfather continued to remind him of his duties as a father. Nothing shook him. His solid faith grew stronger each day as Grandfather switched from simple warnings to menace. Father saw himself already a martyr, like those of Uganda whom he knew better, because they were black. In his mind, being a martyr meant a free ride to Heaven, and, somehow, he wished for that.

In the meantime, two other children were born to him. He baptized them immediately as Daniel and Pascal. Time passed and the children grew to the age of initiation. The missionary warned him against such a practice and he accepted their words. Grandfather, tired of it all, decided to become an outsider. It was then that things started happening, faster than it was possible to take action against.

One morning, Elizabeth caught a fever or a cold, nobody knew what; she died at noon before the missionary could give her extreme unction. In the course of the funeral, Marguerite expired while running wild with sorrow over the departure of her twin sister. The funeral intensified. The sudden death of Marguerite affected Father beyond repair. The funeral, however, was brief. People knew what was going on. Twins don't die the same day. In ancestral law, that was the beginning of the end, an apocalyptic moment which was irreversible.

People asked my father to perform an armistice rite. It might have been his fate not to listen. Instead, he prayed to the Lord harder than ever, offering Him his pain as a present. To him, this drama was willed by the Lord as a test to his faith. So, he often repeated the famous sentence of the Lord's prayer, "Thy will be done."

And the Lord's will was done, beyond his expectations. Daniel, the first son, expired two weeks after the funeral of Elizabeth and Marguerite. Nobody knew what killed him. He had been playing with his friends when he cried out loudly that he was dying, and he did. Julia, the unfortunate mother, died of sorrow during the funeral of her son. She was already too worn out by the shock of the death of her two daughters. There remained only Pascal and my father.

Father wondered how many "Ave Marias" and "Paternosters" he would have to recite to end the evil. The missionaries counseled him to pray, and to pray harder, attributing the calamity to the thinness of his faith in God. He spent nights and days praying, yet things became worse everyday. The ghosts of his wife and children were haunting his sleep with the same question: "Why did you do that to us?"

After a few days living in the terror of another ghostly visit, Father went up to the hill to seek the spiritual assistance of Catholicism. He returned home with a ghastly air, an empty look, as if his own soul had already gone out of his body. He had received the same counsel: prayer. Ruined by pain, eroded by continuous effort, he discontinued all social activities and voluntarily ostracized himself for months. He would leave his quarters to check that the only survivor of the holocaust was still alive.

Then Father disappeared. Consumed by restlessness, he had suddenly fallen in love with adventure. People said later that he was in the Gold Coast. And, in truth, he had gone to Takouradi, then to Sakounde, where he thought he would cleanse the pain which had taken hold of his body and soul with the help of a favorable environment. He worked in the gold mines. Later on, released and relieved from the weight of the past with the gift of a brand new family enlarged by eight children, Father took pleasure in recounting his experience as a mine worker. He came back from the Gold Coast three years later, apparently less torn by psychological traumas, but seriously ill. His face was emaciated, his chest was swollen and grew bigger with every air intake. His eyes were injected with blood, and his look was ghastly. He walked like a drunken man, zigzagging randomly. His legs looked more like sticks than parts of his body.

His dying physiognomy caught Grandfather's attention. Grandfather never missed a chance to remind Father of his pending duty whenever the occasion availed itself. But Father, as if accursed, always answered the same way, saying he would think about it. He was proud of his English bicycle which he had successfully smuggled into the tribe. He paid more attention to it than to his health, which was deteriorating every day. He opted for a new marriage first. Then he returned to his religious activities as if nothing had happened. But things went downhill, until Father became completely debilitated. Incapable of moving around by himself, he used to spend his days sleeping and his nights groaning. He had pain in his chest, pain in his belly, pain in his back, pain virtually everywhere.

One morning, Grandfather announced to him that he had three days and two nights left to conform to his duties, unless he preferred the realm of the ghosts. Panic-stricken at the idea of dying at a time when he had just married and had a bicycle, he ordered the ceremony of the twins to be performed. Two clay pots were bought and filled with water from the underworld. This water was kept on a special shrine at the entrance to Mother's room. Grandfather threw some ash around the compound to keep mal-intentioned spirits away from the house. Then, the ceremony began. It lasted a whole day—mostly because it had been made complicated by Father's constant postponements.

Three days later, Father felt better. His health was improving almost visibly. At the end of the first week, he had recovered his movement, and, by the end of the following week, he decided he was strong enough to return to the farm. His pain had disappeared without trace.

After that Father developed a critical mind in which the new Christian religion lost a lot of its credibility, and the religion of his ancestors gained much. He still went to Sunday masses, was still friends with the missionaries, but he listened more to Grandfather. My sister was born at that time. The happy event revived him, and my sister benefited from it. Yet she was baptized, as was the practice among the proselytes of Christianity in the village.

Three years later, I was born in the cold air of the new year. The birth took place in the open air, halfway between the family house and the modern maternity, built a year earlier by the colonial administration. Mother didn't make it to the maternity. She could not walk the four miles. My father left us, Mother and me, where I was born, and went up the hill to ask his best friend Father Maillot for help. He returned with Father Maillot in his 2 hp Simca and gave us a ride to the maternity.

Before returning home I, too, was baptized like my sister. Father Maillot decided that I would be called Patrice. Grandfather, who understood nothing in this strange name, registered me in the family ledger as Mado, meaning that the accumulation of pain in the past must serve as lessons in the present. Thus, evil actions are good if they serve as teachings in the medicine of everyday life. Grandfather had also baptized me Mado, for reasons pertaining to ancestral law. For him, guardian of the house, link between the dead and the living, he expected his grandson to be recognized by the ancestors. As the first male of a family, his responsibilities were predetermined.

Malidoma Patrice Somé was born in his native village of Dano in the Burkina Faso region of West Africa in 1956. His tribe, the Dagara, are a people known for their spiritual practice and visionary ability. At age five, Malidoma was kidnapped by a French Jesuit missionary and taken to a boarding school far away from his village and family for sixteen years. Malidoma studied politics at the Sorbonne in Paris where he received a Ph.D., and then at Brandeis University where he received his Ph.D. in literature. He leads an ongoing men's group under the umbrella of "The Flight of the Hawk" Center for the study of contemporary shamanism, and teaches initiation wisdom and the value and practice of ritual to individuals and groups. He is based in Palo Alto, California. He is the author of Ritual: Power Healing and Community.

First Loves

by Jeff Beane

Our Frigidaire hummed so loudly I could hear it from my bedroom. When I opened the large white door for my four a.m. glass of chilled water, light sprang out and spilled into the living room. Even though my late night excursion was routine, I was always startled by the great rush of light, afraid it would wake Mom and Dad sleeping in their bedroom ten feet away.

At night the house was safe, unlike days when Dad's loud angry voice, harsh words and unpredictable slaps filled me and the small frame bungalow with tension and fear. My body relaxed at night in the dark; the quiet rooms were filled with peace and calm. Feeling safe and free, I walked around excitedly on the balls of my feet.

On snowy nights, the lone streetlamp at the corner of the cemetery near our home sent shards of light dancing through the dark. I delighted in the magical beauty outside, as snow and light adorned our neighbor's evergreen trees. Occasionally, I'd have my four o'clock water at five and could see faint light through the twin kitchen windows as they peered eastward. The pale morning light gently awakened a new day.

Relishing the safety of the night, I tiptoed past my parents' bedroom. Even though Dad slept, my body remembered its tormentor and tensed up as I returned to my bed.

My six-year marriage to Frances Earhart began in 1953. Together we walked up the aisle which separated the wooden schoolhouse into first and second grade. It was a spring morning recess. The small wooden desk tops were covered with *Dick and Jane* readers, pencil boxes, and pale mimeographed sheets of addition and subtraction problems filled with dark penciled answers.

Frances was a little fat, had a round face and liked me. Her brown curls were short and sometimes frizzy. I thought about getting married all the time, to have someone who would be mine. Our best friends, Shirley and Marie, officiated. Marie lived on Cherry Hill Lane, ten houses and one church from Frances' house.

Mrs. Seldomridge sat at her desk in the Paradise Elementary School on White Horse Road. She was busy correcting papers with her big red pencil, but glanced up curiously during our ceremony. Marie stood in front of the grey-haired teacher's desk with a book open in her hands. As Frances and I walked down the aisle, Shirley threw the wildflowers she had gathered from the fields outside at our feet. I don't remember what we said to each other during our ten-minute recess ceremony.

All the boys were outside. They were playing kick ball, being loud and pushing each other around, stuff I didn't like. By the next day they had heard about our wedding and branded me "Sissy."

We were all looking at a small, pale penis. It was recess in the fall of 1954. We were in the second grade. Someone had suggested we take up a collection to get Mark Hershey to take his pants down. Forty-four cents got us what we wanted. Freckled, red-haired Mark leaned against the back of the girls' outhouse, behind the old wood frame school. Surrounded by dry fallen leaves and autumn smells, we stood in a tight semicircle, waiting. He loosened his belt and pushed his blue jeans down to his ankles. I quivered as he stood there in his white underpants with the tiny bump in front.

He slowly pulled his underpants down to his knees and stood up. There it was, a tiny limp penis underneath a slightly curved white belly. I was breathless with excitement, caught between intense interest and the fear that someone would notice my eager eyes. I wanted to touch Mark all over and feel his smooth skin under my hands. My body was tingling everywhere. The recess bell rang much too soon. I was the last one to leave.

That spring the one-room school was surrounded on three sides by cornfields. Our wooden desks, with wrought iron sides and circular inkwell openings in the upper right corners, were bolted to the floor.

I sat in the row of second-graders next to the wide aisle which separated us from the first-graders. My seat was the second to last one in our row, right behind Jerry Morris. He lived across the Lincoln Highway from my grandmother's house. His close proximity, coupled with his good looks and quiet demeanor, drew me to him as a friend.

His thick brown hair and the smooth, tanned back of his neck were constant distractions during class. One day, I leaned forward and reached my hand inside the place where his shirt met his neck. I loved the feel of his warm, hairless skin under my hand. The muscles of his youthful back were firm, yet supple. My insides were quivering. Leaning forward even more, practically standing up at my desk, I pushed my arm farther down the inside of his shirt until it reached his belt. My heart pounding, sensing no resistance from him, I continued my quest until my hand reached its goal; the soft, fleshy cheek of his butt.

I looked up. Squat, grey-haired Mrs. Seldomridge was standing over me. I felt sick in my stomach. She made me hold out the offending hand and cracked it with her ruler as she said, "Don't let me ever catch you doing that again."

The jungle on the round, 14-inch, RCA TV screen was black and white. Ramar's scantily clad body revealed smooth, muscular arms and legs. My eyes fixated on his dark loin cloth, hoping to see the impossible. In 1955, at age eight, "Ramar of the Jungle" was one of my favorite shows. He was a good guy who helped people when they were in trouble. He protected innocent panthers and tigers from bad hunters and traders. Several times he rescued the boy Joby by physically plucking him from dangerous situations in the jungle. I ached to feel his strong, warm arms around me. I wanted him to protect me from the danger in my life.

Danger, hope-filled fantasies and escape were mine for thirty minutes every Sunday morning, right before Sunday School. The suspenseful jungle music, with its occasional wild animal shriek, terrified me almost as much as my father did when he came into the house. My eyes were glued to Ramar whenever he picked up Joby and held him in his arms. My mind stretched to imagine what it could possibly feel like to be touched by a man that way. Whenever he laid the boy down to sleep on his jungle cot, I imagined how safe and secure Joby must have felt.

I climbed the six steps to my top bunk bed thinking of Roy Rogers again. He was brave, and risked his life to protect others. Sitting astride Trigger, he was powerful and strong. I tried to imagine what a hot, muscular horse would feel like between my legs. I read *The Black Stallion* and every other horse story Walter Farley wrote.

With my eyes closed, I imagined Roy Rogers riding up to our back door and taking me away with him. I sat behind him on Trigger, my small arms wrapped around his firm body. I pressed the side of my head against his back and squeezed. I pushed my crotch as hard as I could against his butt. With my eyes still closed, I would see us riding away together. I must have imagined it a hundred times.

And then I felt my nine-year-old body, penis erect, pushing itself through flannel cowboy pajamas into the mattress. Falling asleep was easy with my mind full of Roy Rogers.

At age eleven, "Dr. Kildare" and "Ben Casey" were two of my favorite TV shows. I dreamed about Richard Chamberlain. He was so handsome, fair, gentle and wise. The only man in my life who came close to resembling him was a gentle farmer who taught me Sunday school. Herman Brackbill was a large, soft-spoken, clean-shaven man who talked of love, even though it was God's. His face was kind, his eyes warm and inviting. His hands were nicked, rough, large and comforting. On Sunday mornings he smelled of soap, Aqua Velva aftershave and a mothballed suit. I felt safe and relaxed just sitting next to him on the hard wooden pew. After church, I often went to the farm where Herman and his family lived. He never raised his voice to his wife or kids. He was fair. The farmhouse was peaceful inside and out. Once or twice I spent the night and imagined being part of his family.

Ben Casey had the largest, strongest-looking arms I had ever seen. They were covered with dark hair from wrist to elbow and then disappeared beneath his white doctor's smock. His deep, strong, firm voice was never harsh. I wanted so badly to be the woman he fell in love with. When I imagined him holding me and kissing me, I felt nervous and excited inside, but didn't know why. I wondered if the others watching TV next to me could tell what was in my mind. My thoughts and fantasies made me very uneasy.

I had pleurisy when I was twelve. In level of pain, it ranked right up there with my excruciating tonsillectomy at age eleven. I don't know how Doc Bauer got to be my doctor. He went to our church and I was in love with him. He was six feet tall, slender and bald, with a soft confident voice. His walk was slow and relaxed. Even though I was sick, I felt excited as he stood next to my small single bed.

When he sat on my bed, I inched my leg closer to him to feel his body against mine. His manner was calm, reassuring and friendly. His warm, soft hands felt incredibly comforting on my pain-filled abdomen. I didn't want him to take them away. Once I captured them by putting my small, frightened hands on top of his. He seemed comfortable with my touch. I cried when he left my bedroom that day.

Dick Whitehead lived next door to Nanny and Grandpa, my mother's parents. He was a large, muscular man in his late twenties with a huge black motorcycle. When he worked on it in his motor-oil-scented garage, I stood daringly close to him, observing him carefully. His dark hair, slight speech impediment and black leather jacket intrigued me.

When I was twelve, I baby-sat his three young boys. If it was an afternoon job, he'd take me for a ride on his motorcycle first. Danger, thrill and excitement filled every cell of my pubescent body. As I sat with my budding crotch pressed tightly against his large, firm ass, I wondered if he could feel me behind him. I longed to reach my hands below his thick belt to see if his crotch was bulging. But I never did. I remember being embarrassed at the end of the ride, fearing he would see my hard-on when I stood up. Secretly, I wanted him to notice my interest and take me in his arms.

It's 1992. About once a year, I visit that old, one-room school, still surrounded by fields of corn, feeling like the boy from 1953. As I walk past the fading structure, I feel empty because there's no lover beside me to listen to me tell my story. I still fantasize about being married one day to a handsome, gentle, caring man. My six-year marriage to Frances remains my longest relationship. I'm still afraid of men. I wonder if I'm too sensitive. The feel of smooth skin under my hands continues to excite me. I have become a do-gooder in the world, a psychotherapist and a gay activist, an amalgam of Kildare, Casey, Doc Bauer, Herman Brackbill and Roy Rogers. Although to a lesser degree, and well hidden, I can be angry and intolerant just like my father. My eye for cute butts and sweet, boyish faces remains. I liked to be touched almost as much as I like having orgasms. I like to be held and sleep like spoons all night long. I fantasize about meeting a man who has small children, falling in love with him and all of us living together. Although I've been gone from Paradise for over twenty-seven years, in many ways I've never left.

Jeff Beane, 1947–1994, was the oldest of four children from a working class family in Paradise, Pennsylvania, a small town in rural Lancaster County. He was a psychotherapist who worked in Los Angeles and San Francisco and an early leader in the feminist men's movement.

The World Crashes In

by Daniel J. DeNoon

"And it may be that a man cannot live unless he prepares a drama, at
least cannot live as a human being against the ruck of the world."
—Robert Penn Warren

Miss Thorpe's feet didn't seem to be touching the ground as she walked
toward me through the heat mirage shimmering over the summer grass
in deep right field. I spit, nonchalantly I hoped, but couldn't resist
peeking over my shoulder to see if she might be watching. She was. I
socked my glove.

There was no breeze on that hot Miami afternoon, but I felt the
sweat on the back of my neck run cold. What was she doing here?
Usually I wanted the batter to hit the ball to someone else, but at that
instant, I wanted to make that one perfect catch of a lifetime. "Hit it
to me," I thought. I wanted to die. I was in love, though I didn't have
words for it yet. "Hit it to me and I'll catch it, or I won't catch it, and,
either way, that's all that will ever mean anything, ever, at all."

The world would never be that simple again.

Miss Thorpe had curly red hair and wore red lipstick. The pumps
she wore were, well, maybe not too sensible, and when she sat on her
desk in front of the class, she would cross her legs and swing one red
shoe with her toes. There were no seams in her stockings.

The year before, in fifth grade, I had the hideous Mrs. Bowers. She
made us write with fountain pens, and even though I crabbed my left
hand around backwards, I somehow always smeared the ink. The
bitter stink of ink eradicator still evokes pain.

But Miss Fleta Thorpe never graded us on penmanship. Every
Friday she would tape up the funny/sad picture on the last page of *Life*
magazine and the class would have to write an essay about it. Miss
Thorpe just about always laughed when she read my essay; she would
often have me stand up in front of the class and read it aloud. Other
days I wrote themes and poems and plays for her. Miss Thorpe learned
to give me advice very, very gently because once she was publicly
critical of me and I cried and wouldn't stop, and had to go outside and

stand in the hall, and later I had to punch out my best friend Bruce Harding—just because. So Miss Thorpe learned to discipline me with extra assignments, encouraging me to practice writing more. I hoped sixth grade would go on forever.

But that June day there was no more action than there ever was in right field—except that she was standing out there with me, just beyond the foul line. That life-defining fly ball never was hit to me. I got a pitch from Miss Thorpe instead.

"Danny," she called, noticing that she wasn't exactly interrupting anything.

Later, when the world and I will have changed, my seventh-grade English teacher will tell me that Dan is a more virile name, and I'll spend months pointedly ignoring anyone who calls me Danny. But that day Danny sounded pretty good to me.

At that moment, and for the first time, I experienced the elated feeling, the dizzying physical sensation akin to weightlessness, that everything in this confusing world was going to be all right. My life up to this point was redeemed, my future would be perfect, my happiness assured. Since then I've known that feeling a few more times: the intoxicating, fallacious belief that I wouldn't have to struggle any more. Each time I thought, "This is it." Finally it's going to be easy. When I fell in love for the first time I thought, "This is it." Then I had to learn, painfully, about relationships. When I got accepted by a fancy college I thought, "This is it." So, when Miss Thorpe told me that I was sixth-grade valedictorian—you guessed it—I thought, "This is it." "Citizenship in Our Community": just another theme, only this time a chance to show all of Sunset Elementary, my whole world, how clever I was. I didn't know that the world was a whole lot bigger and a whole lot scarier. I didn't know that, ready or not, I was about to become a citizen. I didn't know that it was going to hurt.

My sixth-grade graduation was in the summer of 1963. Outside Sunset Elementary and the sunny confines of the affluent white suburb of Coral Gables, the world I soon would enter was in trauma. A part of this trauma was what we Southern whites called "the race riots." That summer, blacks using passive resistance—but sometimes rocks and bottles—confronted troopers who used tear gas, dogs, fire hoses and clubs. It took the presence of federal troops to prevent George Wallace from blocking the door of the University of Alabama to blacks. A racist sniper shot Medgar Evers in the back. The war was fought on fronts in Greensboro, Durham, Lexington, Tallahassee, Jackson and

Gadsden, and on the other side of the tracks in every Southern town, Birmingham most particularly. In other news, the Russians would launch the first woman into outer space, President Kennedy would proclaim "Ich bin ein Berliner," the Supreme Court would ban school prayer, Buddhists in Vietnam would riot in protest against the corrupt U.S.-backed Diem regime, there would be a bloody war in the Congo, the Pope would die and a new one would be elected. In the late fall, this age they called Camelot would be shattered forever in Dallas. But beginning that spring, and for years thereafter, especially in the South, even in Coral Gables, all eyes were turned toward the civil rights struggle. Lines were being drawn, sides were being chosen, everybody would be involved for the rest of the decade—even some sixth-grade white boys.

By April, 1963, the civil rights movement had reached virtually every Southern community, but somehow it was Birmingham, Alabama, that stood as the purest symbol of the struggle. The Birmingham Crisis, everybody called it, and every day a new episode appeared in the papers and on the nightly news. In April, black leaders—Martin Luther King prominent among them—began a direct-action campaign in Birmingham. The stated goals were desegregation of lunch counters, schools and school buses, and fair hiring practices. The unstated goal was to portray civil rights as a moral issue by forcing Alabama Governor George Wallace and Birmingham Police Commissioner "Bull" Connor to participate in a morality play enacted before the eyes of the world. And the whole world *was* watching, even an eleven-year-old boy who read the *Miami Herald* and watched TV.

It wasn't just that I was born in the North, because we had segregation in the rural New York town where I lived until moving to Miami in the fourth grade. The only black kids I ever met in Pawling, New York, kept to themselves on the school bus and went to a different part of the elementary school. Things weren't much different in Miami, except I didn't see any black kids at all (unless we gave the maid a ride home), and some of the kids at school used the odd phrase "nigger lover" to provoke a fight.

And it wasn't that my family was radical; we were just kind of liberal. My mother, a Jew, had experienced anti-Semitism as a student. She got a nose job and, after the divorce from my WASP father, became a Congregationalist. She used to tell me, "Just thank God you're white." I learned from her that racism wasn't fair, but that I was exempt.

So when it came time actually to write a speech on "Citizenship in Our Community," I didn't think of civil rights right away. It's just that I was looking for a gimmick. You see, my success as a sixth-grade essayist was founded on taking an unusual approach to my subject. When the assignment was to write a theme on Mohammedanism, I wrote a play titled "Savior of the Islams." When we were asked to write about the highlights of our sixth-grade year, I wrote "Miss Thorpe's Diary." It was even then a well-worn literary device, but to me it seemed shiny and new: for a theme on citizenship, I'd write about what citizenship was *not*.

First, I stayed close to home, writing about how bad teenagers spoiled things for the rest of us by acting up and getting a citywide curfew imposed. Then, for contrast, I bragged about how when our class lost the sixth-grade softball game, we shook hands with the gracious winners. Then, for my finale, as an example of community-wide bad citizenship, I wrote about racism. It worked so well, it seemed, that I was moved to rhetorical excess and called for love and understanding and—well, for good citizenship.

"Citizenship is a funny thing," I began. "It—and it alone—can determine whether or not someone is respectful to others in his community." Next came the part about the teens setting the bad example, followed by the sportsmanship equals citizenship stuff. Then, on page two, I hit my stride.

"Almost everybody is aware of the Birmingham crisis. Everybody knows about how Negroes are not socially accepted. The Birmingham crisis is just the beginning of what might happen if people don't start judging people by what they are, not by an ancient reputation or the color of the skin. Just because of the whims of white people, Negroes are forced to live in slums, go to schools that are no more up-to-date than they were ten years ago, be barred from some public places, and things of that sort. Now remember that this is strictly opinion and that I'm no one to say who's right or who's wrong, but I believe in at least being kinder to Negroes. Who knows? If you set the example, you may be followed by someone else, who will start a chain reaction! Plain, ordinary, everyday kindness and love is the most vital part of good citizenship in your community.

"You, and everyone else, make up a community. The individual is a vital and necessary part of citizenship. You alone can make your community strong or weak. The way you act, the way you feel, and the way you do countless other things will make a difference. You should help build a strong community, not a weak one. Birmingham is a weak community. Make yours a strong one. Your community and you make this a strong nation, a nation to be proud of. Everybody, in a way, is affected by citizenship in our community."

"Who put you up to this?" the principal wanted to know. Miss Thorpe, smelling a teapot tempest brewing, had taken my handwritten draft to the principal. But I think she was surprised by the reaction. The principal, Mrs. Eloise Bates, was a white-haired gentlewoman not inclined to rock the boat. She was at the pinnacle of her profession, after all, and had a pension to think about. She was not amused by my clever approach to "Citizenship in Our Community."

The ground shifted beneath my feet. Was it because I feared criticism? Or was it because I somehow sensed that I just stepped out of the little world of children and, even though still a child, had exchanged that safe place for the colder, wilder world? Anyhow, I cried.

There followed parent/teacher conferences and other meetings with the principal. Finally, as I really had written the speech all by myself and as it was after all the Kennedy years and as, most importantly, Miss Thorpe went all out in my defense, I made the speech. Oh, I had to say, "Now this part is strictly my own opinion" a couple of times, but they let me speak. Miss Thorpe made me memorize it, and then I practiced it in front of our class.

I guess the word got out that something controversial was going down, because the sixth-grade graduation assembly was crowded not just with mothers but with fathers as well: a rare sight in those days.

For some reason my own mother was not there (my divorced father lived in New York and he, too, was absent). I don't know why she wasn't there. It's possible I insisted that she not come, I don't know. But I do remember sitting there all alone. Well, not quite alone. Miss Thorpe, for the very last time, sat behind me. I distinctly remember feeling a chill, as if a door to a cooler had opened behind me.

When I got to the Birmingham part, there were shouts from the audience. "What's going on here?" I remember one man saying. There was both nervous applause and hissing when I was done. Later, in the seventh, eighth and ninth grades, kids who remember the uproar still shunned me, and I more than once had "NIGGER LOVER" scratched on my locker, and spit in my face during fights. Some of my friends weren't allowed to come over any more. But I wouldn't take any of it back—I knew somehow that the speech came from my truest self, and I chose to embrace it.

I felt scared, of course, and I also felt a strange mixture of pride and sadness. Most of all I felt alone. That was the day I entered the world. The world was lonely because, then and forever more, it would be my duty to find my own way. I knew immediately that I'd never be able to go back even if, as I often have, I wanted to. Before my speech, the world was a sea of possibilities. Afterward, I found I had forever closed many doors. New doors would open, but not by themselves.

Did this choice really matter? Consider another, somewhat older Southern boy who at about the same time was assigned an essay on integration. Looking for a novel twist to *his* theme, he found his way to the Klan bookstore and became fascinated with the literature of hate. He wouldn't take back anything he wrote, either. His name is David Duke, onetime Grand Dragon and would-be President.

Two years after my speech I became a believer in the Great Society and handed out buttons in the Johnson-for-President campaign. Still a liberal four years later, I helped organize Teen Dems of Dade County and worked in the Humphrey/Muskie campaign. The world again crashed in on me when the good liberals I supported sold out so blatantly at the 1968 Democratic convention in Chicago. This time I turned on, tuned in, dropped out. But when I moved to a log cabin in the mountains and turned my attention inward, I found the world there, too.

Like the happy fool on the tarot card, I stepped off a precipice in the sixth grade. I began my entry into man's estate and had to put aside my childish things, for they no longer suited me. For the world of the child, whether a good world or bad, is a hand-me-down world not of one's own choice or design. The real world is what we make of what we are given, the choices we have made and the choices we continue to make. When the world crashes in, as it must, we ignore it only at the cost of our humanity. This is the duty of men and women in this world, to choose so as not to drown in possibilities. What we do matters. And in the end, we embrace our true selves only to the extent we embrace the real world. Is this not truly citizenship in our community?

Daniel J. DeNoon was born in Bronxville, New York in 1951 and spent his first eight years in rural New York State and the next ten in suburban Miami. Today, he lives in Atlanta and works as an editor and writer. He is author of AIDS Therapies *and research editor of* AIDS Weekly.

The Names

by Edward Field

In earliest childhood I learned about my name
being changed from Feldman to Field, and before that
in the Old Country it was Felscher, and before that
in the days when Jews only had first names, my father said,
the Czar commanded everyone to take last names too
or assigned them ridiculous ones
to add to the ordinary burden
of noses, circumcision, and dietary laws.

I also learned about the time before that,
more remote, almost mythological, when our name was Cohen,
the name of the priest-class, and before that,
slavery in Egypt, still in our bones, and before that
the wandering of the tribes with tents and flocks
along the caravan routes, out of the heart of the desert,
out of history, even in the time before the sand,
with the burden of The Knowledge—
names and countries
forgotten, but still felt
in bad feet and aching back.

I knew from my beginning that the story of my name
was not just the story of one people
but of mankind, and mine was its name.

Growing up before World War II, Edward Field was one of the few Jews in a WASP community on the south shore of Long Island. He escaped alive, barely, and eventually regained his sanity by means of therapy, love, poetry—and luck. He now lives in New York City, and writes poems, essays, and novels, the latter in collaboration with his friend, Neil Derrick. Most recently, he has been editing the works of the late Alfred Chester: Looking for Genet, *the collected essays, and* Head of a Sad Angel, *the selected stories, both published by Black Sparrow Press, which is also bringing out a book of Field's new poems,* Counting Myself Lucky.

BOYHOOD
AND THE SOUL

"Each event spoke with a cryptic tongue. And the moments of living slowly revealed their coded meanings. There was the wonder I felt when I first saw a brace of mountain-like, spotted, black-and-white horses clopping down a dusty road through clouds of powdered clay . . .There was the faint, cool chill of sensuality when dew came on to my cheeks and shins as I ran down the wet green garden paths in the early morning . . .There was the vague sense of the infinite as I looked down upon the yellow, dreaming waters of the Mississippi River from the verdant bluffs of Natchez . . .And there was the quiet terror that suffused my senses when vast hazes of gold washed earthward from star-heavy skies on silent nights . . ."

Richard Wright writes of the spiritual life of a boy in touch with the numinous power of nature. The Swiss psychoanalyst Carl Jung argues for the existence of the soul as a powerful and animating aspect of all of our psyches. In the life of the male, the time of boyhood is often difficult and perplexing. Fear looms large and the relative smallness and vulnerability of the boy's growing body are often felt in antipathy and accord with the politics of experience. It is here that the boy finds his need for an inner life, safe spaces and secret gardens, fields away from houses and basements, attics and trees where he goes to think and be. Sometimes he is not alone. He goes to a communal hiding place, summer camp, a tent in the back yard or a vacant building to be privately in the company of his peers. No place is more private than his dreams. Boys dream, as we all do, what we dare not or cannot live into being. The boy in a man keeps all his secrets collected, like rocks or stamps or tropical fish. They are watched over by that same angel who set Isaac free. The angel is the guardian who always whispers this: You are the only you that is.

The Rainbow

by Steven Finch

for Miguel

When I was a boy, I often spent
my afternoons singing and dancing
with Bonnie on her parents' back porch.
Bonnie had a record player, and we played
"Somewhere Over the Rainbow" over and over
till our heads were also spinning.

Outside my window this afternoon,
the rainbow brightening the sky,
as it does the heart of San Francisco,
brings that memory back to me.
I no longer wonder why I can't fly
beyond the rainbow—the rainbow
itself, when double, is everything
men like me need to sing.

Steven Finch was born (1955) and raised in Hinsdale, Illinois, a Chicago suburb. "I now reside in Switzerland, where, after several years of teaching English, I'm about to venture into international shipping. I live with my lover of seventeen years, Miguel; our minpin, Nina; and our birds, plants, poetry, and music."

Finding the Light and
Keeping It in Front of Me

by Bob Vance

I am very young, no more than three or four. I follow him around the side of the house that is deeply shaded from the large oak and elm trees. I follow him around the side of the house, through the gate, into the back yard. I have something to say to him, or show him. What is it? I'm not sure. I feel playful, jumping and skipping—perhaps just to keep up with him, perhaps just because I am full of a child's energy and am happy he's home.

He does not seem to notice, at least he never turns around as he walks in front of me.

I want something from him but am not sure what it is, and, as I follow him, I think my awe—of his largeness, of the broad steps he takes, of his silence—impresses me more than the distance I feel is being maintained between us.

I notice his back. He is wearing a white shirt. There is a pattern of sweat, sort of a horseshoe shape, not unlike some Rorschach cards I have seen since. That impresses me the perhaps most of all the things I notice about him at that moment. I make no connection in my child's mind between the sweat print on his back and why he does not turn around to me and, just because I am skipping behind him, pick me up and carry me the rest of the way around the house.

If that is, in fact, what I want.

Something inhibits me from asking him for what I need. I know, if a very young boy can intuit such things, that I am left out of his world and am somehow forbidden to ask him what I can do to have him take me into his world, to hold me playfully or tenderly.

The rift begins here.

This is the earliest memory I have of my father.

My great-grandfather had a farm in Iowa. I am told that we visited that farm several times in my early years. Some of my earliest childhood memories are from our visits to the farm, although they seem to me to be from a single visit.

The farm was somewhat inactive, with the physical manifestations of unused outbuildings and animal pens left from when it was more productive.

In my memory, there were two cows left, some chickens and a field of corn that began not far out the back door of the house. Although the farm had indoor plumbing, there was still an outhouse on the edge of the cornfield which my great-grandfather used almost exclusively.

My interactions with my great-grandparents were filled with an odd shyness on my part, a mixture of awe and fear. I believe I was painfully shy, something I've not gotten over completely to this day. I remember feeling great pressure when meeting and being around unfamiliar relatives, a pressure that made it impossible for me to speak and that persisted even after I met them. Once I hid in my closet for what seemed to me to be an eternity because I was afraid to meet my grandmother's sister-in-law when she came to visit. This feeling never completely wore off when I was around my great-grandparents, however modified it became because of my growing respect and wanting them to like me. They were perhaps the most direct and honestly warm people I had ever met.

My great-grandfather was a very big man, bigger than my father. During visits I recall, or in the composite my memory created, I slept with him in a huge, high, feather bed. I remember it being hard to climb into such a high bed. I remember his snoring; how I would wake up in the morning and he would already be up. I would wake with the feeling that I had been "tucked in" firmly; wake up with the anticipation only a child can feel toward an unstructured day in an unexplored new place. I felt safe, filled with happy excitement, but had difficulty moving from under the heavy quilts because they felt so good over me.

The upstairs of the farmhouse was light and airy. There seemed always to be a window open quite wide somewhere. The angles and shapes of the rooms were not rectangular but, I imagine, like most of the two-story farmhouses of that period, with rooms that angled up under a high-pitched roof and that contained many nooks and corners. This made the house somewhat magical and mazelike to me, a child used to housing built in the fifties with square rooms and rarely a second floor.

I got up. No one else was upstairs. The sun came cool through an open window in the bedroom across the hall. There was always a huge open Bible on the dresser in that room. My memory of that Bible is perhaps the clearest memory I have of my great-grandparents' house.

I doubt I could have lifted it if it was, in fact, as large as my memory makes it.

Downstairs in the kitchen, my great-grandmother was at the sink. The sink had a hand pump. She gave me a glass of raw milk taken from the cows that morning. It was bubbly and thick, almost yellow.

I remember other mornings when I watched Great-Grandpa milk the cows. He let me try to milk. I stood about belly-high to the cow and was not very good at getting the milk from the cow's teat. Great-Grandpa showed me again how to use a relaxed but firm grip, and then he squirted me in the face with milk.

One morning when Great-Grandpa wasn't in the kitchen, I was told he was out back, and then I remember vaguely some discussion concerning whether I should go out to see him. He was in the process of butchering a chicken for dinner. The next thing I remember is being in the back yard walking up to Great-Grandpa, who was sitting near a chopping block with a headless chicken, plucking it. I was not shocked or affected by the dead chicken and I remember his story about how it ran after he chopped its head off. I asked him where he put the head. He motioned over his shoulder toward the cornfield. I recall wanting to run into the cornfield to look for it, and wondering how many heads were out there. I think he told me not to look, or distracted me some other way—perhaps he told me that the dogs or cats got them.

As I delve into these memories of my great-grandfather and they become clearer and more specific to me, I begin to realize the impact he had on me. His directness and the matter-of-fact, understated quality of his interactions with me were what impressed and awed me. I'm not sure I had experienced such uncluttered warmth and honesty from an adult until then. At least I have no early memories of my parents that contain interaction with these qualities.

Some years later, after Great-Grandma had died and Great-Grandpa was himself blind and less healthy (but never frail; he was always a huge man), he came to visit us. I was entering adolescence. I had been taking care of the family garden for several years, and there was quite a production made by other family members the day he was led out to the back yard to inspect my garden. I was a good and productive gardener; however, the onions I grew were something of an oddity. I could never manage to grow them as far in the ground as they are supposed to grow. No matter how large they got (and they were very big) the entire bulb usually sat on top of the soil with only the root hairs down in the dirt.

Great-Grandpa knelt in the dirt to feel these onions (just as he had felt other examples of my green thumb) and while being impressed with their size, he said they were the strangest onions he'd ever seen. He repeated that several times during that visit. I remained struck dumb by my shyness around him, but this effort to tease me, to find some way to speak to me, meant the world to me.

During that same visit, there was a loud, but not violent, thunderstorm of the variety that starts with a good, cool wind and then proceeds with loud thunder, flashes of lightning and a soaking, big-dropped rain. Great-Grandpa sat in our screened porch and listened to this storm. Since he had moved to California with his daughter, he had missed this kind of Midwestern deluge and had talked about hoping there would be one while he visited with us. He got his wish. Not long afterward, he died.

The light switch at the top of our basement stairs turned on two bulbs, one above the staircase itself and one in the hallway directly off the bottom of the stairs that led into the larger part of the basement. Once past that hallway, one needed to feel around in pitch black to find the strings attached to the switches that turned on the bare bulbs. That hallway was the only finished portion of the basement. An opening in its paneling about halfway to the end led to the laundry room, also very dark. Across the hall from that opening was a section of paneling that swung open, almost a secret entrance as it was nearly indistinguishable as a door. Inside that door was the furnace and then another windowless damp room under the front porch of the house. These dark parts of the basement, without lights and far from the safety of the lit stairway and hall, were where our monsters lived.

We spent many early evenings after dark playing endless games of "spook," and daring each other to go further and further into the dark. The "furnace room," as it was called, was generally off limits and so it became the most frightening of the basement rooms. Each of my sisters and I, or whoever else might be involved, dared each other to run into the black void as far as we could go and then ran screaming to the stairs, all the while making up horror stories of things we had seen and felt in the basement. Unearthly ghosts and incarnations of evil itself lurked in that dank lightless place.

These games usually progressed until our shrieks and screams became too loud for our parents to tolerate, or until one of us ran in true tears of fear upstairs to our parents to find safety in the world of light. Invariably one or more of us would be punished for frightening each other—sometimes quite severely.

My sister tells me of one such incident in which I happened to be the child singled out for punishment. Apparently our younger sister had become quite badly frightened during one of our games. My parents decided that a fitting punishment would be to lock me in the furnace room with no lights on. As my sister relates, my screams and pleadings could be heard for quite some time. I myself have no firsthand memory of this, but, oddly enough (or perhaps not so oddly), I remember a similar incident in which the same punishment was meted out to her for a similar infraction.

Another example of this kind of repressed childhood memory was related to me by the same sister (who, at two years older, was closest to me in age of my three sisters). Apparently I was quite young, somewhere between three and five, and she and I were caught playing with matches. To deal with this misbehavior, my mother poured lighter fluid on our hands and lit it. My sister said she still remembers the silent terror on my face before my mother put out the flames.

Our back yard was surrounded by a chain link fence. My best friends during most of my early childhood were the two kids whose yards were on the other side of that fence: Suzie and Ricky.

One of our favorite things to do on summer afternoons was to attach one end of old room-sized rugs, bedspreads and other large pieces of material to the fence, stretch them out and weigh down the other end with bricks and rocks. With a number of these blankets and rugs we could create quite a "house" with a number of rooms and even makeshift furniture. This game even worked well on days we were not allowed to play in each other's yards. We could make tents in each of our respective yards, opposite from one another, hardly even noticing the fence that divided us.

Another favorite game was to take turns telling each other our dreams. Most often the scary ones were our favorites, and sometimes I believe we did not tell dreams at all, but made up stories to impress and scare each other. At least I remember embellishing my dreams. There are even one or two I still recall from this game. Often these "dream telling" times were held in the tents.

These tents were also where we showed each other the private parts of our bodies. This was a genuine "I'll show you mine, if you show me yours." Inside the musty coolness of the tents we shared quick glimpses in curiosity and fun.

I suppose this is child sexuality, but there were never any exchanged touches, just looking. I particularly remember being involved with Suzie in this game. As I recall it now, there was an interesting intensity of feeling involved, different from other childhood moments shared with her. Perhaps these are my earliest erotic memories. Suzie and I would ask each other how it felt to have what we each had, and we were quite intrigued by how our differently equipped bodies worked.

One day we both went into the bathroom in our house when she had to pee. I was to watch. I do not recall feeling we were doing anything particularly wrong; it was all very exciting, stimulating and private. But then, as we were leaving the bathroom (I don't remember the specifics of this), we were caught. Suzie was sent home immediately and I got my mouth washed out with soap. To this day I am not sure how my watching Suzie urinate warranted an assault to my mouth, but then inappropriate punishments were certainly not out of the ordinary in my home. I laughingly (but only half-jokingly) attribute my fondness for the deliciousness of oral sex to this incident.

My relationship with Ricky was less erotic and more adventurous in other ways. Actually my first experience with examining another boy's genitals was with the Italian kid down the street. We went behind his garage one day to check out each other's equipment. He was not circumcised, as I was, and I remember wondering about the small flap of skin that hid the ridge of his glans. Ricky and I had other opportunities to see each other unclothed. We spent many evenings sleeping over at each other's homes and showered and bathed together. There seemed to be no reason to make a point of showing each other our genitalia.

I remember Ricky and me being rather intense with each other, always struggling for dominance and reassurances of our status with each other, always looking out for one another too. I remember riding bikes endlessly, riotously weaving from side to side down the street. Once we suddenly miscalculated each other's moves and smashed together, tangling in a heap by the side of the road. With the wind knocked out of me, I was barely able to speak. Of course, this may be a composite memory of sorts, because there must have been many times we crashed and fell either alone or into one another. We could be quite reckless. In fact, I do remember another incident in which we were riding through an empty tree-filled lot on separate paths. Suddenly my front wheel hit a hole and I was thrown quite far to the ground, again with the wind knocked out of me. This must have occurred quickly because then I heard Ricky's frightened voice calling me. When I was able to respond (or when he found me on the ground), he stated he thought I had disappeared or been taken aboard a passing spacecraft. "One second you were there," he said, "and the next time I looked you were gone." We laughed in relief.

Rick was also with me the day we had an acorn war with the kids from another block in another empty lot on our street. A similar battle—which we had won—had also occurred the year before. We prepared for the rematch with confidence that we could once again be victorious. We climbed periodically into our lookout tree that straddled the back boundary of the lot, watching for the enemy. We built a fort in the middle of the thickly wooded lot by piling up branches against larger trees that stood in a rough rectangle. We collected ammo.

Somehow, our enemies took us by surprise and outnumbered us. They rode their bikes, charging into the "woods" (as we called it). We retreated into our fort. Once there, our acorn ammo did not repel them. They tore down the walls of our fort, surrounded us and threw their acorns painfully hard at our bare arms and legs. We broke and ran into the street. Ricky's lip was trembling. Suddenly, we stopped in front of another vacant lot in which a house was being constructed and in which there were great puddles of muddy water. We proceeded to throw great gloppy glumps until the other gang retreated from our territory.

That empty lot, the one we called "the woods," was also the scene of another incident in which Ricky was involved. One afternoon, Ricky, another friend and I planned that they would tie me up, gag me and then run down the street to report to my parents that I had been kidnapped and thrown in the back of the lot. My parents, not fooled for a minute, came down to get me. I was whipped all the way down the street and into my room. Their major gripe was that Ricky had told my sister that I had been kidnapped and she had run in the house and told them. Because she had been frightened, they felt I deserved the beating.

I recognize that a good portion of these remembrances deal with the often abusive kinds of punishment I received from my parents. At the outset, I was determined not to make this another missive by a survivor of childhood abuses perpetrated by important adults in his/her life. One of the reasons I recall my great-grandfather with such detail is an almost unconscious effort to remember adults who were overwhelmingly positive in my life. I still want to avoid dwelling on the abuses I suffered, but not in any way to deny their effect on me. As I write I am finding that they pop up almost inadvertently, even in my most pleasing childhood memories. And, of course, as was stated earlier, there are some sections of my life I have no memory of at all.

I am confronted with the fact that the abuse demands to be dealt with, even if the memories are only accessible to me through my sister. Perhaps it becomes important for me to admit this: I remember being abused. But, and I think this is even more important, it is essential that I remember surviving the abuse; that, even as a child, I was endowed with some sense of how to survive. I did what I needed to do.

I believe we all have those innate skills. I believe it is important to honor the things we learned to do, or came by intuitively, in order to survive . . . even if those behaviors become counterproductive later in life. One must honor them for what they provided, and then move on. Denying their worth and forbidding their expression (a mistake behaviorally oriented therapies can sometimes make) only serves to further convince the victim of childhood abuses that he/she is incapable of doing "the right thing," and that he/she actually got what he/she deserved. It is also important to understand that taking away a behavior that has, even in its counterproductiveness, provided some respite or shelter from the catastrophic effects of abuse can result in the surfacing of even more self-destructive behaviors. I sometimes think that the therapeutic community can create such things as, say, Multiple Personality Disorder, simply by continually denying the importance of survival behaviors present in a seriously traumatized individual who has been labeled as having a Borderline Personality Disorder.

Perhaps the best thing to attempt to do (as a therapist or in progressing with one's own "self-therapy") is to provide constructive directions when those behaviors rear up; allow their expression in as safe a context as is necessary, respond with empathy and then present safer, less destructive variations on that behavior as options for the future. These variations should serve to connect one with others, rather than serving to deprive one and reinforce the isolation and pain felt as a child.

I recall, perhaps more clearly than any other memory, a particular, very short time-period in one afternoon, when I was about eight or ten, walking through our dining room and thinking that it was the first day in quite a while that I had not been hit. I remember being proud of myself, not so much for being "good," but for simply avoiding being hit. I think I was already aware of the fact that I was being mistreated, although I constantly doubted it. I think this one, very short, memory is an important one to me in my quest to learn what kind of behaviors and attitudes helped me survive.

I am convinced that abusive punishments were more the rule than the exception for children of my generation, regardless of social class, and that they reflected how our parents were raised and the kind of responses we were being taught to expect from those in authority when we broke the rules. Remember, this was the McCarthy era and just after. People were being punished for breaking the rules set by a ruling class in much the same way we children were being punished.

It is also quite possible that, as a little boy, my punishments were harsher and more frequent because I was expected to grow up tough, to be able to "take it," to grow up to be able to protect this country right or wrong, to fight Commies who were any day going to drop atom bombs on us. I was expected to tough it out and save the day for democracy. To do this I could not indulge in any "soft" or erratic behavior.

I now see quite clearly how much the sexual behavior of men in this culture, whether bisexual, gay or hetero, is merely a sexualized attempt to prove that we can "take it." In this way, painful kinds of intercourse, cruising, and some kinds of rape become very connected to what we were taught was masculine. Being able to take it becomes the ultimate expression of masculine toughness in the same way an athlete or soldier is encouraged to endure and ignore pain and "take it like a man." What else could our parents expect?

At any rate, my parents must have been quite frightened when confronted with me, the dreamer child who regularly played with the neighborhood girls and showed no real aptitude or interest in organized team sports. I remember being threatened with military school numerous times as a way to straighten up any behavior not regimented enough or too soft. They forced me into sports I felt were cruel and an extension of other abuses I had suffered, or forbade me to quit when I felt totally intimidated and terrified by what I was subjected to in the name of competition. They also pressured me into the Boy Scouts. However, I grew to like that experience immensely, not because those same repugnant pseudo-masculine virtues and behavioral expectations were absent, much to the contrary, but Scouts taught me to love the woods and to learn about the earth. I find it humorous now that in Boy Scouts (which, as I have said, I was pushed into in order not to lose sight of the fact that I was a boy and had certain boy things to accomplish), I also had some of my first extensive homosexual experiences.

To become more specific about the abuses I suffered is less important than understanding how I survived. A concrete example of how that became more apparent to me is evident in a more recent memory involving my own pre-adolescent step-son and my even younger niece:

During a family Christmas gathering at my parents' home, a disagreement broke out between my stepson and my niece who had been until then playing cooperatively in the basement. They had been playing with a blanket, and my stepson apparently flipped the blanket up in a way that hurt my niece. She ran upstairs to the adults in tears and my stepson was right behind trying to apologize. She would have none of it and refused to look at him or accept his apology. Her parents, my younger sister and her husband, became quite angry with her, demanding that she accept the apology. She, in turn, became more stubborn, continuing her refusal, regardless of what punishments were threatened if she did not verbally accept what was now a somewhat frightened apology from my stepson.

I was in the kitchen preparing dinner for the entire clan as the argument escalated. My sister and her husband were visibly infuriated by my niece's refusal to cooperate. Red-faced and furious, my brother-in-law began to search the house. At first I didn't know what he was looking for. He came into the kitchen, pulled open drawer after drawer, then asked my mother where she kept her wooden spoons. I don't recall whether he found one. By that time, realizing what was to transpire, I was beginning to feel light-headed and leaned heavily on the kitchen counter, mixing whatever I was mixing with a vengeance. I broke out in a sweat.

The next sounds I heard were barely muffled blows from the room on the other side of the house where my niece had been carried into by my brother-in-law. The blows were punctuated by screaming cries from the child. I lost count after four. The room I was in seemed to be swaying. I was having a difficult time standing and was nearly in tears. I remember standing there terrified in the kitchen, pleading that each hit would be the last.

None of the adults said anything to question such punishment. When my brother-in-law came back into the room, I recall my parents giving him support and my sister saying things like "Well, she hasn't had a spanking in a long time, she was about due for one," and the others joining in with statements like "She was asking for it."

It occurred to me at that very moment, in my shaken, internally enraged state, standing over a bowl of meat loaf, that those were the exact words I had heard innumerable times as a child. I even remember getting those so-called spankings only because (at least in my youthful judgment) I "hadn't had one in a while."

My own stepson reacted with horror to this scene and was taken from the room by his mother. Even though a single swat to his backside had been known to be administered at several key moments in his life, he was surprised and confused that adults would treat children this way, as surprised as I was when I discovered that there were children who were never given more than an occasional swat to their behinds.

When my brother-in-law brought my red-eyed niece out of the room where he had beat her, he again insisted she accept my stepson's apology, also insisting that my stepson be present to hear it. In a voice that was barely there, I refused to allow him to be a part of what was occurring. My sister approached me then and hissed that I shouldn't "put her husband down" in front of the children.

My niece was a lovely, creative and intuitive child. In the years since this incident, I've noticed she's become more introverted and less likely to share the products of her delightfully creative mind. I hope she heard my angry words to her parents. I hope she remembers them, even if she can't remember the beatings she received. I believe that her stubborn refusals to apologize in the face of totally demeaning and cruel treatment show that she is a survivor, as I had been a survivor at her age.

I was a boy soprano. I sang in the junior choir in our Lutheran church. I remember music being the one thing I enjoyed that my parents encouraged. In fact, they used to play Mitch Miller records, giving us the word sheets and having us sing with the record, either alone or standing in front of the TV in various combinations. They also did this with the many Rogers and Hammerstein musical recordings they had. As a very young man, I remember liking to sing "I'm Just a Girl Who Can't Say No" and "Surrey with the Fringe on Top" from the musical, *Oklahoma.* "Nothing Could Be Finer Than to Be in Carolina" was my favorite Mitch Miller tune.

I believe my mother was more supportive regarding my singing because her own father, a handsome, unhappy and extremely abusive Irishman who raped and beat her as a girl, had a beautiful Irish tenor which he neglected to develop, even though a priest had offered to support his education in this direction. My mother's father apparently decided that only "sissies" would take singing seriously and went on to become an automobile mechanic who later left his wife and three children (or was finally asked to leave after he fathered a child with a woman other than my grandmother). Encouraging my singing was, in my mother's own indirect and perhaps entirely subconscious way, her way of making right the basic error she felt my grandfather had made in his life.

I'm not sure how I felt about my singing beyond the very pleasant tactile feeling of being able to be as loud as I wanted and making a melody happen. I'm sure I did not think much about the words I was singing. I sang many solos between my eighth and tenth year. I liked the sound of my voice and I liked the attention my singing received. I was something of a celebrity in the church, however reserved and Lutheran that kind of notoriety was expressed to me.

What I liked most was that I could make melodic statements and sing loud enough to fill a rather large sanctuary. I felt unity and autonomy at the same time. My sense of independence and any sense at all I had that I was special came from my singing.

If any one feeling has carried me through the years and has at all been spiritually cathartic it was, and is, this feeling. It is the same feeling I get now when I read a poem and the tension in the room unifies, all the background chatter melts and I know I am moving people. My singing as a child was the first thing I did that opened up that part of my psyche to me. Perhaps all the struggles I had in my adolescence and early adulthood were only the internal wrestling with angels that occurs in the heart when one attempts to repress true gifts or minimize them, denying their importance or integral nature.

I suppose I should thank my mother for introducing me, however inadvertently, to a feeling that I consciously or unconsciously struggled to recapture. A feeling that quite possibly became a major reason I survive with my faculties intact, capable of true joy; a feeling that my entire life seeks out like magnet to steel; a feeling that is my connection to the order of the way of the ten thousand things and my gift to it.

Bob Vance lived his first eighteen years in Mt. Clemens, Michigan, a place where Thomas Edison stopped during train trips between Detroit and Port Huron. He currently works with an assertive community treatment team that helps those who have persistent and debilitating mental illness to live outside of institutional settings. He publishes poetry regularly, has seen several of his plays produced and is poetry editor of Changing Men *magazine.*

Magic, Imagination, and the Loving Male

by Jerry Rosco

Even before I opened my eyes, I was aware of a light and a presence in the room. It was very late at night and, at the age of nine, I was never one to wake until morning. But I was awake. What I saw was my father's mother standing in the far corner of the bedroom. Without lifting my head from the pillow, I blinked and focused my eyes until I was sure it was her. Though I knew very well that she had died several days earlier, there was no doubt about it.

My grandmother's thick braid of white hair adorned her shoulder. Her handsome European face was turned toward me, her eyes smiling joyously, protectively, as if she understood the moment and knew that I did, too. Dressed in her white robe, she was solid and real, and yet I could see somewhat the corner of the room beyond her, through her.

My brief surprise quickly melted in the powerful feeling of love and goodness that filled the room. I've waited all my life to know that feeling again, and perhaps only now do I realize when that shall be.

I sat up to the strangeness of that gentle, luminescent light and the late night stillness of the apartment. To make sure I was awake, I actually pinched myself and looked at my sleeping twin brother John in the bed beside me. I considered waking him but instinctively felt that was wrong, that whatever this moment meant, it was meant for me. I was afraid that it would end too quickly, that she would vanish. Not for a second did I consider waking my half-brother Mike, three years older, who lay turned toward the wall in the bed to my left. I didn't know then that the great enemy of my childhood would one day be a true friend.

This moment was different from the Old-World good-bye of a week earlier. We children, including my two sisters and all my cousins, had been brought to an uncle's apartment in an Italian section of the Bronx. One by one, or in twos, we were led into the large back bedroom to see my grandmother. John and I had stood by her bed and seen her beaming smile.

This visit in my bedroom seemed lighter and happier. I don't know how much time went by. We looked at each other and didn't speak but understood very well. Finally she did leave, fading gradually until I saw only the corner of the room. Only then did I notice the first pale light of dawn at the window behind me.

I woke my twin and told him. To his credit, he believed me even though the early hour pulled him back to sleep quickly. The next morning my other brother and two sisters politely did not believe me. My parents liked the story but soon forgot it. And I was smart enough not to repeat it. Even as a child, I knew the difference between imagination and magic. Others would call what I saw imagination. I knew it was a matter of spirituality, of magic, and I would not argue about it.

On the other hand, imagination was a different but more routine part of my world. My mother was not Italian but came from an old family in the South, with just a trace of Native American lineage that was enough for my Italian relatives to half-jokingly refer to her as "The Squaw." But it was also enough to fire my vivid imagination, and perhaps see the country and society with a different perspective. Of course, I didn't know before puberty that there was a deeper instinctual reason for feeling like an outlaw, a renegade.

When we children played Cowboys and Indians in the vast wooded park near my home, I always fired my plastic musket as an Indian defending my people. Most of my early reading was of books relating to Native Americans, both in fact and fiction. I knew about the last of the war chiefs, Sitting Bull of the Sioux and Geronimo of the Apache. My real heroes were gentle men of peace, Chief Joseph of the Nez Perce, the great speaker, and Sequoyah, who put his Cherokee language into printed words.

This interest in my heritage was sincere enough, but perhaps it was symbolic of my alienation from other boys. I was like them in some ways—but then I wasn't. My feeling of male identity didn't fit the schoolyard pattern of crude words, feigned anger and forced competition. Between the ages of eight and twelve, I retreated deeper into the realm of imagination.

I invented a secret visionary game which I've never mentioned to anyone before. After going to bed, but before going to sleep, I closed my eyes and opened my mind to an ongoing story, one that usually had continuing episodes like any good serial. There were a few set characters, but the main one was an Indian boy about my own age. I experienced the story through his eyes.

The boy had a good loving mother, but she was usually in the background and could do little to protect and teach him. Instead, his protector and teacher was a handsome Indian brave, skillful on horseback and in the field, gentle but firm, with a quiet masculine dignity. It was not his father—the boy had no father—and the man was too wise and noble to be a mere older brother.

Just as creative writing is unpredictable, this imaginary game moved through adventures large and small whose inventive plots often contained surprises. No doubt, these near-dream visionary scenes were rich in symbolism. What mattered most were not the adventures, but the purity of the bond between the boy and the man he trusted and emulated.

This secret game ended at age twelve, but not because my imagination had weakened. In fact, I was a young adult before I finally gave over my scores of toy soldiers, cowboys and Indians to my little nephews, and, in other ways, I've never grown up. No, I gave up my nightly escapes to this rich, logical other-world only because I had no choice. Sexuality was moving from my subconscious and crowding into my consciousness, and it could not exist side by side with my ideal of the pure and perfect older man. As a child, of course, I did not analyze this conflict but I believe I understood it very well. Deliberately, reluctantly, I had to let go of the world of that Indian boy and that great and noble man, his protector and friend.

The early mysticism and spirituality, the visionary night-world of imagination, all of that was a part of me that excluded my father. But the daytime world did not exclude him, even if those hours mattered least to me.

I rejected him early on, simply because he so seldom showed tenderness. Large and powerful, he frightened all of us with his loud temper and, with the boys, physical punishment. After all these years I can remember very well several times when he struck me, when the punishment was excessive and traumatic. It is enough to shake or lightly smack an unruly child. A muscular two-hundred-and-twenty-pound man should never strike a child at all.

Yet my earliest memory is of my father carrying me gently to a window so that I could see and hear an Italian parade in the street below. Recently I learned from my mother that my twin brother and I used to sit on that large front window for hours at a time. Our apartment then was on one side of my grandparents' vegetable store. An uncle's apartment was on the other side. Only in a colorful scrap of memory do I see the store and my grandparents' apartment in back.

I knew that my father was something of a war hero in World War II, and I respected that. A foot soldier in France, he was wounded below the right knee by mortar shrapnel. Field doctors with limited supplies considered amputating his leg but he argued to save it. When he finally returned to the States on an ocean transport, he walked with a cane onto the dock in New York. When he saw his mother in the waiting crowd, he threw away the cane before she could see it.

At the beach in the summer, everyone could see the deep wound in his leg, the evidence of war. At home, there were other mementos of field combat. In contrast to the wide blade and large practical handle of his regulation M-1 bayonet was a chilling souvenir: an ivory-handled Nazi dagger, its twelve-inch blade thin, sharp and extremely deadly-looking. It fit into a decorative self-sharpening steel sheath. On the blade guard was an artistically engraved swastika and the German eagle, spreading its wings.

Despite these and other dramatic artifacts of the European front, my father was no braggart about the War. He told a few stories, but never violent ones, and as a foot soldier he surely knew some. From his eyes and his silences, I gathered that he had killed men, but would never talk about it, and would always regret it.

As young as I was, more than a decade after the War, I understood little about it. I knew the Nazis were evil, that the Japanese had launched an unfair sneak attack, and that Mussolini was a misguided fanatic. (The Italian nation got off a little easy, you'll note.) Even as a child, I somehow never bought the whole ball of wax. The atom bomb was beyond comprehension. Why was it not beyond use?

In the late fifties, we schoolchildren heard air raid sirens and saw well-displayed signs for public bomb shelters. At school, we learned to hide under our desks during the practice drills. But even then, comprehension of a real atomic blast was impossible. I'd look out the window of my classroom and the streets would be quiet. I'd calculate that if the bomb fell a few miles away, downtown, we would be all right and have time to escape to the country.

Talk about Communists, and the hysteria of the fifties, was somewhat over my head, but I couldn't help but be aware of it. I was too young to know about the McCarthy hearings and other Red Scare witch-hunts, but in school the notion of an imminent Communist invasion was instilled in us. We were told that these Communists would take over our classrooms and pressure us to betray our country and the Catholic religion. My vivid imagination turned to daydreams of courage. I'd imagine Communists in bright-colored uniforms taking command from the teacher's desk. I recall now that my idea of myself was greatly weighted by how well I might face that ultimate moment of truth.

Although I was an infant during the Korean War of the early fifties, I have a lasting memory of it in the late fifties. My father had an old-fashioned reel-to-reel tape recorder, on which he played a strange recording of a U.S. general speaking harshly about the shameful performance of American soldiers in Korea, and how it had led to a disgraceful U.S. compromise on the outcome. Not quite ten, I understood my father's feelings clearly. He and his fellow soldiers had been heroic and victorious in World War II. Younger, greener soldiers had failed in Korea and given a foothold to the new enemy—world Communism.

However, listening to the very same tape, I heard a long story about the low morale and bad behavior of soldiers who were deep in enemy territory, starving and freezing and cut off from help. I thought of those boys and their plight, not the angry platitudes of the general. Something about that conflict was complex and terrifying. Of course, it was a clear forewarning of our country's disastrous fifteen or so years in Viet Nam. Naturally, that warning was wasted.

My boyhood instinct against the indignant general and in favor of the supposedly disgraced soldiers was also a personal forewarning. In young adulthood, I would become very involved in the anti-war, anti-draft movement—and that meant years of angry, bitter conflict with my father.

Yet, from a greater perspective, I see my father in a more just light. What scars, deeper than those on his leg, were left by field combat at age nineteen? I remember that he would never again fire a weapon of any kind, not even the smallest target rifle. I silently mocked his stubbornness then. Today, when it is too late to say so, I greatly admire him for it.

Nor would he ever eat lamb, because as a boy he'd seen one slaughtered. Today I compare that to the time when I, as a boy, saw a gray cat get hit by a car. I picked it up and rushed with it to a cellar where I tried to comfort it as it purred loudly in its last minutes. It closed its eyes and died in my hands. How much I revere the life of any animal now.

What conflicts went on in my father's great hulking self between the tender feelings he suppressed and the brutal realities of the hard world he knew? That and a working-class struggle to support his large family had something to do with his bad tempers and stormy moods.

More than nostalgia but perhaps a greater truth lies in the happier moments. One morning, a surprise blizzard left nearly four feet of snow outside our ground floor apartment. Like a girl, my mother opened a window to make a snowball and toss it at my father. Like a big boy, he lifted her, carried her outdoors and dropped her in the deep snow as we all laughed. Surely, it was the most delightful moment my whole family ever shared together.

So many years later, when my father and I were having our last real talk together, I told him again of seeing my grandmother after her death. Whatever else that boyhood vision had meant, it eventually, magically, led to reconciliation, spiritual comfort and peace between my father and myself.

During his early boyhood in the fifties, Jerry Rosco lived in Manhattan's Inwood section, near historic Fort Tryon Park and The Cloisters. A contributor to many journals and magazines, he co-edited Continual Lessons: The Journal of Glenway Wescott *(1991). He is currently writing a memoir/biography of Wescott.*

Dream Branches

by Stephen Silha

The other day I came upon a clear-cut hillside. On one side of it lay a tree, on its side, that the loggers had somehow missed. I lay down on one of its horizontal branches, as I had so often done as a boy in Minnesota. I closed my eyes and the voice of the seven-year-old in me began to tell a story I thought I had forgotten:

I can't remember when we first found the Dream Branches, or when we realized that's what they were. Must have been a year ago, after we moved to the place in the country. I couldn't believe how big this place was compared to our old house. Even when the big kids threw rocks from our yard, they couldn't get 'em all the way across that field to the next house.

On one side of our house we discovered the Rocky Mountains. I thought they were real mountains then, but my dad told me they were just mounds from dirt that used to be in our basement. I love the way you can run up and down them and find red and green and even gold rocks. Some gray ones stick to your lips if you lick 'em. Those mountains fill a whole baseball field between our house and the house next door.

On the other side of our house is a huge rock in the middle of a field filled with grasshoppers that spit tobacco, plus a lot of ladybugs and weeds. A neighbor lady, a friend of Mom's, says that rock is even bigger underground than the part you can see. I try to think about that but it seems crazy. I'll bet the underground part doesn't sparkle like the part that sticks up.

When we moved here I was six; my brother was only three. We still share a room upstairs. When grandma isn't visiting, we have the whole upstairs to ourselves. It's easier to sing songs at night than it was in our old house, with our parents' room next door. Also, if I get up on my brother's bed I can look out at the Rocky Mountains.

I like living between the rock and the Rocky Mountains.

But down *behind* the rock, away from the road where nobody can see, where the field turns into a shady hill and the smells get wetter, a big old oak tree has fallen over. Its roots stick right up and poke at the sky. Its leaves have dropped off, and its branches point down the hill. Those are the Dream Branches. Me an' the neighborhood kids go out there all the time, 'specially after a hard game of tag, PIG, Starlight or Moonlight in the middle of the afternoon.

We lie out on the branches and tell each other our dreams. It's easier to remember dreams when you're lying down. When you bounce on a branch, you feel like you're floating. It's easy to talk about dreams when you're floating. It's a good place to go with friends, or even with your brother. Somehow, when you get out on the branches and start floating, it doesn't matter who's better at baseball or in school. And even if you can't remember your dreams, you can always make them up, floating there on the Dream Branches.

I was always scared to tell about my wolf dreams because I was afraid the wolves, who chased me everywhere in these dreams, would get upset and would come and get me when I waited for the school bus one morning, or when I rode my bike at night or even when floating on the Dream Branches.

But one day, I smelled the moss on the bark of that tree. I looked up at the sky. I felt the sun on my neck. I took a big breath and I told my dream anyway to Jim and Bob and Sherry:

"One day my parents were having a big barbecue in their yard. I was playing across the street with some friends. I got hungry and ran to get some food. I started talking with one of my parents' friends—a man I liked a lot. He was a clown in the Aquatennial Parade and everything. While I talked with him, he turned into a wolf. His teeth grew long. Fur covered his body and face. I knew he was the Head Wolf and that there were lots more. I ran back across the street, still hungry, and he ran after me. I called to my parents but they acted like I was just playing with their friend.

"I woke up screaming and the baby-sitter ran into the room to see what was wrong. I told her the wolves were coming, and bawled. I went back to sleep and had a bunch more nightmares that night. In the last one, a wolf was riding my bike off into the woods. And I've had wolf dreams ever since."

It was quiet on the Dream Branches. There were always quiet times on them. I looked out the corners of my eyes to see if any wolves were coming, or if any of my friends on the dream branches were getting hairy necks. After finally *telling* someone that dream, I felt like the weight of the Rocky Mountains was taken off me as I bobbed on my branch. The bark made funny red marks on my cheeks, I could feel it dig in. But telling my friends about the wolves put them on my side. I thought, for once, I might win.

One day Bob told about a dream where his dad kicked his mom down the stairs 'cause he was upset about the pink color she painted their bedroom. And she tripped on a Silly Putty egg that belonged to him and his twin brother Jim. She got so mad at them she slapped them across the cheeks, all in one swoop like the Three Stooges. That didn't seem so much like a dream to me, but we talked about it and laughed.

Sherry usually tells about flying dreams, or dreams where she meets Annette Funicello. Since she started having her Annette dreams, she hasn't been able to fly as much. She used to be able to fly whenever a monster or something chased her. Not anymore.

We laughed when she told us the one about Annette coming up to her on the beach and having her bikini top fall off when she tripped over a cooler and fell right on top of Sherry!

Jim's dreams are usually about machines. He invents all sorts of machines like the one that makes oranges into orange Lik'M-Aid, and the bed that does your homework while you sleep and the record player that delivers live frogs, cats and snakes from the speaker. Sometimes his machines go berserk and won't stop making snakes or Lik'M-Aid even if you unplug them.

Some days I go to the Dream Branches alone. Once when I was there by myself, they turned into a pirate ship and I jumped from deck to deck and even walked the plank a few times. Then I heard my mother calling me and I took a flying jump off the end where the roots stuck out. Somehow I missed the spot of ground I was aiming for and speared myself in the chest with a root. At least, it felt like that. When I got to the house, I was crying and I took off my T-shirt. There was a big bold stroke of blood across my chest, right over my heart. I never figured out if it was a pirate wound or if it was just the Dream Branches leaving their mark.

The mark is still there after a year. But the Dream Branches are gone. On the way home from the bus stop this afternoon, I saw that they were gone. A big pile of ashes was smoldering in the middle of the vacant lot behind the rock. A bulldozer sat in one corner of the lot, waiting to eat up the grasshoppers that spit tobacco. I couldn't believe it.

"What happened to the Dream . . . to that tree on the hill behind the rock?" I asked my mom. I was out of breath and starting to cry.

"They started clearing that lot today," she said. "A new house is going in there." She hugged me and gave me a Hydrox cookie. She added, "That's progress, Honey." I ran back out to where the Dream Branches had been to see if they were really gone. They were. I ran over to the rock and walked around it a bunch of times. I tried to climb it, but couldn't. I got grass stains all over my pants. I felt my world getting smaller and more crowded. I ran over to the Rocky Mountains and wondered how long it would be before they were turned into somebody's basement.

Stephen Silha grew up in suburban Minneapolis, Minnesota, where he edited his first newspaper at age nine. He went on to become a reporter for newspapers, including The Minneapolis Star *and* The Christian Science Monitor. *Today, from his house on Puget Sound near Seattle, he still writes, consults on public relations, philanthropic and media issues, and often turns over the pen to a new generation of reporters and editors at Children's Express News Service.*

Little Boy Found

by Thomas Moore

"Father, father, where are you going
O do not walk so fast.
Speak father, speak to your little boy
Or else I shall be lost."
—William Blake, "The Little Boy Lost"

One of my early memories is of a Sunday afternoon on Lake St. Clair north of Detroit, a day on which my father's father and I would sometimes go off in a small rowboat, a five h.p. outboard motor taking us a short way offshore to do some lazy, grandfatherly fishing. My memory of this day begins with the unusual sight of my grandfather standing up in the boat and feeling a cold line of water rise up over my ankles, followed by a water's-eye view of seat cushions, a gasoline can and assorted containers floating on the surface of the lake. I can still see vividly the white bottom of the capsized boat and feel my grandfather's arms as he held me to the surface so that I could breathe. I watched my uncle dive off the shore to help us. Then I awoke in a dry, oversized bed in a strange room where people were whispering.

I lay there in the bed feeling the sheets too tight over my shoulders, and I heard someone mention an undertaker. I was four years old, and it seemed entirely logical to assume that I was dead, laid out in this uncomfortable bed, flat on my back, no one near me or talking to me. Later, I found out that my grandfather had died in the water, perhaps from a heart attack, but in my memory and the minds of my family, he died saving my life.

Little boy found.

I think Pluto, Lord of Death, left his mark on me that day, with a fear and a depressive blotch of feeling that is so constant as to be existential in tone. An essential blue emotion that doesn't rise and fall with the vagaries of life, and doesn't swap other emotions either, but qualifies them all with its mere presence, with its memory. I think that mark also fixed my childhood, like a bath that stops a photograph from further development. That child who clung to the bottom ribs of the white boat clings still today. There are moments even now, forty-five years later, when I am swimming or in a boat, when suddenly the smell of engine oil and gasoline wafts in from somewhere, and I see cushions floating on the water and a man diving off a cement pier. That child is still present, not far beneath the surface, ready to eternally replay what he sees in his mind's eye.

Whoever catches a glimpse of Pluto's deathly landscape or waterscape remains like Persephone partly in that place forever. Life goes on and fears become dulled, but the seed of death has been planted and there is no earthly way of getting away from that knowledge. And yet, at the same time, in some way the seed was preordained.

For the past fifteen years, I have been trying to develop a classical yet practical, non-new-age, poetic and prophetic view of astrology. For me, my lessons began in this boat, with water threatening to absorb me, the universe creeping up my ankles from the lower watery firmament. At the moment I was born, the moon was passing through Capricorn, the kingdom of Saturn, who has a preference for dark emotional tones and a familiarity with death. "The undertaker is here," someone whispers, and I, under the stiff white sheets, know with certainty that a Saturnine spirit is in the room.

The reaper has cut down another beautiful, bountiful, loved shoot of human grain. My grandfather, I have been told many times since, was a man of humor, passion, family spirit and friendship. My relation to him is as a child, from before almost all conscious memory, and yet he speaks to me and lets me know that, however deep the waters, I will not be lost. In relation to him, I am eternally child.

I'm not saying that intimacy with death stunted my growth and so I became an eternal boy. No, the bond with death that day evoked an awareness of boyhood's eternal nature. The child is an ever-living person, as much out of life as in it, as much unrelated to life as affected by it, profoundly affecting the soul but neither caused nor conditioned by life. Perhaps through my experience I have felt closer to the body of death than the boy of life.

"It took me a long time to mature," my father once told me when I was about twelve years old. I had no idea what he was talking about. But he spoke, and I listened, and many times since I have pondered the meaning of that confession, to him and to me. In my professional work I have long been interested in the Jungian image of the *puer æternus*, the eternal boy. This is a deep source of identity. In some men and women, *puer* is a minor motif that appears now and then; in others it is an element of character and is inseparable from fate. In still others, *puer* is a problem, a source of pathology—emotional suffering and neurotic experience. Jesus is a typical *puer:* idealistic, spiritually ambitious, detached, self-destructive, homoerotic, wandering, at odds with authorities, revisioning revered traditions, preoccupied with a time to come characterized by peacefulness and love.

When I was thirteen, I was so taken by the saintliness of a parish priest, Father Weber, whose integrity reminded me of my father, that I shipped off to a prep seminary in Chicago, leaving my family behind. Even today people say incredulously, "Why did you do that?" The answer is connected to that fated *puer,* that Jesus-man who could be bitterly tormented by homesickness and yet remain loyal to the *puer* need to soar into the sky, like Icarus up from the labyrinth of ordinary life. Nothing was higher than the priesthood and therefore I had to put on my wings, fly away from home, and reach for the sun.

Leaving home to chase a sunbeam had nothing to do with conscious choice and reasoning. *I* didn't choose. That heliotropic boy insisted. There was no holding him down. Wings of wax may melt in heat, but they carry the spirit upwards with unexpected force. No matter that the seminary program was twelve years in length; no matter that I'd have to renounce my family and a sexual life. To the *puer,* these earthly concerns carried little weight. The only point was the takeoff, the ascent.

Aphrodite, anyway, is leaning against my midheaven in the tenth house in the place of the virgin. The tenth is the house of vocation, and so I tried to make Venus a virgin, finding chaste avenues for my passions. I could transfer my Venereal affections for devotedness to the Virgin Mary, the Mother of Sorrows, as she was venerated in the religious order fate ordained for me. I have often thought of my own mother at the moment they called to say that there had been an accident in the water, and at that first daybreak departure from the train station bound for Chicago. I felt my mother's ache as much as I felt my own. I wonder what my father's feelings were. The *puer* is cruel and doesn't give a damn about tender ties. My own ache is still strong, the child still hoping that there might be a way out of this romance with the sun, some compassion on the part of that ambitious boy.

Little boy lost.

I think what my father was saying is that the *puer* was so strong in him that he felt he would never grow up. Now approaching eighty, he is still in the boy's grip, that boy who is so eternally slow to mature and is helping him age with amazing grace. We feel that the *puer* spirit in us needs to grow up, that one day he will, that soon this immaturity will pass, life will settle down—but the expected change may never occur.

In my practice as an analyst, over the years, I have tried to honor the *puer* spirits that have come to me in distress. Colleagues tell me that the *puer* needs life experience to get grounded. But, if that were the case, then *puer* wouldn't be *puer* any longer because by nature he doesn't like the earth. His element is air; his desire the sun. My friend James Hillman says, as a true father of the *puer,* that the *puer* needs to be taken seriously, on his own terms, and in that way keep his nature while he leans toward maturity. That approach makes sense to me, but it isn't easy to put into practice. A strong *puer* spirit elicits an opposite reaction, demanding maturity and grounding so forcefully that the temptation to move against the *puer* is almost insurmountable.

I feel the tension in myself. Can I resist the temptation to grow up and get grounded as a way of defending myself against my own *puer* fate? Maybe I could be father to this boy, to my own boy, and speak to him so he won't feel lost. It's all right to be a boy. Boyhood doesn't have to be redeemed by adulthood. I don't have to grow up, or, at least, *he* doesn't have to grow up. In fact, if I artificially force him to grow up, he will always be present to me neurotically, and there will be no way to align him with the more mature elements in my soul. The boy Mercury, that rascal *puer* spirit, is in Scorpio, supplied with a stinger and a threat, and in the twelfth house—Pluto's. For me, *puer* and death have a holy alliance, the boy and the undertaker.

The shadow of the *puer* appears in his dalliance with death, his risking his life or his accidents. The boys of myth are wounded: Icarus crashed into the sea. Phaëthon dashed onto the earth, Jesus nailed to the cross, Hippolytus trampled by horses. Our mythic boys have a weakness that leads them to death: Elvis Presley, James Dean, John Belushi, John Lennon, John Kennedy. Maybe my ankles, those tender and vulnerable boy parts, feeling first the arrival of death, gave my boyish spirit its dark base. I learned early on that the dissolution of one's Eden begins at the foundation, from some mysterious, infinitely deep place, and is felt first in the feet.

My *puer* spirit ranges vertically between the infinite depths of my watery grandfather and the infinite heights of my solar father.

The wings of the *puer* are strong, but his constitution is not robust. He has an innate vulnerability and wobbliness. He doesn't live easily on this demanding earth, and he doesn't stand up well to the tough criticisms and weighty values of those around him who are less flighty. He may find it difficult to defend his ways, although he has no choice but to live them. He toys with death because he isn't really comfortable in this earthly life. He'd rather be imagining something more exciting, less boring.

My grandfather held me up out of the water, shouting words of encouragement and instruction to me, talking to me so that I wouldn't be lost. I'm angry at the fathers who refuse to speak to me. The last president who talked to me was John Kennedy, a man who was able to keep father and son in dialogue in his own life and work. The others, except for Jimmy Carter, seem to be corrupted men who disdain my *puer* idealism and my longing for integrity and wisdom. The senators over the years whose words I could hear have almost all been voted out of office. Politically, I feel lost. The way these national fathers spend money and deal with international conflicts has no relation to my values. I've recently made trips to Europe where I found deep patrimony in some of the cultural artifacts some true ancient fathers left for me and, as I stood in the presence of their beautiful gifts of paintings and architecture, I could feel the boy spirit in me come to life and feel secure again. The boy needs to hear the father's words and see his deeds, knowing that he is truly the father and that he loves the boy sufficiently to give his life for him.

Recently a woman told me a dream in which a boy with a badly diseased leg was presented to a priest. I thought of the icy water crawling up my ankles, a sign that the bright Sunday morning years ago was turning dark. The boy needs an association with death, so strong is his attraction for the sun. The *puer* turns pathological if he doesn't experience the tug at his feet; and if he doesn't feel that downward pull, his feet might succumb to some kind of putrefaction. I've known many young men almost wholly constituted by this *puer* who break their legs, hurt their feet, trip over themselves. A young rock-climber never got over a fall in which he broke a foot. A pilot walked with a limp, though he didn't know what was wrong with his leg.

The dream of the rotting foot is a nuisance to the *puer*, but it is his healing wound, saving him from the literalism and monotheism of his sun-worship—his sunny disposition, his dawn-colored lenses, his wish that night would never fall. Oedipus, the "swollen-footed," thought he could solve the riddle of life, but he was tripped up by the most profound ignorance about his own guilt. The feet of Jesus are fixed to his cross by nails that both keep him grounded and torture his spirit.

The undertaker is waiting. I will always be a boy, never grow up to be a man. The sheets are tight around my shoulders, preventing me from all movement, this boy who squirms and runs, who has fast feet and itchy arms. Saturn is in the sign of the Bull, keeping me on earth, constricting my movements. Father Saturn gives me an essential sadness as an antidote to the sun my *puer* spirit sees everywhere. I float easily. A stranger once talked to me for five minutes and concluded that I have my feet firmly planted in the clouds. I need the Bull's heft and Father Saturn's way of making my bed. The little boy knew that this way of lying in bed was death, that the undertaker must have done it.

The little boy was almost lost in water, but his brush with death saved him possibly from disappearing into the air. His inclination is to be lofted like helium, toward Helios, the Sun-god. Then he falls like Brueghel's Icarus into the sea. I saw this painting recently in the magnificent Musées Royaux des Beaux-Arts in Brussels, and even there, inches from the scene, I had to look hard to find Icarus splashing into the water, a small figure in a vast landscape. To the *puer,* his fall is tragic and cosmic, but in context it is fairly insignificant, little more than water rising slowly up a little boy's ankles.

In some versions of the myth, Daedalus is Icarus's father, the craftsman and artist, who knows how far to aim in his flight away from the labyrinth, escaping from the Bull who lives at its center. *Puer* life is vertical, extending between the sea and the sky, a father at each end; one keeping the boy from disappearing into the water, the other from flashing into nothingness in the hot light of the sun.

If the fathers speak to us, we can preserve our golden spirits and save human life from being devoured by the Bull. Fathers and sons need each other, for they sustain each other. We need the tension that is felt in the speech between them. We need to let our fathers be slow to grow up, and thus tend their *puer.* They need to take our childlike foolishness seriously, giving their lives for it, so that we can be fathers ourselves from our place in the sun.

Why did my grandfather hold me high in the air when the water was claiming us both? What is that impulse that is unthought and ultimate? What is the mystery that is being honored when the father speaks encouragement to the son to live on in the midst of danger?

The *puer* loves the soul and women of a particular sort, depending on the nature of the boy. Aphrodite rises to the top of my zodiac, while the sun shines in her face of Libra. She rises out of the water as I was lifted out of the water by my grandfather. For me, she is the sublimation of the water into sunlight; the redemption of the water tragedy where the father was lost. She is the foam and froth of water and air; she is the golden sparkle of the sun, and she is a fitting lover for the *puer* spirit that wants to rise up from the humid and Taurean bottoms in order to live in the yellow sunshine and in the daybreak airs of dawning life. She is the resurrection from Saturn's bed and the guardian of the place between the fathers.

We could do worse, those of us whose boyhood is eternal, than to be in the world in the golden halo of Aphrodite's absorption in beauty and sensation. We don't need more body, more relevance, more effectiveness than what we find in her virtues of love and pleasure. She is generated by the father as he sinks into the sea. And, therefore, she is a resurrection of fatherhood, who can speak to the boy knowingly and compassionately. My grandfather was taking her part when he helped me rise out of the water and live in a humid air.

What a mystery it is to be a boy, so close to death and birth, so uneducated and therefore so fresh and uncynical. We should end our disparagement of this boy, of our own immaturities, of our tardiness in growing up, of our sheer delight in beauty, of our love of the sun, of our vertical inclinations, and of our wanderings and great falls. Aphrodite loves Adonis so much she cries for him annually. We could speak words of encouragement to this boy where we find him—in our friends and students, in our institutions, and in our own hearts. If we don't speak to him in this way, he will be lost, and we will have lost with him all tenderness and grace.

Thomas Moore was born and raised in Detroit, went to high school at a Catholic prep seminary outside Chicago, and spent many summers on a farm in upstate New York. He just ended seventeen years of private practice as a psychotherapist, and is now making his living as a writer. His latest book is Care of the Soul, *and he is almost finished with a new book on the soul of relationship and intimacy.*

The Dream of Pink Dolphins

by *Leandro Barros Vianna*

To Duane, who will be playing with the
pink dolphins in the dark waters of the Rio Negro

I washed his face while he burned with fever. He struggled with his shallow breath, afraid to move because he might start coughing again. I gently moved the soft fabric across his forehead as if I were bathing a child who was passively drifting into the darkness of death. Tears filled my eyes and ran down my tired face.

He fell asleep. I looked out the window and saw an old lady caring for her roses as if they were her only friends. Suddenly I could understand how she felt; she has buried her peers, perhaps even her own child.

Her wrinkled, soft, gentle hands reminded me of Minerva, a lady who lived next to my house when I was twelve. She was eighty-three years old but always had a smile. She often called me over to her house and gave me my favorite sweets while I helped her care for her roses. That was the basis of our friendship. She passed away on a cloudy winter day. While the family mourned, I took care of her roses, knowing that Minerva would be happy to see them blooming next spring.

He woke up and asked for a glass of water. His fever was getting worse. I gave him some water and medication. He looked lost; his eyes were losing their unique brightness. His smile, however, was the last thing that would go. I held his hands and sat looking at him, trying to engrave that gentle face in my memory, as if I could ever forget him. He closed his eyes and I drifted away into my own thoughts.

I remembered several weeks before when I was flying west over the Great Lakes and had a dream about my childhood friend Marcus. When I woke up, I saw his face staring at me through the clouds. His eyes were asking for help as he fell. I pressed my face against the window but could not go any further. He broke the surface of the water and went under; now his face was even sadder. He was trying to talk to me, but only bubbles came out. I screamed his name but he couldn't hear me; he kept going deeper until I could no longer see him.

The flight attendant jolted me out of my fantasy when she asked if I wanted something to drink; I asked for a glass of water. As I drank the cold water and slowly came back to my senses, my mind drifted back to my childhood.

Marcus was walking down the street towards my house. He was my friend, and looking back, my first love. He was kind and warm, his eyes green, his skin brown, his smile radiant and his voice soft like his hands. Every day we went to school together, and on the way we would stop to buy Pe de Moleque, a cake from the northeast of Brazil. We sat on the curb and ate quickly before other kids saw us so we wouldn't have to share.

Every year after Christmas, my family would begin preparing to go to the seaside. This was a week-long process that involved packing clothes, beach toys, books, looking for my swimming suit and saying good-bye to my friends. I remember that period of time; it was something that happened every year like the seasons.

It was December 26, the heat was suffocating and I was sad because in a few days I would have to say good-bye to Marcus. He was going to the farm to visit his relatives and he would stay for the rest of the summer. Late that afternoon I called Marcus and asked him to come over to my house to play with the train I got for Christmas. When he arrived, we ate some leftover fruit from lunch and we played for hours.

The sun was going down when the phone rang. My mother answered it and came over to tell Marcus that his mother wanted to talk to him. He argued with her because he didn't want to go home, he wanted to stay with us. She finally gave in.

Before leaving the room, my mother told us that we must shower before dinner. We went to the bathroom, got undressed and jumped in. Though we had often showered together, something was different that day. I looked at his body, longed to feel his skin and feared his reaction. But in the way that he looked at me, I felt permission. Finally I hugged his wet body and, to my surprise, he held me tight. His hard penis pressed against my leg and his hands caressed my back. I closed my eyes, kissed his lips and he kissed mine. I was thrilled and at the same moment afraid to be caught, especially because we were unusually quiet. Before I let him go, I kissed him again, this time with my eyes open. He looked at me and said, "Don't tell anybody!"

That was the last time that we touched each other. We met one more time at the New Year's Eve party when we hugged, wished each other a happy new year and planned to get together as soon as we returned from vacation. I returned from vacation, but he did not.

Two days after our arrival at the beach house when most of the stuff had been unpacked, we could finally rest. As usual, everybody took a nap after lunch. It was a hot afternoon. In the tropics, even the dogs take a break from the heat. I was in the hammock reading a book. It was quiet and the air was still. The only things moving were the flies hovering overhead. I heard the phone ring but did not get up. The housekeeper finally picked up the receiver and said, "Everybody is sleeping!" There was a pause and then she asked, "You sure you want me to get the lady?" Another pause, then, "Okay, if it is important."

My mother was not happy. She complained all the way from her room, saying that if it was not an emergency, she would be very angry. I stopped reading and waited for her reaction. Suddenly I felt cold and afraid. My mother said, "NO!"

I got up to see what was happening. When I entered the room, I saw horror in her face and tears rolling down. I reached for her hand and asked, "What happened, Mother?"

She looked at me and said, "A tragedy! Why?"

I looked at her and said, "Mama, who is dead?" I took her other hand, "Mama, what is going on?"

She looked at me and said, "I am sorry."

"Why, Mama?" I asked.

She said, "He is dead!"

"Who is dead?"

"Your friend, Marcus, is dead!"

I do not remember what I thought as I ran out of the house and climbed the old cashew tree in the far end of the back yard. My mother came out looking for me and heard me crying. She came under the tree and asked me to come down. I told her that I wanted to stay there. She left because she did not know what to do; she had a very hard time with death.

I spent the rest of the afternoon in the tree. I cried for a few minutes and then looked at the blue sky, wondering if I would see Marcus flying with the birds or floating in the puffy clouds. The air was humid. I knew that it would rain soon and I thought perhaps Marcus was not there because he was afraid of water. He had, after all, drowned in a pond.

As I gazed out the plane window, I could see the same puffy clouds along with dark ones covering the Great Plains, getting ready to storm. Far away on the horizon, I could see the mountains breaking the gentle plains as we approached the western side of the continent.

How many times will I feel what I felt then—the heavy emotion that we call *"Saudade,"* that intense feeling that is overwhelming and painful, like the pain that you might feel when part of your body is removed. I remembered once watching a documentary about elephants. It took place in East Africa in the space of one year, from the rainy season when food is plentiful, to the drought, when competition for food intensifies and death settles in throughout the savanna. The heat burned the plains and the dust swept across the land. Amidst the dust clouds, we saw the elephants slowly walking toward the horizon. A mother stroking her baby was left behind. She was trying to wake him up but he was dead. She hesitated to give up, but the other elephants were slowly moving forward, sometimes pausing and looking back at her. They could not waste much time because the drought was killing them. She tried in vain several times until she realized that she had to move along with the pack; alone she would be defenseless.

The mother moves on but will always remember her child lying on the dry soil. I, too, remember my friends who are gone forever yet they live in my memory.

Looking out the window I could see the Rockies approaching. The high peaks broke the clouds dividing earth from the heavens. Soon I would be in the Pacific Northwest holding the remains of somebody who once upon a time held me while I made love to him. I remember him whispering words in my ears, his moist lips kissing mine.

They are all memories now. I spoke with him the day before and he told me that he loved me, that he needed to take a nap. Next morning, he drank his coffee, smoked his cigarette and left.

I was back to the Pacific Coast to say good-bye to my friend who finally decided to take a nap to rest his weakened body.

Upon my arrival, I realized that it was time to start boxing up things that we had collected through the years, small objects that for many have no value, yet, for me, were the remains of our history.

That night I had a dream. I was traveling on a boat up the Rio Negro. The river was calm and the dark waters moved slowly like a snail. Suddenly I heard an animal sound. I turned around and saw a pink dolphin. (In Amazonian mythology, the dolphins are believed to be a higher form of being. They are people who can transform themselves back and forth from human to dolphin and vice versa. Thus they are sacred.) They were trying to tell me something but I could not understand. I woke up and remembered that my friend Duane wanted to have his ashes scattered over the Rio Negro so that he could play with the pink dolphins.

It is raining out. I sit by the window and watch people coming and going. Sometimes I wonder if there is a purpose to all this. At times I wonder why I have experienced so many losses in my short life. Why am I burying my peers when my parents have not yet buried theirs?

I wait for the spring to come so I can go back to my homeland and take Duane where he wants to be. He will finally rest and play with the pink dolphins in the calm waters of the Rio Negro.

Leandro Barros Vianna grew up in the poverty-stricken area of northeast Brazil. When he was nine years old, in 1964, he came home from school and his father was burning books. He told Leandro they could no longer read. A military coup put an end to the democratic era. This was the end of his happy childhood and the beginning of the development of his social consciousness. Today Vianna is an AIDS activist who has educated prison populations, prostitutes and migrant workers, and has provided case management to people with AIDS, among other things. Presently he works at the AIDS Action Committee of Massachusetts, and coordinates their Speakers Bureau.

The Night When Sleep Awoke

by Neale Lundgren

"And he himself as he lay there comforted,
under the drowsy eyelids of your light form . . .
seemed one well-guarded . . . but within, who
could fend off, protect him from the inner flood-
tides of origin? Ah, there used to be no caution
in that sleeper, sleeping . . ."
—Rainer Maria Rilke, Duino Elegy 3

I remember the early childhood days and nights were such magical ones, brimming over with enchantment. Every moment was fresh, lit up, and brand spanking new. Sleep was a mere void, a waste of precious time, a winter season of non-being. Despite my nightly struggles against the Great Opiate, without fail I was overcome by that senseless, monotonous, breathing in and breathing out. When each day and waking night ended I was carried away, out of the world that mattered. I was abducted out of that conscious sunlight and moonlight world that I trusted, because there even my highest of adventures were somehow predictable. I felt fully alive yet protected in this wondrous world.

On Saturday mornings, I would spend hours riding and falling off my imaginary steed, rolling and tumbling down the hill of a dried-up canal on the corner of Hector Avenue. I would land at the bottom of the grassy hill and look up to the cloud-clad sky from under the dusty, dented rim of my cowboy hat. In the sky I saw noble warriors on chariots and huge, swift-moving birds making their way over jagged and steep mountain lands. In my mind, I walked among these great beings of the sky.

On rainy days after school, barefoot, with my blue jeans cuffed to the knee, I would run outside to the curb of the street. The pouring rain made a little river which magnified into a Mississippi. I singled out and followed some broken twig or ice cream stick making its way down the street. These, I imagined, were great sailing ships; I wished them well, and I helped them navigate the rough winds and waves of the torrential waters.

I loved playing hide-and-seek at dusk with friends on Hector Avenue. Many were the summer nights that my best friend Mike and I lay with our backs atop a blanket of freshly mowed grass. With our feet up in the air, leg to leg, we wrestled like brave Indians and found out which one of us could hang onto the stars by his feet the longest. It felt good to be both alone and connected to Mike, connected to the stars, and to the fireflies, and to the airplane lights that flickered steadily like a rhythmic heartbeat. I remembered life being this way for the longest time, never looking back to see a boy who was often painfully alone with his serious thoughts and intense feelings.

One night I woke up from one of those first dreams children call nightmares. I wonder now whether or not this is one of the ways that Sleep—that wide and deep world where the living gods dwell—first gets a child's attention. I must have been around six or seven years old. I woke up trembling, hearing a continuous buzzing sound. I could still faintly see with my mind's eye many strange and ghoulish faces calling out to me with their arms outstretched from some cavernous ravine. As I sat up in bed startled, I could still hear their voices, the voices I would come to call the "dark mother- and father-gods of the blood." I felt these rumbling voices move inside me like the undertow of the sea, sinister, intending—I thought—to do me harm.

It took me many years to understand just what these inner voices were actually saying and to find the tools to translate their ancient language. These words I would later discover were written upon inner, sacred, family tablets that I, along with my mother, father and sisters, had inherited long ago. It took me more years still to learn that it was my destiny to be the first among my family to decipher and transmute this psychogenetic code that seethed through my veins. But of this I will speak later.

I jumped up out of bed and ran in a cold sweat to my parents' closed bedroom door. I knocked on it hard, and cried out, "Mama ! Daddy! Please, open up !" I could hear them stirring and moving toward the door. They opened it asking with concern, "Son, what's wrong?" My mother gently stroked my forehead, and both attempted to reassure me by saying, "Sweetheart, it was only a dream." But their words only worsened the terror I was already feeling. "Only a dream!" I thought to myself. Why were they trying to tell me what just happened was not real?

Before this night I had always perceived my parents as strong and protecting. Their bigness used to keep me from all life-threatening dangers. I knew now that they didn't know how to save me from this dark, inner world that was now emerging with such relentless force, overwhelming me with fear. I knew they couldn't explain to me the Sleep world which had all of a sudden lit up into being, into strong and strange waves of speaking light.

Deep down inside, I knew that my parents were afraid to see that all of a sudden a separate self was taking shape right before their eyes. It was all a bewilderment to them. I had become more than just an extension of my parents, a being no longer capable of mirroring their expectations. Didn't they have nightmares like this, I thought? Was this the way they dealt with their dreams, by minimizing this huge and undiminishable reality? Why wasn't there a teaching, an initiation into this other world which all mothers and fathers would celebrate with their children? After all, my fascination with the inner world had been sparked, and the seamless, psychological fusion with my biological mother and father had once and for all been torn apart.

This time my entrance into the Sleep world was different from all those that had gone before. This time the eyes of my soul had opened. I had become a child of the gods now. For the first time in my life, I felt the painful solitude of separateness, and I was no longer at home in the "surface" world that I had grown to count on and to love so dearly.

That night I begged to sleep with my mother and father, feeling too big and yet needing to hide in the middle of their bed, between the two of them. Their god-like largeness had always shielded me from the unknown before. In fact, hadn't my mother and father been my only real gods? Since my birth they had benignly governed the realm of my day-to-day existence. I could lean on them; I wanted nothing to do with these other horrible and hideous forces that were pulling me into the terrifying territory within and away from their comforting arms.

I looked first to my left, and then to my right. I lay so close to my father that I could hear his heavy breathing and envied his not being awake. I realized then and there that my father never really welcomed me into his world, even though I felt its importance. I remembered "Daddy" (as my sisters and I called him) was gone a lot on business trips. When he came back he'd sometimes bring little gifts. I don't remember them because they never seemed connected to his heart. Upon entering the door he'd say smiling, "Hi son," and shake my hand, telling me to always grip another man's hand deliberately and strongly. He'd then say, "Where's your mother?"

I recall days when my father, home from the road, would catch me following him out into the garage and into the yard. I was so hungry for his guidance. Instead, he would give me some work to do where I couldn't be near him. In the evening after work, he would call me home from playing with my friends, "Neale Powell . . . Neale Powell, get over here this minute and get busy. Police the front and back yard!" He once taught me how to shine his shoes with a military shine. He'd shout, "With elbow grease, son!" as he brushed the leather of his boots with pride. I was in awe of my father, and it seemed to me that I often sensed he was afraid of me. Perhaps he was intimidated by my heart that was as his used to be when he was a boy: big, full, open, strong and tender.

As I was recounting these memories in the middle of my parents' bed, my father let out a huge snore. I quickly turned away from him and drew near to my mother. She was sleeping, too. I longed for her world: the world of warm, clean and good-smelling kitchens, gardens of flowers, songs on the record player, grocery stores, and her letting me pick out a small toy from Woolworth's department store when I'd go on errands with her.

My mother often told me what a "good boy" I was, that she loved me. I felt I had a golden aura about me, that I was special. I wondered why my mother wasn't that way with my father. I remember feeling kind of sad for him when he put his arms around her while she was cooking at the stove in the kitchen. I didn't understand why she didn't seem to like us seeing his hugs and kisses. She would turn her face away from him and prudishly say, "Neale, not in front of the children." And sometimes I heard fear, anger and condemnation in my mother's voice when she asked my father at the dining room table, "Neale, have you been drinking?"

But now, as I lay there in bed so physically close to my parents, I felt so far away from them. I began thinking of my friends I hoped I would see when the morning came. Surely, they would understand what was happening to me. Maybe Mike had already had a similar nightmare like the one I had tonight.

It must have been just before dawn before I finally dozed off. The monster monotone faded into the distance, melting into the sweet, familiar sound of baby birds in the trees and on the wires, ushering in the first light of day over the horizon.

I woke up to find myself lying awake in my own bed. It was late Saturday morning. My father must have carried me back to my room during the night. The sun shone through the blinds and I could smell sweet cinnamon, eggs and bacon. I looked around me and it felt like all the other weekend mornings. All seemed well. I hardly remembered the goings-on of the night before. In fact, it all seemed light years away. Boy, I had made such a big deal of it. Maybe what happened last night wasn't real after all. Maybe it all was "only a dream."

I got up and immediately headed for the kitchen, and there my mother was, like always, fussing about the kitchen, scrubbing the dishes and wiping the grease clean from the stove tops. My father was seated, smoking a cigarette and drinking his coffee. He had long finished reading the newspaper that was strewn across the table. "Good morning, son," he said, then got up and hurriedly walked out into the backyard to mow the grass. At first it felt as if nothing had changed. But I would find that the next night, and the following nights afterward, would never be quite the same again. Just when I thought I had managed to forget that night when Sleep awoke, those voices would come again, murmuring in my chest, laughing in a language I couldn't understand. When I think about it now, I wonder why I kept silent all those years? Why was I utterly speechless? Why was I for so many years powerless to name what frightened me so?

From the very first morning after that terrible night I rarely remembered any dreams. Still, from time to time, even in the sunlit world of consciousness, I would get glimpses of these menacing figures of the Sleep world and my gut would wrench. Once, I was frightened for no reason by an afternoon shadow made by a tall oak tree in our back yard, and another time disturbed by the sickly, sweet smell of gardenias that lined the front of our house on Hector Avenue. Another day in the hot summer around noon, I felt a nauseating sadness as I gazed upon an oil slick on our driveway made by my father's car. And then again in my mid-twenties, when I was living on my own in the inner city, I would quickly turn away if my eye caught the disease-ridden face of a homeless person. I never let my gaze fall upon these places and faces too long, although they would linger in the corner of my eye and then fade entirely from view.

Soon after that fateful night, I wouldn't go to bed unless the lights were on and the bedroom door was kept slightly ajar. As my mother or father would reach for the light switch, I'd quickly make up some excuse why I wanted the lights on, all the while feeling ashamed of my new-found fear of the dark. Adults didn't like showing when they were afraid of the dark, so I wanted to be grown-up like them. In the summer evenings I'd play outside with my friends. One night I heard one of them cry out, "You better watch out, the bogey man is going to get you!" I shuddered inside and let out a scream, but never made a conscious connection between this "bogey man" and the "dark mother- and father-gods of the blood" in my dreams. I lived for many years like this, into my adult years, dipping in and out of the Sleep world, always relieved when I woke up not remembering anything about my journeys there.

Then it happened early one morning, many years later, long after my father had divorced my mother and then died in middle age a penniless alcoholic. He had lost his family and everything that was dear to him before he turned forty. My mother welcomed few people to her home outside of her immediate family. Uninterested in having a healthy, intimate relationship with a man or with women friends, my mother slowly turned into somewhat of a recluse who did not like going anywhere after dark. My three sisters (geographically miles away from their mother, yet still needing her approval, but avoiding her disapproval for their self-worth) were scattered all over the country, two out of three in second marriages with many unresolved family issues.

Smothered by the excess of female energy in my life and hungering for male energy, I searched for brotherhood by traveling across the country in a professional music group, for several years seeking a father-mentor as a monk in a Benedictine abbey, and again within the intellectual milieu of an academic institution. Just when I thought I had exhausted my search for the father, I began to reach out for therapeutic help. After several episodes of chronic, unexplainable depression, I made a decision to finally stop avoiding the hurt and anger. With assistance and support from therapeutically literate men and women, I began to explore the feared terrain of my wounded heart. I began to grieve past losses and attachments, and took up again the "archeology of soul" I had begun during the monastery years.

And so it happened one morning in the dead of winter, that I heard those ancient, inner voices again, but this time the once loud, cacophonous drone that had all but become a distant ring became both audible and crystal clear for the first time.

One by one each voice took its turn. The first voice sang: "All my children who become the gatekeepers of the Hero shall not speak the family's pain."

Then a second voice rang out: "All my children who become the gatekeepers of the Scapegoat shall not accept criticism for their benefit but only to feed their self-pity."

And then a third voice sounded: "All my children who become the gatekeepers of the Addicted shall not face their fears."

Then a fourth called out: "All my children who become the gatekeepers of the Clown shall not laugh save to distract themselves and others from the search."

A fifth intoned: "All my children who become the gatekeepers of the Lost One shall not challenge the prevailing belief system."

Finally, a sixth voice proclaimed: "All my children who become the gatekeepers of the Coward shall not love with the truth."

As I listened intently to these "commandments," I recognized who they were, who they had been all those years from the time when I was a boy, from the very first night when Sleep awoke. They were the "dark father- and mother-gods of the blood," those ancestors of mine who had not learned their lessons when they last walked upon this good earth. It was as if their voices had been stuck between two dimensions of time, fated to sing to the soul of each new child a condensed version of their lives that had been written in stone.

Flabbergasted at what my heart heard, little did I know that this was only the beginning. After hearing these "family tablets" over and over again until I memorized them, I tumbled out of the Sleep world and beheld the clear, winter sky. A full moon was shining its soft light through the trees and onto my bedclothes. I needed no artificial light to see. I reached for the pen and journal that lay on the nightstand, and began to write down without pause what the "mother- and father-gods of the blood" had just spoken to me.

No sooner had I penned the last word, "truth," when I once again dipped into the Sleep world, only to see a shining figure emerge from beneath my ancestors. I didn't recognize him at first, but soon I saw that it was none other than Hades (whom the Romans called Pluto), the god of wealth and riches. He was carrying in his arms a huge horn of plenty. I had only known Hades in books. My religion teachers told me Hades was a place like hell where the dead went, but where there's no fire or devil, just a void. I had no idea that Hades was not a place but a living god within the self, who the ancient Greeks claimed assisted sojourners through the barren land of depression, then to the lake of grief, and finally to the vibrant country of renewed exuberance and re-affirmation of life within the conscious sunlight and moonlight worlds.

Called "the Invisible One" by the Greeks because the sky gods at that time were in ascendancy (led by Zeus): favoring reason, logic, abstraction and measurement, Hades presided as king here in the murky underworld of the unconscious. His bearded face shone intensely brilliant, not like the radiance of the sun but like the ivory light of a lamplit tent under the desert stars. He addressed the throng of my ancestors who were huddled together, hiding their faces in their hands and muttering words to one another in confusion. Each of this king's words, which were spoken with a quiet strength as powerful as the ocean at eventide, overwhelmed the voices of my ancestors, and soon they, one by one, fell silent.

Then to my amazement, the bountiful basket of fruit which Hades carried was transformed into a golden scroll. He slowly turned his gaze from the "mother- and father-gods of the blood" and looked at me, penetrating to the very core of my being. Then Hades turned his eyes to the gilded page before him and began singing the following words directly to me in a voice more beautiful than I could have ever imagined:

"There is a Warrior world that exists beneath the Hero world you have known. In this world, the Warrior makes the great descent into the belly of the fish and the great ascent into the heart of the bird to receive the power to reconcile all opposites and accept the unacceptable parts of self and other. Welcome, my son.

"There is a Prince world that exists beneath the Scapegoat world you have known. In this world, the Prince daily takes on the dignified cloak of humility that is at the same time the pendant of self-worth. Welcome, my son.

"There is a Lion world that exists beneath the Addicted world you have known. In this world, the Lion learns to face fear and retrieve the power that fear holds within its breast. Welcome, my son.

"There is a Trickster world that exists beneath the Clown world you have known. Welcome, my son. In this world, the Trickster sets about being purposefully mischievous, and incites healing laughter and tears through the telling of tales directed to the hearts of men and women.

"There is a Godchild world that exists beneath the Lost Child world you have known. In this world, the Godchild reclaims the original power that the child lost when it became distracted by the distorted reality of the grown-up world. Full of wonder and a friend of the living gods, the Godchild's relationship with the living gods is not one motivated by fear, guilt, or shame, but rather, the simple desire to be nearer to them. Welcome, my son.

"And finally, there is a Prophet world that exists beneath the Coward world you have known. In this world, the Prophet learns to love with the hard truth despite the powers generated against it, and to reveal the truth always with the soothing balm of compassion. Welcome, my son."

As soon as Hades finished singing these words, the scroll from which he was reading immediately turned back into a horn of plenty. He then turned once again, faced my ancestors and thanked them for a job well done. He told them that their desperate reaching into the sunlit and moonlit worlds of consciousness to prey upon another human soul had instead attracted another initiate into the deeper mysteries of the Sleep world where the Living Gods dwelled. Then Hades, in all his marvelous splendor, sank beneath the "dark father-and mother-gods of the blood," disappearing into yet deeper realms of that awakened world that we human beings mistakenly call "Sleep."

I woke up to a glorious morning in the sunlit world of consciousness, and walked out into the clean day with a renewed sense of freedom and connectedness to the sacred earth, which shone like a brilliant god. As I walked toward the iced-over lake, out of the grey-pink sky, snow began to fall lightly, a symphony of silence. All at once, I was filled with the joyous certainty that I had just made passage through an invisible wall that separates those in this world (and beyond) who are asleep and those in this world (and beyond) who are awake. I knew that I now walked among the living. Without holding back, I breathed a deep "Yes" to all that this new life had in store for me, and I entered the Great Dance.

Neale Lundgren was born in 1951 and raised in Pasadena, Texas. He has worked as a professional musician and spent time as a Benedictine monk. He presently has a private practice in psychotherapy and is Spiritual Director at Ridgeview Institute in Atlanta. His publications include a number of recordings (Time of the Harvest *and* Breathing Open) *and* The Materialization of Spirituality *(Ridgeview, 1990).*

Away from the Shore

by Franklin Abbott

when I was a little boy
standing in shallow water
I saw a fisherman pull in
from the deeper blue
the fin then the head then the tail
of a hammerhead shark
belly to the sand
drowning in air

somewhere under the waves
the sister and brother still swam
the father and mother still spawned
the son and the daughter
    still scanned the current
    for flesh of fish
did they see my tiny ankles too
my mother and father said they did
so I wouldn't go out over my head
in the shallows where I stood
    clams buried themselves
    under the scuttle of crabs
    jellyfish bobbed and minnows
        glistened in schools of jewels
        that broke the surface
        for the pelican's eyes
            and beak and craw

I've gone up to my knees
up to my chest
up to my shoulders
up to my head
my feet letting go of the sure sand

I have floated beyond lifeguards
fooling myself
believing no undertow
stronger than my arms and legs
that stroke wave upon wave
I believe will carry me
without cause or certainty
back to the shallows
and back to the sandy shore

so far
this prayer
has been
answered
so far
every time
I've gone down
I've come up

Franklin Abbott was born in 1950 in Birmingham, Alabama, and spent his boyhood years there, in Buffalo, New York, and at his grandparents' homes in Bon Secour and Shades Mountain, Alabama. He lives in Atlanta and works as a psychotherapist with Ansley Therapy Associates. He is a poet, essayist and editor. His anthologies New Men, New Minds *(1987) and* Men and Intimacy *(1990) are published by The Crossing Press.*

HOW TO USE THIS BOOK

"Genius is but childhood recovered at will."
—Baudelaire

Many of the men who read this book will do so out of a desire to better understand their own boyhood experiences. Some may use it as an adjunct to psychotherapy or recovery, others as a stimulus for writing, journaling or other forms of creative expression. The book and its two predecessors (*New Men, New Minds* and *Men and Intimacy,* Crossing Press: 1987 and 1990) are still subdivided in ways that make them good source material for men's groups or academic courses on gender.

There are a number of helpful techniques that also may be used by individuals or groups. One is "show and tell" which involves bringing photographs and artifacts from boyhood times to share with other group members or to reconnect with in solitary meditation. Photographs can yield a tremendous amount of information and should be handled with care because of the memories they can evoke.

Another technique used in the currently popular "inner child" work is drawing pictures or writing letters with the non-dominant hand. Some people believe that this accesses the right brain or the child within. I have found it a useful tool in psychotherapy and workshop settings for facilitating dialogue with younger parts of the self. Lucia Capacchione has written a manual on this technique entitled *The Power of Your Other Hand* (Newcastle, 1988), and I recommend it.

A list of questions follows that can be used to survey boyhood experiences. It can also be useful in talking with people from that time (parents, relatives, neighbors, peers, teachers, etc.) in order to get more information. Do not be surprised if two people remember events differently. Tape or video recordings of these conversations may be very helpful in further analyzing and understanding boyhood experiences. These questions might also provide the means of breaking new ground with male relatives as experiences of boyhood are shared across generations.

Boyhood Questionnaire

1. At what point were you aware that you were not a girl but a boy?

2. Who taught you more about your gender role? Mother, father, peers or others?

3. Before puberty, what was your awareness of the male body—both yours and others? What was your awareness of the female body?

4. Do you remember any recurring dreams or fantasies from this time?

5. How did you feel about being out of doors? At school? At home with family? By yourself?

6. Who were your best male friends? Who did you look up to among your elders? Whom did you avoid or fear?

7. Whom did you have fights with? How often? Who disciplined you? How? How often?

8. Who would you go to if you were in trouble? Where did you go to be safe? Who cared for you when you were sick?

9. What did you accomplish in elementary school? Did you excel in games, music, school subjects? Were you well-liked? What kinds of problems did you have?

10. What were you told about your race/ethnicity/religion? What were you told about other races, ethnic groups or religions?

11. Who taught you about religion? Did you believe it? What were the hardest parts to believe?

12. Did you go through a time when you didn't like girls? Did you have friends who were girls? Girlfriends? Were you ever called a girl or a sissy? By whom? How often?

13. What toys did you play with? What games did you play?

14. What were your clothes like? What kinds of haircuts did you have?

15. What TV shows, movies or stories did you like?

16. What did you want to be when you grew up?

17. Did you have heroes or idols?

18. Did you have sex play? With whom? How often? Were you ever caught? Punished? By whom? How?

19. Were you ever forced to have sex or seduced by someone older than you? How did you feel about it? Was there anyone you could talk with who would help you?

20. Did you hunt, fish or garden? Who taught you how?

21. Did you have pets, hobbies, special treasures?

22. Did you have favorite teachers or relatives? Teachers or relatives you disliked or feared?

23. What was one of the best things that happened to you as a boy? What was one of the worst?

24. What happened to you as a boy when you reached puberty?

25. Assuming you have or could have a son or foster son, how would you want his boyhood to be different from yours?

Be patient with yourself in answering these questions. Get support if painful memories surface. Every question holds a story that needs to be told carefully. Add questions or amend these to represent the issues of your boyhood more accurately.